Temple Emanu-El
of Dallas 1872-1997

The Chisholm Trail Series
Number Seventeen

Elissa Sommerfield
Contributing Editor
for
A Light in the Prairie

a LIGHT in the PRAIRIE

**Temple Emanu-El
of Dallas 1872-1997**

by **Gerry Cristol**

TEXAS CHRISTIAN UNIVERSITY • FORT WORTH

Copyright © 1998 by Gerry Cristol

Library of Congress Cataloging-in-Publication Data

Cristol, Gerry.
A light in the prairie : Temple Emanu-El of Dallas, 1872-1997 /Gerry Cristol.
p.   cm.
Includes bibliographical references and index.
ISBN 0-87565-184-4 (alk. paper)
1. Temple Emanu-El (Dallas, Tex.)—History.
2. Jews—Texas—Dallas—History
3. Dallas (Tex.)—Ethnic relations.
I. Title

BM225.D35E49   1998
296'.09764'2812—dc21
97-3705
CIP

All photos are from the archives of Temple Emanu-El
unless otherwise indicated

Design/Margie Adkins Graphic Design

IV

To my husband Charles

CONTENTS

FOREWORD

Dr. Levi A. Olan, one of Temple Emanu-El's most beloved and erudite rabbis, once devoted a radio sermon to the question "Does History Teach Us Anything?" His answer was unequivocal—a resounding 'yes'— and he focused on three of its most significant lessons. First, he explained, "history must be read so that we may learn from the experience of generations who struggled and suffered. If we truly remember them, we can avoid making the same mistakes." Second, "history must be read so that we may recognize that this heritage of our life was bought and paid for by our fathers of yesterday at a great cost and sacrifice. We ought not to treat it scornfully. Finally," he concluded, "history ought to be read so that we may take hope that the future is not in our hands alone. There is God whose purpose and plan we only help to fulfill."[1]

Gerry Cristol's authoritative history of Temple Emanu-El bears out Dr. Olan's message. The product of years of research in primary sources, this is a history full of significant lessons concerning Temple Emanu-El, Dallas, the Reform movement, and the American Jewish experience as a whole.

The volume begins, as so much of American Jewish history does, with migration—the arrival in Dallas of ambitious, venturesome young men, among them Jewish immigrants from Europe. In 1872, the city's first Jews formed a benevolent association; in 1875, they went on to found a synagogue, Congregation Emanu-El. Like its namesake in New York (established in 1845), but somewhat atypically for its time, the congregation identified from the very start with Reform Judaism. The fifty-one men who on September 30, 1875, pledged their support to the new synagogue adopted the *Minhag Amerika* prayerbook of Isaac Mayer Wise, probably in the mistaken belief, shared by Wise himself, that it would become the standard for all American Jews. The rabbi of Cincinnati's Temple Bene Yeshurun, Wise at the time was the most visible and articulate leader of Reform Judaism. Just three days after the establishment of Emanu-El, he presided in Cincinnati over the opening exercises of Hebrew Union College, soon to become the prime training seminary for Reform rabbis. This coincidence, if not providential, was certainly propitious. From the beginning, destiny seemed to link Temple Emanu-El with the development of Reform Judaism in the United States.

Through the years, some of America's foremost rabbis have served Temple Emanu-El, bringing with them Reform Judaism as they understood it. The temple experienced as part of its own history many of the Reform movement's critical turning points—the full cycle that carried Reform into its so-called classical period and then back toward greater appreciation of Jewish tradition. Change, however, has necessarily been tempered by the congregation's firm sense of its own heritage and tradition. Throughout its history, Gerry Cristol shows, it has seen itself as the voice of the Jewish community of Dallas, speaking out forcefully on issues of contemporary concern and working closely with its non-Jewish neighbors for civic improvement and social reform. "Temple Emanu-El's leaders and rabbis were representative Jews as they enacted their civic roles in the community," she explains. "How the temple leadership conducted themselves imprinted the image of the Jews as perceived by the larger Dallas society."

It is important to remember while reading this volume that the history of Temple Emanu-El reaches beyond the story of its rabbis and officers. The men, women, and children found on the membership roster and the additional multitudes who, through the years, have fallen under the temple's sway form part of its history too. Their changing needs and interests—the prayers, classes, and rituals that have inspired them, the activities and causes that have drawn them in, and the irritants that have sometimes driven them away—all have played a formative role in shaping

Temple Emanu-El. As a voluntary institution, its survival and success have always depended on keeping attuned to the expectations of those it serves.

Does this history teach us anything more? Like Dr. Olan, another modern student of American religion, Professor E. Brooks Holifield, responds affirmatively. "Painstaking examination of religious congregations," he writes, "promises to alter our perceptions of both religion and of community in America. To explore the congregation is to penetrate to the grass roots of American religious culture. . . . Most of all," he observes, "the study of the congregation clarifies an enduring dimension of community in America. More Americans have belonged to a church or synagogue than to any other private association. That fact alone," he concludes, "makes the congregation a resource for a deeper understanding of America."[2]

Gerry Cristol's history of Temple Emanu-El contributes to this "deeper understanding." A valuable resource for temple members and for all who seek to understand the congregation's place in American Judaism, it is a history that both teaches and inspires.

Jonathan D. Sarna
Joseph H. & Belle R. Braun Professor
of American Jewish History
Brandeis University
Waltham, MA

ACKNOWLEDGEMENTS

During my time as archivist at Temple Emanu-El, many people encouraged my commitment to preserve and record the history of the temple and of the Jewish community. One person in particular—Elissa Sommerfield—provided invaluable help and advice during the four years we worked together on *A Light in the Prairie*. Elissa, a former English instructor who heads an extensive tutoring service for students and would-be-writers of all ages and for college board preparation, taught me the importance of descriptive, expressive, and clear writing. Her understanding of the temple as a former staff and board member, her familiarity with Dallas history, and her enthusiasm for the project immensely improved the strength and vigor of the undertaking. I am most indebted to Elissa for contributing her professional and personal knowledge and skill.

At the suggestion of Rabbi Sheldon Zimmerman, I sent the first draft of *A Light in the Prairie* to Jonathan D. Sarna, Joseph H. and Belle R. Braun Professor of American Jewish History at Brandeis University and 1990 Sam R. Bloom lecturer at the temple, a scholar who generously and kindly agreed to look at my work. To my profound gratitude, Professor Sarna analyzed each chapter and offered constructive suggestions for revision in order to bring forth "the major themes and conceptual ideas that make sense out of all the detail." Professor Sarna's interest in Temple Emanu-El's history and his attention to my efforts focused the direction of the book and spurred more extensive research in order, as he said, "not to pass judgment," but to "show with the retrospect of the historian what clamorous arguments were really all about—what the key issues underlying the debates were." In addition, Jonathan Sarna has honored our temple by writing the introduction to its history.

When I sent the manuscript to Judy Alter, director of Texas Christian University Press, she gave the work professional standing by selecting it for publication. My grateful thanks to her for recognizing its merit as regional history and insisting upon necessary revisions to create a more readable book.

From the beginning of my research I added credibility to the project by telling everyone, and especially any person I wanted to interview for the book, that Hortense Sanger was reading all my chapters. For the past fifty years Hortense Landauer Sanger has participated in or thoughtfully observed most events central to the history of both Temple Emanu-El and Dallas. Willing to make herself available to discuss at any length any subject I thought pertinent to Emanu-El, the city or the philosophy of life in general, she offered me a wealth of information.

Because of her interest in the history and her family's relationship to William Greenburg, rabbi of Temple Emanu-El from 1901 until 1919, Hortense secured his voluminous papers for the temple archives. This material filled a twenty-year historical gap in the growth of the temple and of the city, and its significance is well documented in the footnotes of *A Light in the Prairie*. For the most part, all primary material in the book derived from sources in the temple archives. Records of the congregation's first twenty years were lost or destroyed, but subsequent minutes, annual reports, letters, and photographs were conscientiously retained. I also relied heavily upon Rabbi David Lefkowitz's correspondence covering his thirty-five-year career at Emanu-El as well as Rabbi Levi Olan's letters and scrapbooks dating from 1949-1970.

Interviews completed over several decades played a crucial part in my interpretation of events. I am most appreciative of the more than fifty congregants who allowed me to record their recollections and of other members and rabbis of the congregation who were previously taped as part of the oral history program led by Joan Loeb and Evelyn Eldridge. Rabbi Gerald Klein, Rabbi Sheldon Zimmerman, and Rabbi David Stern contributed a great deal of information about themselves as well as insight

into the workings of the congregation. All interviews are listed in the bibliography.

The four-year span of time that I spent researching and writing *A
Light in the Prairie* may be viewed as the inevitable culmination of a twenty-
five-year absorption in the history of Temple Emanu-El. I became the
archivist at the temple in 1973 after Dorothy and Henry Jacobus generously donated funds for an archives room in celebration of the temple's
100th anniversary. Fortunately, Edna Flaxman became the first archives
chairman. By showing unflagging interest, offering concrete suggestions,
and being available for consultation on an almost daily basis, Edna
encouraged me to plan exhibits and create an archives accessible for
research and study. Rabbi Levi Olan, a member of the first archives committee, was interested in sponsoring a history of the temple, which he
insisted must be an "interpretive" history. As years passed and the written
history was still in the talking stage, Edna Flaxman would say to me,
"You'll be the one to write the history."

Many other talented people have contributed to the preparation of
the book. Barbara Zale, whose artistic flair has enhanced and enlivened
exhibits in the archives, helped to choose photographs to illustrate the
book. Frances Steinberg diligently typed the archives' card catalogue organized by Carol Sandfield, thereby ensuring an invaluable research tool.
Rose Biderman, former archivist at the Dallas Jewish Historical Society,
graciously put its resources at my disposal, lending photographs and offering her insight into the records at the society. Andy Reisberg carefully
copied old photographs and lent his selective eye to help choose the best
examples for the book.

Several members of Temple Emanu-El read the manuscript before
publication in order to catch errors in style or content. My appreciative
thanks to James R. Alexander, Rose Marion Berg, Lee H. Berg, Edna
Flaxman, Josephine Goldman, Irwin Grossman, Suzi Greenman, Adlene
Harrison, Harold Kleinman, Ruth Kleinman, Carmen Michael, Joseph
Rosenstein, Buddy Rosenthal, Rhea Wolfram, and also to Rabbi Sheldon
Zimmerman, Rabbi Gerald Klein, Rabbi David Stern, Rabbi Debra

Robbins, Rabbi Charles D. Mintz, my sister-in-law Bernice Selman and brother-in-law Dr. Joseph Selman—all of whom took their tasks seriously and offered well-taken comments. I also want to thank Laura Wilson for her interest in the project. Last, but certainly not least, I would like to express my appreciation to my daughters, Freda Toppel and Amy Cristol, for their encouragement and my gratitude to my husband Charles, to whom this book is lovingly dedicated, for his patient, understanding, unconditional support and good advice. 🕎

CHAPTER 1

ON THE TRAIL OF THE IRON HORSE

We're not only on the map but we are on the railroad now. Hurrah for Dallas.

Robert Seay, 1872

On July 16, 1872, a small, wood-burning locomotive pulling eight freight cars and one passenger car steamed up from Houston to the frontier town of Dallas. There it was met at the depot one mile from town by a "jubilant, cheering throng of 5,000 Texans," by far the largest crowd ever assembled from Dallas and the surrounding communities.[1] Robert Seay, a young lawyer from Tennessee who had arrived in Dallas just six months previously, described the excitement:

> Hardly realized [there were] so many people in this little place, but long lines of them, horse-back, in buggies, on foot, streamed from every direction, converging in one spot like ants in a drop of honey. . . . About 9 A.M. some sharpsighted folks, gazing south, yelled "there it comes." First a wisp of smoke, and then the outlines of the engine shaping up, growing larger, whizzing toward us. The crowd went wild. Men whooped, woman screamed, or even sobbed, and children yelped in fright and amazement.[2]

This triumph, the capturing of a railroad connection for an undistinguished town much like any other small village in North Texas, catalyzed Dallas' unprecedented growth. As an inducement to insure the line's proximity to Dallas (the officials of the Houston and Texas Central originally planned to build it eight miles east of town), Dallas citizens donated $5,000 and a right of way to the railroad company.[3] The advent of rail connections—first the Houston & Texas Central Railway chugging up from Houston and then the intersecting Texas & Pacific Railway bringing goods and people from the East—transformed a landlocked Texas town into a bustling commercial and industrial center. A few days before the first train, the *Dallas Herald* noted that "our city is graced with a continual arrival of strangers prospecting for homes and business."[4] The railroads would help stoke economic prosperity, provide access to the markets of St. Louis and the East, and energize the westward sweep of trade and immigration to Dallas.

Dallas had been founded in 1841 by John Neely Bryan, a wilderness scout with a wanderlust, a lawyer and town developer fresh from establishing the town of Van Buren, Arkansas. Originally, Bryan, riding his Indian pony Neshoba Tenva (Walking Wolf) and traveling with a Cherokee Indian named Ned and a bear dog called Tubby, came to the Three Forks of the Trinity in 1839 with the idea of setting up an Indian trading post. At the site he marked as Dallas (possibly for his friend Joseph Dallas), Bryan staked his claim at one of the few natural fords across the picturesque, though unnavigable, Trinity River, which rolled through hundreds of miles of virgin territory.[5] Bryan's land appeared to be a prime spot for a trading post as it lay at the crossroads of two major Indian traces leading to buffalo country, one of which, the Preston Trail, later became a major Dallas thoroughfare, Preston Road. But by the time Bryan rode back to Arkansas and then returned to Texas in 1841, the Indians, the last barrier to the Republic of Texas' encouragement of colonization, had been driven away. Accordingly, the former town developer turned his attention to a much larger project—promoting the townsite of Dallas.[6]

Bryan's town grew slowly, even after 1845 when Texas joined the Union as the twenty-eighth state. After the first Texas legislature established Dallas County, the designation as county seat was a prize sought not only by Dallas but also by the neighboring communities of Hord's Ridge, located across the Trinity River in what is now Oak Cliff, and Cedar Springs, three miles north of Bryan's settlement. When Bryan donated a plot he had tilled as a corn patch—land bounded by Houston, Main, Jefferson (now Record), and Commerce streets—for use as a courthouse square, his wily gift convinced county residents in 1850 to select Dallas as the county seat.[7] This public square became the centerpiece of the new city and county.

As the county seat and the center of a prolific crop-producing area—mostly cotton and wheat—Dallas began to attract settlers from the states of the Old South, primarily from Kentucky and Tennessee. In a misguided attempt to found an idealistic and idyllic agricultural cooperative community, some 200 French and French-speaking Swiss and Belgian colonists also arrived in 1855 to establish "La Reunion." In the next year these Europeans, artisans unprepared for farming, suffered through a blizzard in May, a devastating summer drought, a plague of grasshoppers, and a winter so cold that the Trinity River froze into a solid sheet of ice.[8] The utopian experiment gradually failed, commemorated only in name as Reunion Sports Arena. However, the "shaggy little village" of Dallas with its log-cabin courthouse benefited from the variety of occupations the accomplished newcomers brought to the predominantly agricultural community.[9] By 1859 the town of approximately 775 persons could boast a French tailor, a milliner, a photographer, a dancing master, a naturalist, and a brewer among more practical business ventures such as several general merchandise stores, two hotels, two livery stables, a blacksmith shop, and a saddlery. As in so many western towns, all stores and houses were clustered tightly in primitive wood-frame buildings around the public square, an area that was, depending on the weather, either unbearably dusty or mired in black clay mud. One of the dry goods warehouses on the dirt-packed square belonged to Alexander Simon, the first known Jew to settle in Dallas.

In all probability, Simon, like other Jews who had emigrated from Europe and journeyed to Texas in the mid to late nineteenth century, sought an opportunity to better himself economically in a land free from

3

inhibiting and oppressive laws. Jews were part of the great German migration to the United States which began in 1815 after the Napoleonic Wars and stretched into the twentieth century. Understandably, ambitious and progressive young men initially abandoned the impoverished, reactionary German states of Bavaria and Prussia, as well as nearby places under German cultural influence—Poland, Austria, Alsace, France, and parts of Russia—to escape restrictive edicts. Often the ruler of these countries limited his Jewish subjects' choice of occupation, living quarters, travel, and, in Bavaria, even the opportunity for marriage. Furthermore, many young boys left at age sixteen to escape conscription into the army. Most of the emigrants were the poorer classes. The more prosperous Jews and Gentiles moved to the larger cities in Europe.

Upon arrival in America, a Jewish immigrant from central Europe had two advantages that helped him cope successfully in his new environment. He usually could read, and he had experience as a middleman and peddler, the only occupations allowed the majority of European Jews. Now he was entering a country which sorely needed literate middlemen who could hawk goods from one part of the population to the other, whether from the East to the West, from the cities to the farms, or from the manufacturer to the customer.

Many immigrants traveled from one town to another looking for a promising place in which to make a living. As they made their way across the United States, sometimes staying with relatives who had come earlier, the newcomers learned the language and sharpened their business skills. Before coming to Dallas and opening a store on the town square, Alex Simon, originally from Poland, had spent time in Houston. While there, he married fifteen-year-old Julia Levy, twenty years his junior. His bride's parents, Louis and Mary Levy, had moved to Houston from Philadelphia when Julia was a baby, perhaps persuaded to relocate in Texas by Louis' brother, Dr. Albert M. Levy. Dr. Levy came to Texas in 1835 with the New Orleans Greys, a volunteer regiment formed by Sam Houston, and fought in the Siege of Bexar (now San Antonio) for Texas' independence from Mexico, a battle which preceded the siege of the Alamo. Appointed by Sam Houston as his surgeon general, Dr. Levy also enlisted in the

Texas Navy in 1836 and later settled in Matagorda County.[10] Although Louis Levy had established roots in Houston (he was a founder of the Houston Hebrew Benevolent Association), his daughter Julia and her husband Alex Simon decided to settle in Dallas. Apparently they were well situated in the city by 1858, the year Alex Simon ran for the city office of alderman. He lost that municipal race, garnering eight votes and finishing last among the six men competing for five places.[11]

Possibly earlier, but definitely by 1858, Alexander Simon had opened his warehouse on the northeast corner of the public square. Simon dealt in a multitude of items such as dry goods, groceries and hardware, cutlery, saddlery, ready-made clothing, crockery, wood and glassware, and paint and oils—articles which he cannily advertised in the May 8, 1858, *Dallas Herald* as being "cheaper than the cheapest." In June of 1860 Simon opened a new store, Caruth, Simons & Company, in partnership with Walter and William Caruth. Their emporium, advertised as "New Store— New Men—New Goods," sold staple and fancy dry goods, including all kinds of shirts and ready-made clothing, boots, shoes, and hats.[12] William Caruth had come to Dallas in 1848. Joined by his brother Walter, the Caruths not only pursued mercantile interests but also accumulated land. Their property of 5,000 contiguous acres grew to encompass the largest plantation in North Texas: farmland where Southern Methodist University, NorthPark Center, and Temple Emanu-El would eventually stand.[13]

Unfortunately, on a searingly hot, dry July day in 1860 a devastating fire ripped through the entire tightly connected wood-frame Dallas business district and engulfed everything in its path. Incinerated in the blazing ruins were Simon's warehouse and the new store. After the fire, according to his advertisements in the *Dallas Herald* in the fall of 1860, Simon rebuilt his store and reopened for business under his own name. The next year the Civil War broke out. When Texas voted early in 1861 to secede from the Union, the hostilities refocused the community's attention and slowed the pace of rebuilding the business district. Dallas writer A. C. Greene has described the interval from 1861 to 1865 when Dallas "embraced secession, the Confederacy, and war with fervor" as a time when the citizenry brooked no tolerance for dissent.[14] The city became a distribution center for the Confederacy, and its economy eventually suffered from the Union blockade. In 1863 Alex and Julia Simon with their three young children left the city for Brenham, perhaps anticipating a more promising business climate in a town on the planned path of the railroad.[15] Alex Simon prospered in his new location, but he missed the commercial boom engendered ten years later when the railroad terminated in Dallas. Even though the business judgment of the Simons may be questioned, the impact of the railroad upon them as entrepreneurs and the example of their resilient mobility is a story reprised throughout the West.

More Jews may have come to Dallas during and just after the Civil War, but the only record of their presence is a traveler's description of Dallas in 1865, which appeared in the French bi-weekly literary journal, *Archives Israelites*. "In Dallas all along Main Street, the shops are closed for Rosh Hashanah. A stranger going by and seeing the shop doors closed, remarked that if the Jews ever left the city, nothing would any longer deserve the observer's notice."[16] But who were these Jews? The 1870 U. S. Census lists a few names that have been borne by Jews, but in this case their bearers do not appear at a later date as part of the Jewish community. The likelihood is that they were transients, or had decided not to retain their Jewish identity, or were not Jews. The next Jewish settlers to arrive in Dallas after the Civil War entered the city about 1871. There is no mystery why these Jews elected to make up-and-coming Dallas their home base—the railroad was on its way.

Emanuel Kahn, who would serve as president of Temple Emanu-El in 1894, epitomized the ambitious, venturesome young men who made their way to Dallas. As a very young boy in Trimback in Alsace, France, he and his brother Leon peddled merchandise in the countryside to eke out a living after their father's business failed. Then, the father died when Emanuel was just eleven, and the orphaned children were separated. Leon went to America, a sister went to live with relatives, and Emanuel was adopted by another relative who sent him to school to be trained as a cantor. At age sixteen he found a position as a cantor and schoolteacher in a small French village, but he later observed that he "had scant ambition for the job." When his singing voice broke from overexertion, he "conceived the notion of going to America."[17] In a memoir written for the fiftieth anniversary of his very successful "gents clothing store," E. M. Kahn and Company, he recalled his excursions in America until he took root in Dallas:

> I landed in a small village in Georgia. Not being able to speak English, it was a hard life in these new surroundings, but by dint of earnest application, a happy smiling disposition soon won me many friends who felt a personal interest in me. Possessing a violin which I played indifferently, in company with a one-legged Negro who played on the banjo, we nightly amused the boys and directly became exceedingly popular. Completely assimilating with the natives, I led a very pleasant but quite a narrow life. I lived there over five years. Being ambitious for a larger field and Texas being considered a promising field for an ambitious young man, sold out [he must have peddled or become a merchant] with the view of locating either in Dallas, Paris, Sherman, or Waco. These four towns numbered about similar in population and prospective future. Landed in Dallas when about twenty-one and beholding the hustling ambitious atmosphere of its citizens, population about forty-five hundred, I concluded to settle here, and a very happy selection I made.[18]

Like many merchants who came west, Emanuel Kahn came to the place of his second settlement, Dallas, with enough capital to start a business immediately upon arrival. Coincidentally, he arrived in Dallas in 1873 at the beginning of the railroad boom and the inestimable impact of the merchants' arrival in the city at the end of the railroad line.

Merchants followed the Houston & Texas Central Railway's path through Texas, setting up shops in towns northward from Houston to Dallas as the line made its way up through central Texas. The Sanger brothers started moving with the railroad in 1865, when Lehman Sanger opened a store in Millican, a town just northwest of Houston. The Millican store was the fourth store in Texas opened by a Sanger brother, after McKinney, Weatherford, and Decatur. As the Houston & Texas Central's terminus from 1861 to 1866, Millican became the bustling locus for all freight bound for North and Northeast Texas, the central destination for passengers who disembarked from the daily stagecoach to take the train south, and the last stop for folks stocking up before moving out to Brownwood, Weatherford, and points farther west. Lehman later wrote "the staple articles with us proved to be revolvers, shotguns and musical instruments . . . sold generally for gold.[19]

In 1858 Lehman's older brother Isaac had opened the first store in McKinney, housed in a rickety wood-frame cracker-box building typical of those thrown up overnight along the frontier. The first member of his family of seven brothers and three sisters to emigrate from Obernbreit, Bavaria, Isaac had landed in New York in 1852 at sixteen. For about five years he apprenticed in his uncle Jacob Heller's small retail store in New Haven, Connecticut, performing mundane chores and receiving valuable bookkeeping experience. On the modest stipend he earned he ventured to New York, where he worked as a bookkeeper in a men's clothing factory. Shortly thereafter, assisted by his firm which provided a Mr. Baum as a partner, Isaac ambitiously set out for McKinney, the county seat north of Dallas whose population of 450 made Dallas seem small in comparison. In 1859 Lehman Sanger joined his brother Isaac in the McKinney store, and one year later the brothers moved their store to Weatherford.

When the War Between the States erupted, Isaac and Lehman dissolved their business and enlisted in the Confederate Army. Isaac served in a frontier regiment, and Lehman joined the Twenty-first Texas Infantry. Their younger brother Philip, who had settled in Savannah, signed up with Company G, Thirty-second Georgia Regiment. He fought in various battles in South Carolina and was wounded in the battle of Ocean Pond, Florida. When the war was over, Philip left for Texas to help Lehman in the new store in Millican. Then, "to retain [their] trade," the three brothers determined to move northward with the Houston and Texas Central and transferred their stock to Bryan, the new railroad depot twenty miles away.[20] As other villages along the railroad's path became the temporary end of the line and the center of trade for the area, Sanger Brothers relocated in the Texas towns of Hearne, Calvert, Bremond, Kosse, Groesbeck, and Corsicana.

Emulating his older brothers, Alexander Sanger arrived in Texas in 1871. Then twenty-five years old, Alex had been in the dry goods business from the age of thirteen as an apprentice to a merchant in Bavaria. Impressed by a visitor returning to Bavaria from Cincinnati, he resolved in 1865 to join his brothers in America. His employer thought enough of him to give him money for steerage fare on a small steamer, and after a stormy ocean voyage to New York he immediately set out for Cincinnati, where Philip met him. Both brothers secured jobs in a large notions firm, but shortly after Alex's arrival Philip left for Texas.[21] When Alex decided to join Philip in the Corsicana store, he fortuitously arrived just before the crucial move to Dallas with the railroad.

In Dallas Alex Sanger would soon encounter the "merchants, professional men, gamblers, and floaters" who had tracked the railroad all the way north from Houston.[22] The *Directory of the City of Dallas* for 1875 may be forgiven for its hyperbole concerning the role of these merchants: "With the Texas Central Road came the Terminus Merchants from Corsicana and with them a destiny for Dallas that is unprecedented in the history of this country." Despite the poetic license and exaggerated civic pride, the hard fact is that in one year the activity engendered by the merchants (and gamblers) drew so many people to the town that according to the 1875 and 1878 directories the population ballooned from 1,500 to 7,063. In 1873 alone, 725 new buildings and residences were constructed, launching Dallas' first real estate boom.[23] Later Alex Sanger said of his coming to the new town, "I never felt the least touch of homesickness. I believe it was because I was associated with a jolly crowd of businessmen; some were single, some were married, but all united on all questions that affected the prosperity of Dallas."[24]

Alex Sanger rented a tiny twelve-by-twelve-foot cubicle for himself in the rear of an unprepossessing one-story frame building on Elm Street.

Sanger Brothers leased a similar building on the courthouse square and advertised in the *Dallas Herald* on March 23, 1872, that it would open with the "most complete and assorted stock of Dry Goods (staple and fancy), clothing, hats, boots and shoes ever brought to this market." Moreover, in an astute bit of promotion, the firm added that Dallas citizens would benefit by Sangers' "having a brother in New York constantly looking out for bargains." Brother Isaac had opened what would become a permanent buying office in New York. The following year Alex Sanger built a frame building on Elm Street between Austin and Lamar streets. Ten thousand square feet of floor space made the store the largest dry goods retail center in the state. In 1874 Philip Sanger joined Alex in the Dallas store, taking charge of all retail operations. Philip's presence freed Alex to devote his efforts to directing the wholesale end, supervising employees, and entering wholeheartedly into Dallas civic affairs. Together the Sanger brothers, including Samuel and Lehman then in Waco, ran the most successful and prestigious mercantile business in North Texas.[25]

As soon as he arrived in Dallas, Alex Sanger began to participate in local affairs. He immediately became involved in Dallas' effort to have the western route of the Texas & Pacific Railway cross the Houston and Texas Central tracks within city limits, thereby ensuring the city's future as a major marketing center. Otherwise, Dallas, which had secured the Houston and Texas Central in July 1872 would be just another one-line terminal town, bypassed in a few months when the railroad moved northward. The proposed direction of the Texas & Pacific from the East closely followed the thirty-second parallel, a path which would place its tracks near Corsicana, approximately fifty miles south of Dallas. Dallas' business leaders plotted to have the Texas legislature fix the new line's intersection with the Houston and Texas Central within one mile of Browder Springs. When the outmaneuvered railroad officials realized Browder Springs was a mile from Dallas, they decided to lay the tracks one mile south of Browder Springs instead of directly through town. To make the route through Dallas more palatable to the railroad officials, the city business leaders, with Alex Sanger as chairman of the finance committee, subscribed $100,000 and supplied a wide right-of-way, now Pacific Avenue, for the Texas & Pacific Railway to move through town on February 22, 1873. That same year civic leader Sanger also ran for office and was elected Democratic city alderman from the First Ward, winning seventy-two out of seventy-three votes—he had gallantly voted for his opponent.[26]

In addition to engaging enthusiastically in business and civic enterprises, gregarious Alex Sanger, on July 1, 1872, also joined a gathering of ten young Jewish men who met to form a Hebrew benevolent association.[27] In America a benevolent society was often the first Jewish organization in a community. Then, as their numbers increased, Jews felt the need for a more structured religious body. The Dallas Hebrew Benevolent Association was the first Jewish organization in the city, and its members proudly noted that it "will be no boasting spirit nor empty honor to claim that we are one of the first in our Lone Star State that unfurled the banner of Benevolent to the God of Israel."[28]

When Dallas was just a frontier settlement, early Jewish pioneers had gravitated to the southern and central parts of Texas and formed communal societies in Galveston, Houston, and San Antonio. In the thriving port of Galveston, where Jews had started to settle in the 1830s, a Jewish cemetery association existed for several years before its members received a charter for a benevolent association in 1866 and organized Congregation B'nai Israel in 1868. Houston Jews met as a cemetery society as early as 1854, but Beth Israel, the only Reform temple in Texas that began as an Orthodox entity, did not officially incorporate as Texas' first synagogue until 1859. The Jews of San Antonio associated as a Hebrew benevolent association in 1856 until its members formed Temple Beth-El in 1874. Following this classic progression, the Dallas Hebrew Benevolent Association organized in 1872 was the forerunner of Temple Emanu-El, established in 1875.

Because in Europe the name "Jew" was often used disparagingly, when Jews organized their societies in America they substituted the word "Hebrew," a name that connoted the prophets of the Bible, who were more acceptable to their Christian neighbors. At the initial meeting of the Dallas association, chaired by Emanuel Tillman, the eleven founders of the organization—Moses Ullman, August J. Rosenfield, A. Dreyfuss, A.

11

Prince, H. Goldstein, L. Jonas, G. Burgower, F. H. Baum, B. Meyer, Alexander Sanger, and Tillman—pledged their honor to help the sick and distressed as a "duty we owe to our merciful God, our children, and ourselves." They also maintained that the "spirit inculcated by our holy religion and inherited through a long line of ancestors, who were never known to refuse comfort and aid to a distressed co-religionist, should stimulate us in this noble work."[29] The new organization welcomed any Israelite of good moral character between the ages of eighteen and sixty who was recommended by two members of the association. Nevertheless, a prospective member had to be approved by ballot by a committee of investigation and, in the practice of the day, could be rejected by three black balls. The group scheduled meetings for the first Sunday of each month and approved a $5 initiation fee for new members, $1 for monthly dues, and semi-annual elections.[30]

Officers of the Association—President Moses Ullman, Vice-President Alexander Sanger, and Secretary August J. Rosenfield, along with Emanuel Tillman—were established Jewish businessmen in the rapidly growing town even though they, like their fellow members, had lived in the city for less than a year. Moses Ullman, born in Herglorch, Germany, arrived in Dallas in December of 1871, the year he located his wholesale and retail grocery store on the north side of the public square. M. Ullman and Company also sold tobacco and cigars, liquors and wines, "which they put up in bottles for private families and medical use."[31] Ullman employed Emanuel Tillman, who had also arrived in 1871. An 1865 Heidelberg University Ph.D. graduate, Dr. Tillman had been trained as a chemist in Germany and had mastered seven languages, including English, before coming to America. Initially he had immigrated to Natchez, Mississippi, where he entered the drug business and was also appointed assistant state geologist. Resigning because of ill health, he ventured west and came to Dallas when he was thirty-one years old.[32]

August J. Rosenfield, who worked for Sanger Brothers, had left Cincinnati to join the firm in Bryan, Texas, in 1867 and participated in its trek to Dallas, taking charge of loading the wagons that transported merchandise from the Corsicana store to the Dallas location. Like Tillman,

Rosenfield had also attended Heidelberg University, and he was related by marriage to Alex's brother Sam, who opened the Waco store in 1873.[33] Clearly, a feeling of belonging and camaraderie developed rapidly among the initial Jewish settlers in Dallas, most of whom were born in Germany and had business, family, or school ties.

Community solidarity was a cornerstone of the Benevolent Association, and its members earnestly asserted that "we all must observe the rapid increase of our population of the Jewish faith, and the too often fatal acclimating ordeal through which so many must pass, and it will be apparent to you all, that a society of this kind has become a serious want."[34] In fact, the genesis of the Dallas group was most likely a reaction to the sudden death in late June 1872 of a young Jewish man named Adolph Deutchner and the pressing necessity to make arrangements for his burial. Hastily, the Association acquired a plot on Akard Street from Mayor Henry Ervay for its cemetery, land which was adjacent to the Masonic Cemetery, Independent Order of Odd Fellows Cemetery, and Old City Cemetery. Just one month later at the next meeting on August 7, 1872, Alex Sanger reported that "the fence on our burying ground is fixed" and that the association had notified Deutchner's parents "all that was necessary about their deceased son." Since the first burial was that of a "stranger in our midst," the organization paid the hack bill to the cemetery, and the president took charge of the arrangements for a decent burial, calling on the treasurer to collect fifty cents from each member. If the deceased had been a fellow member, the Hebrew Benevolent Association would have supplied a hearse and two carriages without charge.[35]

One year later the president directed Moses Ullman, Alex Sanger, and David Goslin (who would be the first president of Temple Emanu-El) to "wait on our mayor and see what arrangements they can make for more ground to our cemetery," called the Hebrew Burying Ground.[36] The second parcel, which augmented the cemetery land to a plot seventy-five by ninety feet, was deeded in 1874 to Emanuel Tillman as trustee for the association by Captain George M. Swink. (Captain Swink is noted for his establishment in 1872 of the original mule-drawn line which took passengers from the train depot to the courthouse, over a mile away.) In 1956 all the graves in the Hebrew Benevolent Association Cemetery were moved to the Temple Emanu-El Cemetery, established in 1884 on Howell Street near Lemmon. But no matter what its later location, the original cemetery was an emblem of community and stability to Dallas' earliest Jewish population.

The stated aim for founding the Dallas Hebrew Benevolent Association emphasized the members' responsibility to help those in distress, and the membership did on occasion contribute sums of $10 to two needy young men (which they repaid) or $20 to a destitute family or took up a collection for some fellow Jew reported in grievous condition by the Relief Committee. But philanthropy was not the predominant concern of the members.[37] They were more involved with attending to their immediate needs as Jews by first establishing a cemetery and then making preparations for the New Year Holidays of Rosh Hashanah and Yom Kippur. Their second objective for associating together as Jews was fulfilled in September 1872 when the association prepared to hold the first Jewish services during "our Festival Days." President Moses Ullman selected a committee of three—F. H. Baum, A. Dreyfuss, and Alex Sanger—for the important project of finding a room for services and borrowing a Torah.[38] The committee made arrangements to hold the services in Masonic Hall, then situated on Commerce Street.

Since colonial times some Jews had belonged to the Masons or Odd Fellows fraternities and Jews often used Masonic halls as their first places of worship in America. But, "when these organizations began to systematically reject Jewish applications for membership" in the 1840s, twelve young German men in New York started B'nai B'rith, which means Sons of the Covenant.[39] Four of the original members (one was Julius Bien, brother of Temple Emanu-El's second rabbi Herman Bien) belonged to the Masons or Odd Fellows. The founders of B'nai B'rith "expropriated the secret handshakes, passwords, codes, regalia, and insignia" of Masonry and created the first nationwide secular Jewish organization in the United States.[40]

Both the Hebrew Benevolent Association and Temple Emanu-El established close ties with the regional B'nai B'rith lodge in New Orleans.

The secular organization sent a Torah for the benevolent association's first services in 1872 and three years later lent Temple Emanu-El $4,000 for the erection of its first building.[41] Most of the Hebrew Benevolent Association members belonged to the Dallas B'nai B'rith Lodge, founded in 1873, and David Goslin, Dallas B'nai B'rith's second president (after Charles Kahn), was Temple Emanu-El's first president. Both organizations stressed fellowship, but the local Benevolent Association directed its efforts toward mutual aid in Dallas, establishing a cemetery, and holding services. The national service organization offered a young man nationwide assistance—interest-free loans, burial insurance, and widow and orphan annuities for his survivors amounting to $1,000. These benefits were applicable even if a newcomer left the city, as by 1861 B'nai B'rith had expanded its lodges to every major Jewish community across the United States. In the later part of the nineteenth century the organization turned to philanthropic work, founding orphanages and administering hospitals, and in the twentieth century bolstered organizations such as the Anti-Defamation League, formed to protect Jews' human rights everywhere.

For the first Jewish services in Dallas, the Hebrew Benevolent Association engaged an Orthodox layman, Aaron Miller (whose grandson Henry S. Miller, Sr. and great-granddaughter Carmen Miller Michael later served as presidents of Temple Emanu-El) to conduct services.[42] Since the members had raised $65 by selling "Mitzvahs" (honors related to holding and reading from the Torah) and expenses only totaled $10.65, it could afford to send a then rather handsome $25 to B'nai B'rith in New Orleans for the privilege of borrowing the Torah. The remainder of the sum stayed in its treasury. The following year the members purchased their own Scroll for $50, for which they asked fellow member David Goslin to fashion a "closet."[43]

As the only Jewish organization in town, the association invited "all the Israelites" to participate in a Purim Ball in March 1873 and advised a committee of invitation "to invite all those that they see proper" to a picnic in May. The members budgeted the grand sum of $75 to plan the picnic but then had to solicit $3.50 from each member to make up the slack.[44] By September 1874 the association could claim almost thirty members, most of them new arrivals in the city; only four of the original eleven men still belonged: Alex Sanger, Emanuel Tillman, August J. Rosenfield, and F. H. Baum. Moses Ullman, the first president, relocated to Galveston, and others may also have left the city. Nevertheless, although individuals may have been in flux, the community endured.

According to the 1875 city directory, approximately forty-two men recognizable as Jews because of their involvement with the Dallas Hebrew Benevolent Association, B'nai B'rith, or membership later in Temple Emanu-El, were living in Dallas. By far the greatest number, twenty-three, listed their occupation as merchants, a designation which usually translated as owning a dry goods store, and the next largest group, eleven, described themselves as clerks. Of the remaining eight residents, two were tobacco dealers, two were peddlers, and the rest were engaged as baker, tailor, and grocer, with one man unemployed.[45]

Naturally, the prime concern of these men was their ability to make a living. Professor Jacob Marcus has described the priorities of the American Jew living in the nineteenth century:

> In principle the Jew had to have a community in order to survive; this he knew and never forgot. Yet remaining a Jew was probably not his highest priority; that was allocated to the job of making a living. Next came the obligation to be a Jew, albeit a permissive one, and close on its heels was the fervent wish to become an American.[46] ॐ

Lehman Sanger opened the fourth Sanger store in Texas in 1865 at Millican, the northern terminus of the Houston and Texas Central railway.

Philip Sanger joined Alex Sanger at the Dallas store in 1872. A founding officer of Temple Emanu-El in 1875, Philip was president from 1889 until 1894.

Following the railroad north, Alexander Sanger opened the Dallas branch of Sanger Bros. in 1872, the same year he helped found the Hebrew Benevolent Association. Immediately plunging into civic affairs, Alex Sanger was elected city alderman in 1873.

CHAPTER 2

Reform Judaism American Style

The ritual then at the disposal of the Israelites of the city was altogether in Hebrew, and there were a considerable number of young American Israelites who did not understand the language, and to make the services interesting to them was the serious question.

American Israelite, February 4, 1887, Dallas, Texas

The American version of Reform Judaism became the cornerstone upon which Temple Emanu-El laid its foundation. The Reform movement in Judaism, which began in Europe in the late eighteenth and early nineteenth century, took root in Hamburg, a German commercial center with a large Jewish community. In 1818 many of Hamburg's Jewish inhabitants, who had become highly acculturated and wanted to "express religious feelings within an acceptable setting," formed the New Israelite Temple Association.[1] These reformers wanted to modify their service without compromising their "aesthetic and moral sensibilities" as they became more like their Christian neighbors and entered into social relationships with non-Jews. Accordingly, they altered their service to include the recitation of some prayers in the vernacular, a sermon in German, and choral song accompanied by organ music.[2]

Shortly after the inception of the German Reform movement, the first stirring of the Reform movement in American Judaism appeared in the old Sephardic (Spanish and Portuguese) congregation of Beth Elohim in Charleston, South Carolina, which had been founded in 1750. By the early nineteenth century, estimates of the Jewish population of the United States ranged from 3,000 to 6,000. Approximately 600 Jews, the largest concentration in any city in the United States, resided in Charleston. The southern city had a tradition of religious liberalism and pluralism completely different from the "all pervasive pattern of Jewish thought, action, outlook, and association" the original Jewish settlers had left behind in their tightly knit ancestral communities of eighteenth-century Europe.[3]

In this American setting of equality and social interaction, some members of Beth Elohim "desired to become in their worship more like their friendly non-Jewish neighbors, particularly the Protestants who were in the great majority."[4] The problem for these intellectual and modern Jews was how to "change their Judaism to suit their changed circumstances, feeling that otherwise it would not survive; and, if to change, what changes to make." Other members of the congregation balked at tampering with the Sephardic service which was in Hebrew interspersed with some Spanish—even though a great many descendants of English, Portuguese, and German immigrants understood no Hebrew or Spanish. They "thought it ironical that their religion, which had survived centuries of persecution, should in the end be changed in a country where they were free to worship as they pleased." Although the Charleston Jews were aware of efforts in Germany to modify the worship service, Charleston had attracted few immigrants for the previous twenty years and had no contact with groups from abroad. Their inclination for reform apparently arose from their own initiatives. In 1824, forty-seven members of Beth Elohim presented a petition asking for adjustments in the traditional ritual. They sought to shorten the service and add an English sermon as well as to eliminate some Hebrew prayers, stating, "the principal parts, and if possible all that is read in Hebrew, should also be read in English (that being the language of the country) so everyone could understand each part of the service."[6] When their petition was rejected as unconstitutional and unworthy of discussion, about twelve of the petitioners organized The Reformed Society of Israelites. In two years the society grew to about fifty members who with their families numbered 200 people, a sizable group comparable to the 300 congregants belonging to Beth Elohim. In the manner of their fellow advocates of reform in Germany, the society's "way of thinking" progressed far beyond just wanting to shorten and Anglicize the service. The reformers, deciding to incorporate relevant liturgy useful to them and the society in which they lived, assembled their own prayer book, which included some passages from the old ritual and a few original prayers. They also worshipped with their heads uncovered and introduced instrumental music into the service, both significant departures from the old tradition.

Not quite ten years after the rift, the zeal for a separate organization faded. The Society of Israelites quietly disbanded, and some of its members returned to Beth Elohim. Its leaders who remained in Charleston (which began to decline economically at the same time the city of New York began its commercial emergence) were instrumental in Beth Elohim's relinquishing Orthodoxy for Reform Judaism, winning controversies concerning the introduction of an organ, and the abandonment of the second day of holidays. Just as the reformers had once departed Beth Elohim, now the objecting minority resigned to form a new Orthodox congregation, Shearith Israel, splitting Charleston Jewry into Reform and Orthodox factions.[7] During the period in which Charleston reformers tried to retain the basic beliefs of their religion while modulating Jewish practice to appeal to their Americanized co-religionists who lacked a knowledge of Judaism, their timing was ahead of their fellow Jews. In a few short years the Reform movement they inaugurated would be bolstered by a wave of reform-minded immigrant Jews from Germany.

The leader of the Reform Jews, particularly of those in the South and Midwest, was the redoubtable, dynamic Isaac Mayer Wise. In 1846 Wise, then a young man, set out from Bohemia intent on leaving behind religious authorities he deemed antiquated and charting a new direction in a new land. Once in America, as rabbi of Bene Yeshurun in Cincinnati, he developed "one consuming passion, to make the Jews absolutely at home as equals in America."[8] In his community he challenged every slur on Jews and fought valiantly for the separation of church and state in the public schools and every public institution.

Isaac Wise's most telling contribution to the Reform movement was

21

his successful effort to "stimulate, unify, and give direction" to American Reform Judaism.[9] To achieve his goal of modernizing the service and making it conform to religious customs in America, Wise shortened the service, allowed male and female members of the family to sit together, and introduced an organ and a choir. He advocated using English in the synagogue and abolishing dietary laws, stating, "As citizens we must not be different from the rest. In religion only are we Jews, and in all other respects we are American citizens."[10] In 1865 he introduced a new prayer book, *Minhag America*, "the American way," whose American-Jewish code of ritual practice underlined the theology that "doctrines inconsistent with reason are no longer tenable."[11] In one of his autobiographies Wise remembered that "nothing new was created; the old was shortened. . . . We had to sacrifice everything related to throne, crown, and dynasty (the sacrificial cult, the messiah, the return to Palestine) and lifted the narrow nationalism as much as possible to universalism."[12] For instance, instead of inserting a prayer for the return of Israel to Palestine, Wise substituted a prayer for the deliverance and brotherhood of all nations.

In competition with a more radically reformed prayer book in Hebrew and German, Rabbi David Einhorn's *Olat Tamid* (Perpetual Offering), Wise's liturgy was popular in small towns able to support only a single congregation embracing and bridging both Orthodox and Reform Judaism and requiring a compromise liturgy incorporating Hebrew and English (or German). *Minhag America* soon became the dominant liturgy of congregations in the Midwest and South, where Wise had the greatest influence. In the 1870s and 1880s it was the most widely used Reform prayer book before the adoption of the *Union Prayer Book* in the early 1890s by the Central Conference of American Rabbis.[13]

Isaac Wise's grand dream was to unite American Jews through their rabbinic leaders in a "Union of American Israel" which would found and operate a college to train American rabbis. However, Wise's attempts to reconcile the conservative and liberal factions of American Jewry failed and would have been completely stymied but for the efforts of the lay leadership of congregations in the West. These enterprising laymen had built synagogues, orphanages, and hospitals. In order to ensure rabbinical leadership, scarce everywhere in the United States but particularly so in the West, these pacesetters were now ready to support a seminary that would educate native-born preachers and teachers to broadcast the message of Judaism easily and effectively. The clarion "call for a convention" was issued from the Jews of Cincinnati to every known congregation in the West and South. From thirteen states, thirty-four congregations possessing close to 2,000 members responded to the summons in 1873 to form the Union of American Hebrew Congregations. Two years later Isaac Wise began his duties as the volunteer part-time head of Hebrew Union College, which ordained four American-trained rabbis in the first graduating class of 1883.[14]

More than a hundred congregations sent delegates to the ceremonies for the ordination, which were marred by the inclusion of shrimp at the lavish graduation dinner. This "terefa (unkosher) banquet" was totally unacceptable to those rabbis who observed the dietary laws. In his autobiography, David Philipson, one of the graduates at the first commencement who later filled the pulpit in Dallas for a year, remembered that "terrific excitement ensued when two rabbis rose from their seats and rushed from the room."[15] Other traditionally minded rabbis may not have walked out that evening, but they never returned to the umbrella organization founded by Isaac Wise. The dietary issue was just one example of divergent viewpoints between the liberal and conservative factions that spurred the establishment of a Conservative rabbinical seminary and made the unification of Jews in America an impractical dream.

The founders of Temple Emanu-El were an integral part of Isaac Mayer Wise's immigrant generation of German Jews who established Reform congregations across the United States. At the dedication of the first temple in 1876, President David Goslin, a native of Prussia, stated that "this great United States is the land we recognize as our country, and glorious Texas and our prosperous city of Dallas as our home," underscoring the members' desire to meld into the fabric of American and Dallas culture.[16] His remarks echoed those delivered in 1841 to the first Charleston reformers by their minister, Gustavus Poznanski: "This synagogue is our temple, this city our Jerusalem, this happy land our Palestine, and as our fathers defended with their lives that temple, that city, and that land so will their sons defend this temple, this city, and this land."[17]

The movement for a permanent congregation in Dallas was vigorously pressed by the Ladies Hebrew Benevolent Association, which "sprang into life" in January of 1875 to "supply a long felt want . . . of regular religious services and of instruction to their children in the religion of their fathers."[18] The women "gave a series of entertainments and with the proceeds, purchased the lot on Commerce Street" as the site for a permanent building.[19] Just before the New Year holidays their efforts "began to attract attention," and "the necessity for some organization which should accomplish the aims of the ladies became so apparent to everybody" that David Goslin, a trustee of the Hebrew Benevolent Association and president of the B'nai B'rith Lodge, was asked to lecture in English at the New Year service to discuss the need for a congregation.[20]

As a prominent and representative member of the two extant Jewish organizations in the city, Goslin issued a call to his fellow Jews to organize a congregation, to erect a house of worship, and to establish a school for the education of their children. That very day, September 30, 1875, his words inspired fifty-one men to pledge their support to a *Minhag America* congregation.[21] By adopting Isaac Wise's prayer book, *Minhag America*, the founders of the congregation allied themselves with the Reform movement in Judaism as expounded by Rabbi Wise. The members proceeded to elect David Goslin president of Congregation Emanu-El, translated from the Hebrew as "God is with us," and chose Philip Sanger, Emanuel Tillman, Alexander Sanger, August Israelsky, and Henry Loeb as officers.

Almost immediately, the new congregation decided to engage a minister (in England and America a term interchangeable with rabbi), allowing $1,500 for his annual salary, and asked Rabbi Isaac Wise to send a prospective rabbi to Dallas. The correspondent for the *American Israelite*, a weekly newspaper founded and edited by Wise, reported the rabbinic auditions:

> Jewish circles were in a state of excitement; a congregation has just been formed, and a minister was wanted. For this position there

were two candidates, the Rev. Mr. A. Suhler, formerly of Akron, Ohio, recommended here by Dr. I. M. Wise, and the Rev. Mr. Rosenspitz, formerly of San Antonio, Texas. Both these gentlemen had been requested to remain until a final decision could be arrived at and it had been agreed that on Friday evening, October 29, both should deliver a sermon, the Rev. Rosenspitz in English, and the Rev. Suhler in German, and from these sermons the merits of the candidates should be judged.[22]

Mr. Rosenspitz, dressed in traditional head covering and prayer shawl, uttered a forty-five minute homily in English, followed by a selection of prayers. Mr. Suhler, dressed in plain clothes, delivered a brief discourse in German, "short, earnest, and impressive, carrying the audience with him from the start and virtually electing himself."[23]

Rabbi Aaron Suhler, who was born in Germany, had graduated with honors in 1866 from the Jewish Seminary in Wurtzburg, Germany, and then taught German language and Hebrew literature in Mainz. Before assuming the Dallas post, he had acted as rabbi in Akron, Ohio. On May 28, 1876, just seven months after coming to Dallas, Rabbi Suhler dedicated Temple Emanu-El, the first Jewish house of worship in North Texas. Helping Rabbi Suhler officiate at the ceremony was Rabbi Chajim (Heinrich) Schwarz, the first rabbi to settle in Texas, according to Professor Jacob R. Marcus. Born in Prussian-occupied Poland, the older rabbinic scholar was the patriarch of a large family and had recently joined his children at Hempstead, the county seat located just north of Houston. One of his daughters later married Rabbi Suhler, and his great-grandchildren would include brothers Robert and Theodore Strauss and Bernice Rosenwasser Davis, all subsequent members of Temple Emanu-El.[24]

The Moorish Revival synagogue designed by Carl De Grote was located on Commerce Street near Field across from St. Matthew's Episcopal Cathedral. The *Dallas Daily Herald* printed four commendatory columns on May 30, 1876, describing the dedication:

The chaste and beautiful building just finished by the Israelites of Dallas was dedicated on Sunday evening. At an early hour the building was crowded with the largest congregation assembled in our city, and embraced members of every congregation in the city who had been invited to be present. The auditorium was brilliantly illuminated by gas chandeliers and decorated with a profusion of the choicest hot-house flowers and plants. The vast audience, all expectation, preserved the greatest decorum. The main entrance was closed after the audience was seated. A few moments afterwards a knocking was heard at the door. The Rabbi, the Rev. A. Suhler, who had approached the door said: "Who comes there" to which Mr. D. Goslin, president of Congregation Emanu-El, responded: "Your delegation bearing the Holy Scroll, the Torah, the banner of light and truth."[25]

David Goslin proceeded down the aisle ahead of two little girls, Sophie Goez and Hattie Bauer, who carried a flower-bedecked cushion holding the keys to the temple. Next marched Jacob E. Wolf, representing the Ladies Benevolent Association; M. Goslin carrying the Holy Scroll, the Torah originally purchased by the Hebrew Benevolent Association in 1873 and given by its members to their new congregation; then Rabbi Suhler and Rabbi Schwarz; and last Philip Sanger, vice-president of the congregation. The *Herald* article continued mellifluously:

At the close of the sermon [The Lord is in His Holy Temple] the Rabbi delivered the beautiful Hebrew prayer of invocation to the Deity to consecrate and bless the temple to His divine worship, which was followed by a hymn [sung by the choir accompanied on the organ] and benediction when the congregation was dismissed.

By 1876 Dallas Jewry had established a religious house, an emblem of their permanence in the city.

One side of the temple, which cost approximately $14,000 to build, was devoted to services. Entered by a door on the left side of the vestibule, the sanctuary contained rows of pews with seating for 160. The other part of the temple housed the free Congregation Emanu-El School, where Rabbi Suhler taught the children of temple members. Some question exists whether Emanu-El's day school, which later employed some non-Jewish teachers, continued to be a free school supported by the congregation or whether it charged a small fee to compensate the teachers and to defray expenses.[26] Apparently the congregation could not support both itself and the school, so the Ladies Hebrew Benevolent Association took the initiative to overcome a major financial hurdle—a debt of $3,000—by holding a fair. The *Israelite's* Dallas correspondent, writing under the intriguing pseudonym of "Czar," reported the success of the undertaking in 1879:

> The committee [men and women] went to work with a vim, obtained reduced rates on all the railroads centering at this point, advertised the affair, interested all our prominent Christian friends by putting them on various committees, and on the 4th of February, everything being in readiness, the fair opened, and such a fair was never seen in Texas before. . . . Of course it was in the largest hall in the city, and the decorations were gotten up in the best of taste. About 3,000 feet of lumber and nearly as many yards of blue and white material were used. . . . Well we cleared the debt from the temple and are satisfied.[27]

After four years Rabbi Suhler left Emanu-El for Hebrew Sinai in Jefferson. The Reform temple in East Texas had been founded in 1875, ironically just as Jefferson was coming to the end of its economic boom as an inland port. As long as the barrage of logs, brush, and mud had clogged the Big Cypress and created a high-water bayou at Jefferson, the city enjoyed a shipping passageway to the Gulf and served as the trade center of Northeast Texas. When the Federal Corps of Engineers dynamited the dam and sent the water flowing freely to the Gulf, lowering the water level and making reliable boat passage impossible, Jefferson declined economically. Shreveport, which was closer to the Gulf, became the favored commercial port, and railroad-rich Dallas strode on the scene in its role as distribution center. As the population of Jefferson dwindled, most of its Jews left. Rabbi Suhler returned to Dallas for a brief stint in the cigar business and then journeyed to Waco in 1883 to serve as rabbi of Congregation Rodef Sholom. A man of many turns, he later became a life insurance agent and edited Waco's German-language newspaper.

By September 1879, when Herman M. Bien became Emanu-El's second rabbi and the Superintendent of Congregation Emanu-El School, the school had changed from an institution open to only Jewish children to one welcoming the community. The approximately seventy-five to 100 young pupils enrolled for the school term were taught by the rabbi and two assistants. Young Sally Dysterbach's father, Abraham Dysterbach, who owned a dry goods store on Main Street, could be proud of her report card for the 1879-1880 term, noting her perfect deportment and her proficiency in reading, spelling, arithmetic, German, and Hebrew. In 1885 the school opened with seventy-eight pupils, but with the city's inauguration of public education, the congregation closed its school the next year, leaving its religious school as the only educational facility at the temple. Emanuel Tillman, then an officer of Emanu-El, was one of the three men who met to organize the Dallas public schools, serving as the first secretary of the Board of School Trustees.

Rabbi Bien, who officiated at Temple Emanu-El from 1879 to 1883, had the most interesting, varied, and peripatetic career of any rabbi associated with the early congregation. Born and educated in Germany, he received a master of philosophy degree from the University of Rostock and completed the requirements for rabbi at the Rabbinical College in the city of Cassel before emigrating in 1856 to New Haven, where he became minister of the Reform congregation. In 1858 he went to Temple Emanu-El in San Francisco, the home of two of his five sisters and four brothers living in the United States. He then moved on to Virginia City, Nevada, where he was elected to the first legislature and sponsored the bill forming the educational system of Nevada. During his residence in Nevada President Abraham Lincoln appointed him consul to Frankfort-on-Main, but while he was on his way to the consulate via New York, Lincoln was assassinated. Bien's commission was revoked. He then spent the next thirteen years in New York where he edited a Jewish Reform newspaper called the *Progress*. In 1877 he was called to Chicago by the Rodef Sholom congregation to be their rabbi and had his then famous controversy with the preacher of agnosticism, Robert J. Ingersoll. Refuting Ingersoll, Bien "delivered his well known lecture, 'Lying Made Easy,' in response to that noted infidel's address on 'Moses and his Mistakes.'"[28] Rabbi Bien's answer was quickly published and sold 5,000 copies, a brisk circulation for that time. After Herman Bien came to Emanu-El in 1879, the notoriety he derived from the clash with Ingersoll probably prompted John Henry Brown, a noted early Dallas historian, to include the rabbi in *The Encyclopedia of the New West*. Brown described him as a man standing five feet eight inches tall and weighing 180 pounds with "an affable and engaging manner" whose duties besides preaching included supervising 100 students at Congregation Emanu-El School.

The early days of Congregation Emanu-El were beset with problems. Within three years after the temple declared itself a *Minhag America* congregation and adopted Issac Wise's prayer book, apparently not everyone was pleased with *Minhag America* as the form of worship. The ever eagle-eyed "Czar" reported the friction in the *Israelite*:

> Every Friday night and Sabbath morning during the year services were held in our beautiful temple, which were attended by a fair number of the congregation who take interest in such matters, and no grumbling would be heard, but at the approach of the holidays signs of dissatisfaction would appear and there would always be some, those who had not attended divine services since the last holidays, who would feel sore about the way things had been carried on, although they had taken no part in it. During the holidays the outsiders, non-members of the congregation, would hold service in some rented hall in the way their fathers did in the old country, and the disaffected portion of our congregation would be with them.[29]

When several of the more traditional members resigned, new members took their place. Thus the congregation was not hurt financially (although Czar gloomily concluded that the congregation "had gone to the dogs"). But some members thought that the conflict should be resolved and the parties reconciled. Most predictions pointed to the breakup of the congregation, but a committee of members and non-members solved the dispute by creating a statesmanlike compromise, *Minhag Dallas*. The congregation printed its own prayer book (or "programme" as it was called by some of the members) which was adopted almost unanimously.[30]

The "Temple Emanu-El Ritual" was used by the congregation for almost twenty years until Edward Chapman, rabbi from 1885 to 1897, asked the board of directors in 1896 to replace it with the *Union Prayer Book* as adopted by the Central Conference of American Rabbis.[31] This first official liberal prayer book was designed to supplant individual liturgies like the "Temple Emanu-El Ritual," which were written and reproduced by rabbis of individual congregations. The *Union Prayer Book* was based primarily on David Einhorn's *Olath Tamid* (Perpetual Offering), first published in 1858 in Hebrew and German and then in Hebrew and English, which triumphed over Isaac M. Wise's *Minhag America*. Until his death in 1879, Einhorn "was America's strongest voice for radical, uncompromising Reform Judaism" as opposed to Wise's more conciliatory and conservative approach.[32] Unlike *Minhag America*, the *Union Prayer Book* represented not just the voice of one man but rather expressed the consensus of sentiments of the Central Conference of American Rabbis.

Deciding upon an acceptable prayer book was not the only controversy confronting the Temple. After Rabbi Herman Bien departed in 1881, a serious quarrel erupted concurrent with the arrival of the Reverend Mr. Schuhl from the Mound Street Temple in Cincinnati. Initially, Schuhl's appointment caused quite a stir concerning his qualifications. The *Israelite* reprinted a letter from the columns of the *Cincinnati Enquirer* which expressed reservations about Schuhl:

> In the religious notes of to-day's paper, I have noticed that the Rev. Dr. Henry Schuhl was leaving for Dallas, Texas. You will oblige a great many Jewish citizens and readers of your valuable paper by correcting a grave error, as Mr. Henry Schuhl is by no means a DD [Doctor of Divinity] or a rabbi, but only a reader who recites prayers

and assists thereby the Rev. Dr. M. Lilienthal, the regular rabbi of the Mound Street Temple.

"An Old Israelite"

The *Israelite* retorted by defending Schuhl's credentials:

The fact that Mr. Schuhl was for two years reader in the Mound Street Temple does not tell that he or is not a rabbi or a DD. Nor did Mr. Schuhl ever claim to be either, and the congregation that elected him did certainly not intend to elect a rabbi or a DD. They advertised for "a minister" and did elect one to their satisfaction, one we think, who will discharge his duties well, although he be less learned than either Rabbi Akiba or Moses Mendelssohn. Hitherto we have no DD among Jewish scholars here or abroad, because Jewish authorities never conferred that degree. The title of rabbi, according to Jewish custom, is claimed by those who hold a diploma to this effect by some acknowledged authority. Whether Mr. Schuhl is in possession of such a diploma is one of those things which "An Old Israelite" does not know nor do we. But it is nobody's business at present to know it except that of the congregation that elects him. The congregation does not advertise for a rabbi, it wants a minister: hence all the controversy on the subject is of no avail. Let Mr. Schuhl depart in peace, he has done you no harm; let him try to do as much good as he can with or without title. He is a young man of talent and enthusiasm; whatsoever he does not know he may learn. Do not discourage a man who tries to rise in the world.[33]

Perhaps Isaac Mayer Wise, the editor of the *American Israelite*, wrote the rebuttal to the charges of "An Old Israelite" with his own situation in mind. Starting out in the United States in just the same manner as Schuhl, Wise must have identified with a young "minister" coming west in the middle to late nineteenth century to be "rabbi" to an embryonic congregation in far away Texas.

Apparently Henry Schuhl was not a good choice as religious leader of Temple Emanu-El. According to a history of the congregation written in

31

1914 by its rabbi, Dr. William H. Greenburg, his ministry caused a rupture:

> There was a tremendous upheaval among the Jewish people, and a
> large number of the most representative men withdrew from the
> congregation and immediately resolved to organize a separate
> Congregation of their own—though they formed a minority of the
> membership of Temple Emanu-El.[34]

Included among this dissenting group were Philip Sanger, plus past
presidents David Goslin and Emanuel Tillman. At a meeting on July 22,
1883, these former mainstays of Emanu-El started Congregation Ahavas
Shalom which ironically translates as the love of peace, "a name well chosen
and that spoke volumes as to the attitude of this newly formed congregation towards the older."[35] The rival congregation adopted the constitution
and bylaws of Temple Emanu-El and held its meetings in what was then
called Mayer's Hall, above Simon Mayer's Beer Garden on Ervay Street,
which advertised in the 1882 *Dallas City and County Directory*, "None But
the Proper Characters Admitted."

The new congregation engaged Rabbi David Philipson, who had
just graduated from the first class of Hebrew Union College, to conduct
its High Holy Days services. In his autobiography, *My Life As An
American Jew*, Philipson remembered the disturbing circumstances that
led to his arrival in Dallas:

> This group had seceded from the congregation, owing to their dis-
> satisfaction with the antics of a minister of the congregation. This
> man, who had no rabbinical training but who was endowed with a
> good singing voice, had led the congregation for a number of years.
> His disgraceful conduct so chagrined a number of leading members
> that they seceded and formed a new congregation. When I reached
> Dallas, which was at that time a city of moderate size but growing,
> I found a disrupted community. The group that had secured my ser-
> vices had rented a hall in which the holy-day worship was to be con-
> ducted. A number of singers had been engaged as a choir. As this

was my first experience in the pulpit, I had my hands more than full. I had to guide the rehearsals of the choir. Fortunately I had written the sermons before I left Cincinnati. I say "fortunately," for I would scarcely have found the time in Dallas. I was overwhelmed with the hospitality of the members of this new congregation. I was the house guest of Dr. and Mrs. Tillman, a most gracious couple.[36]

Later in his career as rabbi of K. K. Bene Israel in Cincinnati, Philipson had a considerable influence upon Classical Reform Judaism.

The breach in the congregation was shortly healed after Henry Schuhl left Emanu-El in 1884 and Rabbi Joseph Silverman was elected minister. Congregation Ahavas Shalom relinquished its separate identity and "became one again" with Emanu-El.[37] Also, that year a small group of Orthodox Jews in the city organized a congregation which they named Shearith Israel, the Remnant of Israel, and in 1892 its members built a synagogue on Jackson Street. Rabbi Silverman stayed in Dallas for one year and then accepted a position in Galveston before returning to New York, where he eventually became rabbi of Temple Emanu-El. A colleague writing about Silverman's life said that Silverman's first holiday position, Dallas, and his next pulpit, Galveston, exemplified communities far beyond the pale of Jewish influence.[38] The writer was absolutely correct. In fact, Dallas was still a frontier town—the buffalo hide capital of the world in 1875. Until about 1890 it was very much a part of the Wild West and persisted as a destination for cattle drives and a haven for gamblers who operated so openly and flagrantly that they formed a major industry. Not until the early 1890s did Dallas start to shake its cow town image, opting for "clean" industry—banking, finance, and insurance.[39] ᛩ

David Goslin, president of the B'nai B'rith Lodge, issued the call for a Jewish congregation and became Temple Emanu-El's first president.

Aaron Suhler served the congregation from 1875 to 1879 as rabbi and as director of the non-denominational Congregation Emanu-El School.

Temple Emanu-El's first building on lower Commerce Street was located across the street from St. Matthew's Episcopal Cathedral.

Emanuel and Franceska Tillman were mainstays of the early temple. Emanuel Tillman was a founder of the Hebrew Benevolent Association and officiated as president of Temple Emanu-El. He was secretary of the first Dallas school board and served as mayor pro-tem under Ben E. Cabell.

CHAPTER 3

PASSAGE TO MATURITY

In doing their good deeds, the Jews are no halfway people.

Dallas Herald, September 27, 1873

In order to maintain any semblance of Jewish life on the frontier, each small Jewish community tried to organize itself and stand firmly together in the face of poverty and the need for mutual aid. Newcomers were eagerly welcomed and accepted if they offered to do their share. The Jews' efforts to take care of themselves and their willingness to help others were commended by the *Dallas Herald* which editorialized on September 27, 1873, "Never, perhaps in the whole history of this country, has the generous kindness of the Jews been more substantially demonstrated than now, when a great scourge has fallen upon the people of our sister city, and had laid them at the mercy and charity of their neighbors." The scourge was a virulent, disastrous yellow fever epidemic. In a relief effort, the Jewish communities in Jefferson and Dallas each raised $1,000 to help "the sufferers" in Shreveport, prompting the *Herald* to trumpet:

> They open their purses and give to the extent of their means, never inquiring whether their contributions are destined for the relief of Jew or Gentile. Furthermore, they are organized for the successful prosecution of their charitable enterprises. Their societies and benevolent associations, they always keep intact and at no time do their beneficent lights shine more effulgently than when calamities

befall us. We honor our Jewish citizens for their magnanimity and commend their praiseworthy example as deserving of the highest emulation by us all.[1]

It became obvious that, for the Jewish people, sharing and mutual aid enhanced the sense of community and, for the newly arrived, was a survival mechanism to combat isolation.

Jews, like other Americans in the nineteenth century, were "joiners." Banding together with others of like nationality or religion eased the immigrants' loneliness. Newcomers bonded to help each other and to feel comfortable among people with common interests and backgrounds. Dallas Jews also undertook civic responsibilities for the benefit of their new community. As early as 1873, Hook and Ladder Company Number 1, the first volunteer fire brigade in the city, listed most of the men in the Hebrew Benevolent Association as members. In 1878 Abraham Dysterbach was the treasurer of Hook and Ladder Company Number 32; Alex Sanger, former president of the Fire Department in 1875, was president of Dallas Steam Fire Engine Company Number 1; and Lee Cohn was its treasurer.[2]

Jews who wanted to socialize in a casual way formed organizations devoted to social and cultural pursuits. A secular organization that sprang up spontaneously among Jews in communities across the United States was the Young Men's Hebrew Association (YMHA), which evolved simultaneously with the Young Men's Christian Association (YMCA), but was more social and less religiously oriented. A group of young men formed the Dallas YMHA in 1879. When the organization was chartered in 1881, prominent grocer Sigmund Loeb became its president. He also served as president of Temple Emanu-El from 1883–1884 and as city alderman from 1882–1891, two of those years as mayor pro-tem. Temple member Ben Irelson, a city alderman as well as a member of the board of education, also served as president of the YMHA. In 1886 he chaired an "Entertainment" for the "literary, musical, social improvement, and pleasure" of its members at the YMHA Hall above Mayer's Beer Garden. The program featured three musical solos—piano, flute, and violin, two recitations, a singer, and a scholarly address on "Judaism of Today" by David A. Eldridge, a lawyer who became secretary of Temple Emanu-El in 1901 and served until 1914. The association's hall was also a popular place for wedding receptions and balls, such as the 1886 Purim Masquerade Ball held by the Ladies Hebrew Benevolent Association.[3]

To raise money for a permanent building, in 1886 the YMHA building committee sold stock at $10 per share, bearing eight percent interest. The *Dallas News* reported the assured construction of a building on Ervay and Jackson streets to house a gymnasium and club rooms in the basement, reception and dining rooms on the first floor, and a large hall with a stage on the second floor:

> The YMHA's working committees are composed of the best element of our Jewish society and the *News* can safely predict that ere the close of the year the city will see one of the best equipped and most elegant club houses in the South. . . . The association is in a very prosperous and healthy condition, and with the officers who are now at the helm, it will always be in the future as in past—an honor to the growing city of Dallas.[4]

In 1890, three years after the clubhouse was built, the organization changed its name to the Phoenix Club, which in 1906 evolved into the Columbian Club.

Members of Temple Emanu-El often joined other fraternal organizations in town, particularly the Masonic lodges. Frequently these same men served as alderman in the city government and on the boards of civic organizations. The lodges represented an intertwined network which contributed greatly to the business and philanthropic dealings of the city. When David Goslin, manager of The China Hall, a chinaware and household goods store on Elm Street, died in 1899, "the several lodges in which he was a member were present to do him honor." For the funeral of this first president of Temple Emanu-El, president of the B'nai B'rith Lodge, and founder of the volunteer fire department, the *Dallas News* was not surprised that "carriages in the procession extended for a distance of over a mile" as the funeral "was among the largest attended ever witnessed in Dallas . . . the sorrow for the departed was not denominational but seemed to be shared in common by Jew and Gentile."[5]

When Samuel Klein, president of Temple Emanu-El from 1879 to 1881, came to Dallas in 1873 and went into the liquor business, he joined B'nai B'rith, the Masons, and the Knights of Pythias. At the time the new city charter was granted in 1893, he was serving as city alderman and was chosen the first president of the city council. He was also the founding president of Dallas' first baseball club, "The Brownstockings," organized in 1883.[6] Emanuel Tillman was another temple president, as well as a B'nai B'rith and YMHA officer, and was active in civic affairs before the turn of the century. He was the secretary of the first Dallas School Board of Trustees in 1884, served as alderman from the 4th Ward and mayor pro tem under Ben E. Cabell, and was also secretary of the Scottish Rite Masonic bodies.[7] Charles Kahn, owner of a bakery, was the founding president of the B'nai B'rith Lodge in 1873. An officer in the Odd Fellows organization and the Dallas Turn Verein, a German gymnastic society, he served as chief of the volunteer fire department from 1881 to 1884, when the city converted it to a paid department. Kahn was also elected an alderman from the 4th Ward, as was Leo Wolfson, secretary of Temple Emanu-El from 1889 to 1901. In fact, from 1881 to 1904 there was a Jewish seat on the city council from the 4th Ward, the South Dallas residential area where most Jewish people lived.[8]

Alex and Philip Sanger were involved with, or consulted about, virtually every civic project in the city. According to his great-nephew, Joseph Sanger Linz, Alex Sanger loved the spotlight: "He wanted to do it all, be it all."[9] A founder of the Texas State Fair and Exposition in 1886, which became the largest fair in the nation and is still located in South Dallas at Fair Park, he served as its officer and president. He handled the funds for the Dallas Public Library, to which Sanger Brothers contributed $1,000 after Andrew Carnegie in 1901 had donated $50,000 for its original building. A "compulsive" civic booster and "a good mixer," Alex Sanger headed up banquets or committees for out-of-town investors like "the large party of eastern capitalists prospecting in Texas for investments," and he capped a long civic career by becoming a regent of the University of Texas in 1917.[10]

If Alex Sanger enjoyed the limelight as Sanger Brothers' representative in the community, Philip Sanger was content to work quietly behind the scenes, supporting worthy organizations such as the Buckner Orphans Home or the Industrial School for Boys. Philip was rarely visible at public gatherings, except those he considered absolutely essential.[11] When the devastating depression of 1893 to 1897 cried out for some attempt to establish regular, systematic aid through a city-wide charity, Virginia K. Johnson, a leader in promoting recovery work for needy young women, began a drive to collect clothing for destitute families. She consulted Philip Sanger, who quickly grasped the dire need, and they decided jointly that the city, with no public funds for the needy, should help with leadership and public appeals. Together they visited Mayor W. C. Connor and Police Chief J. C. Arnold, who joined them in a major drive for donations, selecting Sanger Brothers as the central place for the distribution of the much-needed food and clothing.[12] This combined effort served as a model for several businessmen, including the Sangers, on which to base the United Charities, the city's major source of public aid and the precursor of Dallas' Community Chest, founded in 1924, later called the United Fund and then the United Way.

Before the financial panic of 1893 plunged the country into a depression, Dallas' business enterprises were "thriving." But business and agriculture both suffered when the price of cotton dropped and five banks failed. People began leaving the city.[13] Ludwig Philipson, president of the temple in 1897, characterized the lengthy economic downturn as "unequaled in the annals of this country—commerce paralyzed and a feeling of unrest and gloom prevailing in all avenues of trade."[14] The population of Dallas, which had peaked at 44,000 in 1882, declined to less than 39,000 by 1894 and would not regain its previous high mark for several years.

The bleak economic picture contributed to serious problems at the temple, mainly diminishing membership and consequent financial instability. In one year, 1884–1885, the temple lost sixteen member families, leaving just eighty-three paying members, some of whom were delinquent in their dues. Moreover, its income of $5,873 did not meet its yearly expenses of $6,198, much less pay off a $7,050 debt incurred by the leadership. At the 1895 annual meeting, Emanuel M. Kahn, president of the congregation, gloomily announced he could find nothing "of an encouraging nature to report. . . .[w]e continue to exist in a very precarious condition." He chastised the congregation for its "utter indifference to services on Friday night and Saturday morning," and he continued his lament: "Most deplorable" was "the utter indifference of the parents to their children's religious education," for "it is one of the rarest events in the history of the scholastic year that one of the parents of the pupils sets his or her foot in the schoolroom to encourage both the teacher and the pupil."[15] Religious apathy, then, accompanied the economic distress, although it was not necessarily a consequence of it.

The president of the temple attached some of the blame for the congregation's indifference toward attending services and disinterest in the religious school upon the involvement of the members in their secular social club, saying, "Phoenix Club must be charged up, to a considerable extent, with this part of our neglect."[16] The Jewish lodge and club, especially B'nai B'rith, had long been rivals of the synagogue, allowing, by their very existence, the lay leadership in a community to emanate from an organization not tied to the synagogue. The popularity of service organizations like B'nai B'rith and social organizations like the Phoenix Club made ethnic solidarity and fellowship seem more important as a criterion for Jewish life than religious obligation and education.

The solution to the problem? President Kahn decided to engage the women:

> [I] pondered earnestly in what manner to meet the issue and [had] come to the conclusion that there is only one practical way to get out of our dilemma, and that is by enlisting the assistance of our ladies to form an Emanu-El Aid society, through whose influence and work, I hope and believe will bring about a new and more satisfactory condition of affairs.[17]

The women responded to Kahn's plea by forming the Ladies Emanu-El Aid Society and electing Lillie B. Kahn as president. The aid society attempted to alleviate the situation by earning money for the temple, contributing sums such as $223.20 garnered from items sold at a booth at the Texas State Fair held annually in southeast Dallas. But the efforts of the women, no matter how strenuous, could hardly solve the multiple problems facing the congregation.

The rabbi at this time was Edward M. Chapman, a native of London. He had attended Jews College in that city and received academic degrees from London and Oxford universities. Arriving in New York in 1874 at age twenty, he became assistant superintendent of the Hebrew Orphan Asylum and then served as rabbi in Hartford and Brooklyn. After accepting the Dallas position in 1885, he did his best to attract new members, advising the board of directors in 1894 that "I am in treaty with the communities of Ennis & Mineola, looking to some sort of a union with the Temple . . . through which, I trust, the finances of the congregation may be considerably enhanced."[18] Rabbi Chapman's hopes for an increase in the religious school, which had seventy-three pupils enrolled in the religion department and forty-seven in the Hebrew department, were more realistic than was his prospective membership solicitation.

After ten years with the congregation, the rabbi's health deteriorated, and he wished to escape the "long and excessively heated Texas summer" with a sea voyage in the summer of 1895 and a leave of absence in the summer of 1896.[19] By February of 1897 the board of directors had to grapple with "a deplorable condition that has of late existed in our Congregation," which had culminated in the withdrawal of members and the resultant insolvency of the congregation. The board was convinced that "the unfortunate physical condition of our rabbi [was] the primary cause of this state of affairs" and recommended that the congregation cancel its contract with Dr. Chapman and pay him $2,025, the sum of his $225 monthly salary for nine months.[20] After Rabbi Chapman left for New York, the hard-pressed congregation could not afford to hire another rabbi until the fall of 1897. The temple's financial dilemma understandably left the members adrift for nine months, a void which President

Ludwig Philipson attributed "to the complete indifference of a great many of our members." Saturday services had to be discontinued because there were too few men for a *minyan*, the quorum of ten needed for a synagogue service, and Friday night services without a rabbi were very poorly attended.[21]

In the midst of this gloomy scenario for the future well-being of Temple Emanu-El, the congregation advertised in the June 1897 *American Israelite* for "a competent English scholar as Rabbi and Lecturer for $2,000 a year." The *Israelite* noted that the position deserved the attention of a worthy applicant:

> The stipend offered, $2,000 is not very great, but a young, active, zealous, and ambitious man could soon so increase the membership that the congregation could afford to be much more generous.

The man who answered this call, George Alexander Kohut, was a Hungarian who in 1885 came to America as a young boy. He studied at Columbia University and the Jewish Theological Seminary in New York, but ill health resulting from pulmonary disease interrupted his studies, and he received private instruction from his father, the noted rabbi and scholar Dr. Alexander Kohut.[22] The son left for Germany to study and regain his health, but when his physical condition did not improve, he returned to the United States. Shortly afterward, Kohut accepted the position at Temple Emanu-El, possibly lured by the warm, seemingly salutary Texas climate.

A contemporary portrayed George Kohut as blessed with a "radiant and lovable personality," possessing rare charm and bubbling over with enthusiasm—in effect "a Hungarian rhapsody."[23] Upon arriving in Dallas, he "created an era of good feeling" in congregational life, attracting some new members and encouraging the leaders of the congregation to proceed with plans to build a new temple.[24] Just before Dr. Kohut's arrival, Mr. and Mrs. Philip Sanger threw a lawn party "at great expense" and donated the entire proceeds to reduce the debt of the temple and to "get the ball rolling" for a new building.[25] Realizing that the current structure was unsafe as well as too small, the members, upon the recommendation of merchant Adolph Harris, had decided to sell the temple and had already purchased a lot in South Dallas some time before their present difficulties.[26]

The Sangers, always staunch and generous supporters of the temple, put their considerable weight behind the drive for a new temple building. Since 1872 when the first Sanger Brothers store opened in Dallas, the business had grown with the city. Not only were Philip and Alex Sanger considered the leading merchants in Dallas, but Sanger Brothers was known as the premier retail enterprise in the Southwest. One of the reasons for its thriving business was its use of technological innovations for both business and public relations promotion. Sangers' was the first company in the city to use gas lighting and the first, along with Mayer's Beer Garden, to have electricity. In 1881 when the first telephones were installed in Dallas, Sanger Brothers purchased eight, six for the store and two for the mansions of Philip and Alex Sanger on South Ervay Street.[27] Herbert Marcus, one of the founders of Neiman Marcus in 1907, started his retail career in the shoe department of Sanger Brothers under the tutelage of Philip Sanger; years later his wife, the former Minnie Lichtenstein, would warmly remember the Sangers as "the finest people" and the "very epitome of royalty."[28]

Philip Sanger had been president of the temple from 1889 to 1895, and Alex Sanger was perpetual chairman of the new Emanu-El Cemetery established in 1884 on Lemmon and Howell streets, just as he had been chairman of the Hebrew Benevolent Cemetery downtown on Akard Street. In the spring of 1899 Philip Sanger was designated chairman of the Building Committee for the new temple, and Alex Sanger was elected president. Mrs. Alex Sanger, the former Fannie Fechenbach of Cincinnati, undertook the presidency of the *Jahrmarkt*. (*Jahrmarkt* was the name of an annual fair held in various small towns of Germany, to which peasants, merchants, and tradesmen, costumed in quaint national dress, flocked to display and sell their wares.)

On her many trips to Europe, Mrs. Sanger often traveled to Bavaria. Inspired by the indigenous *Jahrmarkt* she conceived the idea of

45

welcoming the citizens of Dallas and visitors from neighboring towns to a week-long German fair in order to raise money for the building fund.[29] Mrs. Sanger's committee of ladies staged a replica of a fair held in a German village that even boasted booths depicting faraway places like Alaska and Japan.

In her memoirs Mrs. Adolph Metzler, who managed the *Jahrmarkt's* ice cream parlor, later exulted over her good fortune "in obtaining scenery from the Dallas Opera House" representing "the snowcapped Klondike mountains and glittering icicles." The illusion created by the backdrop made the seating area seem cooler and more comfortable in Dallas' warm spring weather. According to Virginia Metzler, the leaders of the German fair were "pleased to hand in a nice amount of cash towards building our second Temple."[30] The fair committees involved virtually every member of the ninety-nine families in the congregation, whose efforts accrued $3,500 of the entire $11,000 raised for the new structure. At the close of the *Jahrmarkt*, reigning Dallas society writer Mrs. Hugh Fitzgerald rhapsodized in *Beau Monde* about the "sweeping social and financial success that was not only a credit to the Jewish people but to all the people of Dallas."[31] Plainly, Rabbi Kohut's era of good feeling had generated a sense of cohesion that was largely responsible for the fair's success.

However, to the members' dismay, after only two years with the congregation, Rabbi Kohut decided to leave Dallas in the spring of 1899 for reasons which he would only vaguely intimate in writing to the directors: "I must obey a holier impulse than that which has led me hither among you."[32] The board of directors was loath to accept his resignation and pleaded with him to remain in Dallas. Even after Kohut left for New York, the board persisted and finally persuaded him to stay another year. When he returned to Dallas to dedicate the new temple on November 30, 1899, Philip Sanger praised him for fostering a congenial, cooperative atmosphere conducive to building the temple: "It is largely due to his efforts in bringing peace and harmony to our congregation and his subsequent good work in helping and encouraging every committee" that assured the building committee's success.[33]

The temple's dedication ceremonies, as well, were an example of

Kohut's spirit of fellowship. Predictably, he had invited a rabbi, the Reverend Dr. Samuel Sale of Share Emeth Temple in St. Louis, to give the sermon, but he had also asked representatives from the Christian community to deliver "fellowship addresses." The Right Reverend A. C. Garrett, Episcopal Bishop of Texas; the Reverend Dr. George C. Rankin, editor of *Christian Advocate*; and the Reverend D. C. Limbaugh, pastor of the Unitarian Church, all spoke at the dedication. After the service, members of the congregation drove their carriages to Phoenix Hall, their club just two blocks away, where they celebrated at a dedication dance.

Unfortunately, while speaking from the pulpit at the dedication ceremonies, Rabbi Kohut suffered a severe choking attack and had difficulty catching his breath.[34] Because of their rabbi's incapacity, the board had no choice but to accept his decision to relinquish the Dallas post and return to New York. Even though his poor health prevented him from accepting another rabbinical position, Kohut continued his career as teacher and professor. He later established Camp Kohut in Oxford, Maine, and founded and served as the principal of the Kohut School for Boys in New York.

The new temple, Rabbi Kohut's legacy to Dallas, was "a handsome and imposing structure of red pressed brick with white stone trimming designed by J. Riely Gordon, H.A. Overbeck, and Roy Overbeck."[35] Just south of the business district, it was located in an area originally covered with "a magnificent forest of oak and red cedar trees," which became known as The Cedars.[36] With the coming of the railroads to Dallas in 1872 and 1873 and the resultant surge in new residents, the southern area's residential development had accelerated, for the spurs of the Texas & Pacific Railway along Pacific Avenue effectively blocked the town's growth northward. The first homes built in The Cedars were mostly small, wood-framed Victorian cottages. But as Dallas flourished, its more affluent business and professional men, including Alex and Philip Sanger, began to erect elaborate Victorian mansions along South Ervay Street. Philip Sanger's residence, on the northeast corner of St. Louis and South Ervay streets, was located across the street from the site of Temple Emanu-El. Alex Sanger lived a few blocks away, across from St. Matthew's Cathedral, on South Ervay and Canton streets. The neighborhood was attractive: "The jewel of Ervay Street was, of course, the City Park with its languid lagoon, its forest of willow, oak, and cedar, and its fragile pavilions and gazebos from which open air concerts were given on summer nights."[37]

For about ten years, from 1880 to 1890, The Cedars reigned as an elegant and fashionable residential area. In 1884 two Jewish real estate speculators, Gerson Meyer and Max Rosenfield, had opened a new housing subdivision. They sold lots mainly to Jewish families who settled in an area bordered by Akard, Corsicana, Browder, and St. Louis streets. Then in 1888 two rapid transit companies extended their lines out to Forest Avenue and South Boulevard, opening up the whole South Dallas area for development. Not surprisingly, the influx of people lessened its appeal as an exclusive neighborhood. By 1905 South Dallas was home to most of the 1,200 Jews in the city. "Yet the community was by no means a Jewish ghetto; they [Jews] constituted less than half of the population of The Cedars in 1890 and an even smaller percentage of South Dallas as a whole."[38] By relocating in South Dallas the synagogue had followed the congregation, establishing a pattern that would continue as the Jewish population of the city moved even farther south before it turned north to follow the main stream of residential development in Dallas. ☙

Retail entrepreneur E. M. Kahn found the
temple's finances in a precarious
position during his presidency in 1895.

When Alexander Kohut became rabbi in 1898, he stayed with the Sol Loeb family on Pocahontas
Street. Next to Rabbi Kohut are Mr. and Mrs. Emil Stern, Mr. and Mrs. Loeb and their son Jerome.

Fannie Fechenbach Sanger, Alex Sanger's wife,
led the drive to raise money for a new temple by
organizing a week-long fair, the *Jahrmarkt*.

The second temple housing the congregation was built on the
corner of South Ervay and St. Louis streets in 1899.

Rabbi Kohut, standing at the pulpit of the Ervay Street Temple, inspired the congregation to erect the new building.

CHAPTER 4

Coming Of Age

This congregation is the reform body in its city and represents a very large, intelligent, and well-to-do community.

American Israelite, June 10, 1897

At the turn of the century Dallas was recognized as the "provincial capital of a 250,000 mile empire—the railroad, business, agricultural, and entertainment hub of North and West Texas, Oklahoma, and Arkansas."[1] The original central business district around the courthouse square had expanded eastward, running along the length of Elm, Main, and Commerce streets. By 1900 Main Street was defined as the banking district, and Elm Street would soon be heralded as an entertainment mecca replete with movie houses and vaudeville palaces such as the gilded Majestic Theater. Furthermore, Dallas had become a regional market center for fresh fruit and vegetable dealers who congregated to sell their produce on Market Street.

Electric streetcars charged up and down the streets transporting people from the suburbs—neighborhoods way out on South Dallas' Forest Avenue or in the northeast part of the city near St. Paul's Sanitorium at Bryan and Hall—to shop downtown at Linz Brothers, Sanger Brothers, A. Harris & Company, and Titche-Goettinger: all substantial business emporiums owned by members of Temple Emanu-El. Moreover, Dallas' claim as the hub of North Texas was also validated by the advent of interurban railroads linking Dallas and surrounding smaller towns like

Richardson, Plano, Grand Prairie, and even Denton, Waco, Terrell, Corsicana, and Fort Worth. In short, the electric trains transported thousands of people to work, to bank, and to shop in downtown Dallas.

The first automobile, the tangible harbinger of the twentieth century, appeared on Dallas streets in 1899. By 1901 Dallas' few automobiles were prohibited from "speeding" more than seven miles per hour on downtown streets. Nathan Mittenthal owned a Cadillac whose purchase in 1909 numbered it the 665th car in the city. Blanche Mittenthal Lefkowitz remembered her father "forever jumping out and cranking it up and having just lots and lots of trouble. He hated that car and finally sold it the day after her baby brother, M. J., fell out of the front seat."[2] The car had no doors to restrain M. J., but of course Jackson Street was not paved so no permanent damage was done to the child.

At this time the Jewish population of the city was probably less than a thousand persons. Figures compiled by the *The American Jewish Yearbook* indicate 1,200 Jewish inhabitants in the city by 1905.[3] Inasmuch as the temple's membership numbered about 104, the affiliated Reform Jewish community probably totaled five hundred or more adults and children in a city of about 42,000. The Orthodox community was not nearly so large. Shearith Israel, organized in 1884 with twenty members, did not build its synagogue on Jackson Street until 1892, and the congregation did not reach one hundred families until 1913, when it joined the Conservative branch of American Judaism. Another small Orthodox group, Tiferet Israel, was formed when some traditionalists who "intended to join Shearith Israel Congregation but were deterred from doing so because the sexes were not separated" constructed a synagogue on Highland Street.[4]

In comparison to the size of the Reform congregation in Dallas, Beth Israel in Houston, the oldest and next largest Reform temple in the state, claimed ninety-two members. Therefore, when Dr. Oscar J. Cohen of Mobile, Alabama, left his congregation in El Paso to become rabbi at Temple Emanu-El in May 1900, he advanced to the prestigious pulpit of the largest Jewish congregation in Texas. Dr. Cohen was another rabbi who, like Dr. Kohut, had settled in Texas for his health. The *American Israelite* reported that "the invigorating climate of El Paso having done for

Rabbi Cohen all that it was hoped it would, he is now prepared to re-enter a larger field where the duties are more arduous."[5] Unfortunately, after serving only a few months at Emanu-El, Rabbi Cohen died in Dallas. In deference to Cohen's memory, Rabbi Henry Cohen traveled from Galveston in April 1901 to officiate at his colleague's funeral.

Once again Temple Emanu-El initiated a rabbinic search. Alex Sanger, the president of the congregation, wrote Rabbi William H. Greenburg in Albuquerque, New Mexico, to ascertain whether he would be interested in coming to Dallas, only to learn that Greenburg had recently accepted an offer from a Sacramento, California, congregation. But a tenacious Alex Sanger repeated the temple's offer. Sanger wired Dr. Greenburg that "your election is unanimous, which of course may be attributed to the fact that all inquiries we made regarding your character and ability were in all respects satisfactory; and since I am responsible for the happy selection of our spiritual advisor, more so than any one else in the congregation, I congratulate myself upon the result of my work."[6] No doubt flattered by Sanger's persistence and kind words, Rabbi Greenburg made plans to come to Dallas.

William Henry Greenburg was born in London in 1868, the youngest of six children. Like Rabbi Henry Cohen of Galveston, he was educated at Jews College in London, the only seminary for Jewish religious leaders in England, most of whom received ministers' diplomas and called themselves Reverend. Greenburg studied simultaneously at University College and won a scholarship to Montefiore College for postgraduate work in philosophy and Semitic languages and literatures. There he was granted his rabbinical degree; then Greenburg matriculated at the University of Heidelberg to study for his Ph.D. While he was pursuing his studies, two favorite professors, one a perfectionist and the other an idealist, made a permanent impression on his development.[7] Tellingly, he would later exhibit the characteristics of his mentors, demanding an elevated standard of excellence of himself and his contemporaries throughout his life.

Upon returning to London, William Greenburg met Dr. Gotthard Deutsch, a visiting professor from Hebrew Union College, who noted

Greenburg's "very liberal tendencies in religion as opposed to the prevailing thought in England" and suggested to Dr. Greenburg that he might like to come to America, which would be "fertile soil" for his "advanced opinions."[8] Greenburg was charmed by Dr. Deutsch, who displayed "one of the most attractive personalities of his day," and the young rabbi readily agreed to sail to America if Dr. Deutsch could arrange a "call" from a Reform pulpit.[9] Shortly thereafter, Greenburg accepted the invitation to be the rabbi of the small Jewish community in Albuquerque, New Mexico, where he spent two very happy years. The friendliness of the community and the stimulation offered by the University of New Mexico at Albuquerque as well as the fascination of the Southwest, including the opportunity to observe the ways of the Pueblo Indians, made life intriguing and pleasant for the English scholar. However, Greenburg left Albuquerque to lead a larger Reform congregation in Sacramento and had lived there just a short time when Alex Sanger convinced him to come to Dallas.[10]

Dr. Greenburg was a thin, red-haired, scholarly man who had a passion for music and a thirst for intellectual company. When he joined the Sacramento Critic Club, a discussion group composed of intellectual and professional men who met monthly, he eagerly anticipated and savored the monthly meetings with kindred souls.[11] Nevertheless, in 1901 the thirty-three-year-old bachelor left California on the Texas and Southern Railway for the more expansive opportunity promised by Alex Sanger. In his unpublished autobiography Dr. Greenburg recalled his first perception of Dallas and Temple Emanu-El:

> It was distinctly a small town with no particular ideas. Yet I did seem to discern a slight ferment in the minds of a few outstanding citizens I soon had the good fortune to meet. It was not long before I met some of the ministers, particularly that genial, eloquent Bishop Garrett, Father Hayes, dynamic George Truett. The congregation to which I was called was comparatively small though I thought the house of worship was very attractive. I found the Jewish people as a whole most responsive and a few individuals with vision and progressive ideas.

The congregation had been worshiping in the new temple for just two years when Rabbi Greenburg arrived, but he was the congregation's third rabbi in four years. Toward the end of this unstable and discouraging transition period, services were so poorly attended that the president of the temple, Alex Sanger, rather peevishly complained that since "the officers and directors are devoting much time to the management of this congregation, the least the members could do is come once a week to participate in the service and thus encourage your rabbi and directory."[12] Thrust into this somnolent and nearly paralyzed environment, the new rabbi was supposed to revitalize and inspire the membership to attend services, a monumental undertaking. Yet a year after Dr. Greenburg's arrival, Rudolph Liebman, then president of the temple, sorrowfully had to admit that "attendance is not as large as we would like," a refrain that would be echoed throughout Rabbi Greenburg's ministry.[13] During the decade of Rudolph Liebman's stewardship as president, the increased temple attendance so profoundly desired by the rabbi and the directors never materialized.

For the first time in years, Emanu-El's chronic financial problems could not be blamed for the members' lack of interest. Fortunately, the directors in 1904 finally sold the old Commerce Street Temple to C. A. Keating, a farm implement distributor and investor, for $20,000 and paid off the $5,846.67 mortgage held by B'nai B'rith District Grand Lodge No. 7.[14] The building had been leased to the University of Dallas Medical Department in 1900, which remained as a tenant until the structure was demolished in 1906. Rudolph Liebman, president of the temple, was the president and general manager of Texas Paper Company, a manufacturer and jobber of paper products. He considered Emanu-El's monetary affairs to be in "an eminently satisfactory condition . . . due to the conservatism and business-like administration of the Board of Directors."[15]

During the years from 1901 to 1912 when Rudolph Liebman was president for ten years and Victor Hexter for one term in 1903–1904, ten to twelve directors perpetuated themselves and thereby ensured stability and continuity. Alex Sanger and Emanuel Tillman seemed to have permanent seats on the board. Max J. Rosenfield, the credit manager of

Sanger Brothers, and Seymour Myers, a vice-president of that firm, also kept their seats as directors, as did attorney Victor Hexter and Edward Titche, president of Titche-Goettinger, a department store. Jacob Kahn, a cotton merchant with a Liverpool firm who had married Alex Sanger's niece, was a continuing board member along with Morris Liebman, Rudolph's brother. These men and others who had been directors of the temple at different times were businessmen of some stature in the community, executives who headed successful enterprises of their own or who had secured important positions in businesses owned by their fellow temple members. When the Chamber of Commerce invited President William H. Taft to visit Dallas and honored him with a banquet at the Oriental Hotel in 1909, the prestigious Dallas reception committee listed several temple members on its roster.

Clearly, financial probity and stability were desirable, but the directors still faced other problems. The quandary over poor attendance at services was by no means a Dallas phenomenon. In general, Saturday morning services in Reform congregations across America were sparsely attended, drawing mostly women whose husbands were otherwise engaged in diligently shepherding entrepreneurial businesses. But congregants who avoided Friday night services, a Reform innovation starting in the 1860s that quickly spread across America, could tender no such excuse. Rabbi Isaac Mayer Wise chided the defectors:

> It has been objected that many prefer the theater and the opera to the temple, and will go to those places of amusement in preference to the house of worship. Good bye to you, ladies and gentlemen, we will see you again. Persons who have no higher than fictitious ideals, who prefer play to reality, self-deception to self-elevation, fiction to truth, amusement to instruction, the fleet shadows of the moment to the rock of eternity, persons who worship selfishness in lieu of the Eternal God, will go almost anywhere.[16]

Pursuing a viable solution to the problem, some Reform congregations had introduced Sunday services to replace Friday night services. As early as 1874 Rabbi Kaufmann Kohler initiated them at Temple Sinai in Chicago but later abandoned the concept as a dilution of Jewish tradition.[17] In 1891, Emanu-El trustee E. M. Kahn supported a change to Sunday evening services. Although his recommendation garnered the approval of the board of directors, which was searching for an answer, the members voted down the rather radical innovation.[18]

Nonetheless, over a period of several decades dozens of "Sunday congregations" throughout America chose Sunday instead of Friday night for Sabbath observance.[19] But as usually seemed to be the case, Isaac M. Wise had the last word, and eventually Friday night uniformly became "temple night." Writing in the *American Israelite* Rabbi Wise enumerated several reasons for instituting evening services: they were more "impressive and solemn" than day services, they were cooler than morning services in the hot summer, and they would attract men freed from their business affairs. Moreover, they can be more easily attended by "our Gentile friends who have overcome many an inherited prejudice against the Jew and Judaism and desire to have a better and more correct knowledge of our mode of worship and our form of faith."[20]

In an effort to increase attendance at Friday night services, the directors of the temple in 1903 asked their wives and sisters to form an auxiliary board, the Guild of Temple Emanu-El, and appealed to the wife of temple president Victor Hexter to head the group.[21] Hexter, a lawyer born in Baltimore, had become a member of the Dallas bar in 1892. Active in civic affairs as well as in Jewish organizations, he was a member of the Dallas school board for fourteen years and its president from 1906 to 1910. When his wife Minnie Wertheimer Hexter accepted the presidency of the temple Guild in 1903, she began her long career of steering influential Jewish women's organizations, serving in 1915 as the second president of the newly formed Dallas Chapter of the National Council of Jewish Women and as the temple's first Sisterhood president in 1920.

Seriously acknowledging their charge from the directors, the women of the Guild attempted to address the attendance problem at services, along with the underlying lack of interest in religious affairs. Rose Titche, Edward Titche's sister, stated her desire that "the Jewish people refuse to attend any and all entertainments on Friday night" in order to free themselves to come to temple.[22] The ladies pledged to attend services themselves and resolved to discontinue shopping on the Sabbath. To make temple worship more inviting, the Guild planned to decorate the pulpit on festival days; to make services more compelling, they asked for an occasional exchange of pulpits between Rabbi Greenburg and other rabbis and speakers, including those from relatively far afield who could proffer fresh spiritual insights and provide a more global perspective on life's crucial issues.

Through the years different lecturers were invited to occupy the pulpit of Temple Emanu-El. Speaking at the temple on several occasions, Dr. Gotthard Deutsch, Rabbi Greenburg's mentor from Hebrew Union College, stirred the congregants. Another inspiring speaker was Sadie American, one of the founders of the National Council of Jewish Women, who toured Texas in 1913 and established branches of the organization in Dallas, San Antonio, Houston, Galveston, and Waco. The National Council of Jewish Women was founded in 1893 at the Jewish Woman's Congress held at the World's Fair in Chicago. Hannah Solomon, a Chicago clubwoman, headed the Jewish Women's Committee, which was part of the women's committees representing each religion at the fair. Her committee decided to organize a Jewish Congress and corresponded with women in the larger cities across the country and in England to urge them to elect delegates. In their search for participants, the women's committee sent out over two thousand letters and described its intent to form an organization of "thinking Jewish women, who have the advancement of Judaism and Jewish interests at heart."[23]

In their attempt to organize and publicize the first nation-wide gathering of Jewish women, Solomon and the Jewish Women's Committee created a great deal of excitement and anticipation. At the meeting, delegates listened attentively as female speakers gave voice to the need for Jewish women to involve themselves in the Jewish community as part of their obligation to their religion. Ada Chapman, whose husband was rabbi of Temple Emanu-El at the time, was one of the speakers emphasizing religious commitment. She urged the audience to emulate the women of the Bible: "We women of Israel must not forget that a great part of this religious task lies in our hands, and we, conscious of our responsibility, ought to make it our pride to follow the example of our mothers in the wilderness, who worked with enthusiasm to build the Tabernacle. Let our sanctuary be our homes, and let us beautify them with the undoubted, holy influence of our beloved faith."[24] The crowning speech was social welfare worker Sadie American's call to organize the first national religious Jewish women's organization in history.

After resolving to call themselves the National Council of Jewish Women, the delegates rose their feet to elect Hannah Solomon president by acclamation. The enthusiastic women formed local chapters in cities throughout the United States, centering their agenda to emphasize a membership "becoming Jewishly educated, fighting anti-Semitism and assimilation, and solving society's problems through social reform work."[25] In the wake of Sadie American's successful swing throughout Texas in 1913, Grace Goldstein became the Dallas section's first president. Later, this "unusually intelligent and active young lady," as described by Dr. Greenburg, accepted a position as secretary to Rabbi David Lefkowitz, Greenburg's successor. [26]

Throughout the country, women who founded chapters of the National Council of Jewish Women were also active in temple auxiliaries. At their synagogues they were well aware of the lack of interest shown by businessmen trustees in the religious aspect of the organization. Men controlled congregational policies but left the women, who attended worship services in greater numbers than the men, to carry on the religious activity. In 1909 Alex Sanger asked the Guild of Temple Emanu-El to call a special meeting, without disclosing its purpose for fear of scaring away an audience. Still determined to prevail over the membership's lethargy, Sanger was seeking suggestions whereby the trustees could "devise ways and means to secure a larger attendance at Temple."[27] The women responded with several creative recommendations designed to make temple-going more appealing. Their first proposal, a volunteer choir supervised and drilled by organist Mrs. J. H. Cassidy, languished. Undaunted, the guild successfully sponsored musical recitals at Friday night services and supported another cultural program, The Temple Literary and Musical Society. Officers and members of the society took part in a series of programs presenting musical solos and readings on current events and historical and cultural subjects of Jewish interest. A typical evening in 1912 included a piano recital by Miss Amanda Hexter, the daughter of J. K. Hexter, a reading by realtor Henry S. Miller, an essay by Titche-Goettinger vice-president (later president) Horace H. Landauer on "Jewish Merchants of the Middle Ages," and a song by Lovie Freshman, daughter of saloonkeeper Sam Freshman. A short story by Mrs. Elihu A. Sanger, daughter-in-law of Alex Sanger, a talk on current events by lawyer Alex F. Weisberg, and a violin solo by A. Harris and Company president Arthur Kramer rounded out the program.[28]

With full knowledge of most of the temple members' whereabouts on Friday night, the Guild also suggested that the temple ask the Columbian Club to refrain from renting its hall for balls or parties on Friday evening. The "competition" between the temple and the Columbian Club for their joint membership culminated in 1915 when New Year's Eve fell on Friday. In a letter to club president Herbert Marcus, Dr. Greenburg expressed his deep chagrin:

> The news reached me yesterday that the Columbian Club has decided to hold its New Year's ball on Friday night, December 31. I confess I was utterly amazed that any such idea could for one moment be seriously entertained. . . . As a minority, we have always been solicitously careful of preserving our dignity, and maintaining a high reputation for ourselves, not only as citizens but as Jews. . . . Can we afford to mangle our consciences; can we afford to flagrantly disregard the sacred thoughts and traditions of thousands of years regarding the Sabbath for the sake of gratifying one evening's amusement?
>
> We must, as a body be prepared to make *some sacrifice* for the sake of *principle.* . . . I would ask you to reconsider your decision and reverse it. The change is not of supreme importance to us as individuals—it is as a body, representing as it practically does, Congregation Emanu-El.[29]

After the rabbi's condemnation of members' public disregard of Friday night Sabbath observance, the club had no choice but to accede to Greenburg's request and move its New Year's Ball to Saturday night, January 1, 1916.[30]

As stringent as were his demands for attendance at Friday night services, Rabbi Greenburg held liberal and progressive views about the Jew's role in improving society and participating in a universal religious ecumenicism. Like his fellow Reform rabbis, he was imbued with the tenets of the Classical Reform movement as "the last decade of the nineteenth century and the first years of the twentieth witnessed the widest swing of the Reform pendulum away from traditional Jewish belief and practice."[31] For instance, the earliest Reformers discarded the traditional Bar Mitzvah in favor of a confirmation ceremony. Rabbi Kaufmann Kohler, one of the leading architects of Reform Judaism, felt that the Bar Mitzvah rite had grown meaningless. Since many members accepted into a Reform congregation could not read the Torah in Hebrew, a boy becoming Bar Mitzvah was not joining a company of learned men conversant in the Hebrew law because the practice of "calling up of the members of the Congregation to read from the scroll of the Law [each Sabbath] has been abolished in the Reform Synagogue." Rabbi Kohler branded the ritual of requiring a thirteen-year-old to ascend to the pulpit for a one-time reading of Hebrew "a sham." He maintained that "the Bar Mitzvah rite ought not to be encouraged by any Reform rabbi as it is a survival of orientalism like the covering of the head during the service, whereas the Confirmation—when made as it should, by the rabbi, an impressive appeal to the holiest emotions of the soul and a personal vow of fealty to the ancestral faith—is a source of regeneration of Judaism each year."[32] Adhering to Kohler's reform, Dr. Greenburg substituted for the Bar Mitzvah an important coming-of-age ceremony, confirmation, that initiated and sanctified older adolescents of both sexes, who studied with the rabbi and affirmed their commitment to the temple.

Besides altering and streamlining its rituals to accommodate congregations whose members had become assimilated into the surrounding society, Reform Judaism began to focus on societal problems rather than on questions of form or custom. The rabbis advocated a Reform Judaism in which "moral action took precedence over religious observance" and "presented its adherents with specific moral objectives that would be as Jewishly significant for them as ceremonies were for traditionalists."[33] Issues of social justice were linked in part to the rise of two outside influences: the American Progressive movement and the Christian Social Gospel. In the years before World War I the Reform rabbinate earnestly endorsed the social reform program of President Theodore Roosevelt, who believed that humanity, governed by a fundamental moral law, could remake society for the better. In fact, the Central Conference of American Rabbis in 1908 joined the campaign against child labor and in 1918 set forth Reform Judaism's first social justice program, arguing for the rights of labor and the special needs of women and children in the work place. At the same time the Progressives were advocating the moral uplifting of society by political intervention, the Christian Social Gospel movement insisted that moral conduct and virtuous deeds, not dogma or ceremony, constituted "the supreme and sufficient religious act." The regard of these tolerant Christians for the prophetic message of the Hebraic seers—Amos, Micah, and Isaiah—shared by both Christians and Jews, instilled in some Reform Jews a feeling of kinship with liberal Christianity as both faiths espoused a common cause.[34]

In 1911 Dr. Greenburg urged the formation of a federated Jewish charities organization and recommended to Godcheaux Levi, who was organizing the planning, a number of congregants Levi should include at the first meeting, held in the Assembly Room of the temple.[35] Godcheaux Levi had come to Dallas from Victoria, Texas, around 1900 to open a Dallas branch of his family's investment bank, A. Levi and Company, in which Godcheaux, his brother Charles, and their brother-in-law Jules K. Hexter, all old acquaintants at the University of Virginia, were associates.[36] "Mr. Levi had not been here more than a few months when he became the moving spirit of nearly every Jewish activity of Congregation Emanu-El," wrote Dr. Greenburg about the first president of the federation.[37]

Representatives from Temple Emanu-El, Shearith Israel, and Tiferet Israel as well as from Jewish charitable organizations such as the

Men's and Ladies' Hebrew Benevolent associations and the Free Loan Society gathered at the temple and selected officers. The Federated Hebrew Charities originated as a dues-paying organization and expected each male member to contribute $12 annually. Wives of members could vote with no added assessment, and single women could join for just $3. The Federated Charities also established a day nursery for women who had to work. Initially, one of the main objectives of the organization was to tender loans to the needy as well as to provide some relief to the destitute. From the fall of 1915 through 1916, applications for aid totaled 477, including 153 immigrants from war-torn Russia.[38] Eventually the goal of the organization crystallized into helping the numerous applicants find work and become self-sustaining.

Ever since their marriage in 1905, Rabbi Greenburg and his wife, Blanche Cahn Greenburg of New Orleans, had been in the forefront of the social service movement in Dallas. Problems involving the welfare of the city, and in particular those of women and children, drew together concerned Dallas men and women of all faiths. Many of these activists already belonged to literary and culture clubs, whose members added deliberations about sponsoring charitable projects to their regular weekly discussions of books, music, and history. Both Dr. and Mrs. Greenburg were officers of the Dallas Free Kindergarten Association, organized in 1900, which operated free kindergartens in poor neighborhoods. The association also sponsored Neighborhood House, a settlement house on Cedar Springs near Harwood. It was an institution whose nonsectarian kindergarten enrolled children from Polish and Russian Jewish families living near downtown who had immigrated after the turn of the century.[39]

Blanche Greenburg knew the needs of immigrant children firsthand from her work at the Dallas Free Kindergarten Association. In 1910 she urged a few personal friends to donate milk for the nursery at the Dallas Free Kindergarten Day Nursery in the cotton mill district in East Dallas. Mrs. Asher Silberstein, whose late husband had been a successful businessman and a director of the Chamber of Commerce, E. M. Kahn, and Godcheaux Levi responded to her request for free milk. Then she began to solicit donations for a more ambitious project, a milk station. By 1913 she had established the Dallas Infants Welfare and Milk Association, modeled after The New York Milk Committee, which had been operating for a few years. The Dallas Association not only distributed free milk to indigent mothers and sold milk at cost to other distressed citizens at its Milk Station on Corinth Street opposite the cotton mills but also operated a free medical clinic which treated 881 children during its first year. (The setting for these philanthropic projects was most appropriate since Dallas was the largest inland cotton market in the United States.) In the interest of teaching effective health care procedures, a nurse was also engaged to make home visits to the poor. By 1914 the Infants Welfare and Milk Association was one of six organizations supported by the Dallas Federated Welfare Finance Committee, the parent organization of the United Charities.[40]

Dr. Greenburg's ministry was characterized by his expansive vision for ecumenical fellowship. One of his cherished dreams was to champion a large gathering of people of all creeds and nationalities drawn from all churches and synagogues "for the purpose of giving thanks as the children of one God at least on one occasion during the year."[41] In November 1907 he invited representatives from Christian churches in Dallas to participate in the first "People's Thanksgiving Service." The *Dallas Morning News* described the packed house at Bush Temple of Music on lower Elm Street: "The temple was crowded to the doors and many were turned away unable to find standing room either in pit or gallery."[42] Eight ministers, including Dr. Greenburg, sat on the platform in front of a great scroll inscribed, "Have we not all one Father?" Reverend M. M. Davis, pastor of the Central Christian Church, gave the invocation. Dean Harry T. Moore of St. Matthew's Cathedral, Reverend Marion F. Ham of First Unitarian Church, Reverend J. Frank Norris of McKinney Avenue Baptist Church, and Dr. William Greenburg read from the Scriptures. Then Reverend James W. Hill of First Methodist Church, Father James M. Hayes of Sacred Heart Cathedral, and Reverend J. Frank Smith of Central Presbyterian Church each addressed the gathering. For years the People's Thanksgiving Service proved to be such a phenomenal success that in 1916 Dr. Greenburg asked Mayor Henry D. Lindsley to recognize the service as a permanent event on the municipal calendar. The mayor assured the rabbi that the board of commissioners had unanimously agreed to take over the People's Thanksgiving Service on Thanksgiving Day "of this year and thereafter."[43] Its impact was acknowledged by the tremendous crowd gathered at the coliseum at Fair Park on Thanksgiving Day in 1918 to celebrate the end of World War I.

Another of Dr. Greenburg's progressive ideas was the organization of a Critic Club modeled after the one he had enjoyed in Sacramento. Early in 1908, Dr. Greenburg called on George B. Dealey, the forty-nine-year-old general manager of the *Dallas Morning News*, to enlist him as a prime member of the group. Inasmuch as Mr. Dealey thought an elite discussion club was too highbrow, Dr. Greenburg then presented his ideas to Caesar Lombardi, the ranking executive officer of the *News*. Lombardi, who had belonged to a similar club in Portland, Oregon, agreed to join Greenburg in persuading Dealey to acquiesce to their plan.[44]

The founders invited six other men to the first meeting at Dr. Greenburg's home on South Harwood near St. Louis Street. The select few included Captain William Preston Wooten, U. S. Corps of Engineers, who was in charge of surveys for Trinity River Improvement and Navigation; Dr. Pierre Wilson, a surgeon; the Reverend Marion F. Ham, pastor of the Unitarian Church; Edwin J. Kiest, president and general manager of the *Times Herald* and president of the State Fair of Texas, who brought Hugh Nugent Fitzgerald, his editor-in-chief; and Yancy Lewis, lawyer and former federal judge and University of Texas Law School dean. At each meeting the host presented a paper on a timely subject, very often civic improvement, and opened the floor for discussion. For the first meeting Dr. Greenburg read his paper, "Factors that Determine Educational Progress." Ironically Dealey had been correct in assuming the Critic Club would be elitist. During its sixty-five-year existence the Critic Club deliberately kept its membership of illustrious Dallasites small and selective, and Dealey, as secretary, was the only officer. When one member wondered to another what the fifteen or so men had in common, he was told, "They are men Mr. Dealey likes."[45] They were also men of some intellectual weight and civic presence who not only provided intellectual stimulation for each other but also supported many ventures for civic betterment.

Music was another of Dr. Greenburg's passions. A fervent lover of classical music, Will Greenburg had played the violin since he was nine years old. While in Dallas he "became intrigued with the idea of organizing a permanent Symphony Orchestra" in a new, vigorous, commercial city which was then "through the vision and enterprise of many citizens reaching out for the cultural aspects of life" to parallel its mercantile success.[46] Actually, the Dallas Symphony had been founded at a meeting in the temple on Ervay Street, which, according to the social directory of 1900–1901, "Messrs. Sanger, Liebman and Harris" allowed the embryonic organization to use. Felice Kahn, the artistic daughter of E. M. Kahn, played the violin during the first Dallas Symphony Club concert May 22, 1900. Hans Kreissig, a "cultivated young German musician" who acted as the director and organist of the Temple Emanu-El choir, conducted the musicians' first performance.[47]

Along with a few music devotees, Rabbi Greenburg attempted to establish a permanent orchestra. As a self-professed "symphony addict," he wrote a letter in 1912 to the *Dallas Morning News* lauding the benefits of an enduring orchestra that would "raise the whole tone of the city and place it among the larger centers of music and art and give it a most enviable prestige." Greenburg helped raise $20,000 for a season of concerts, and the group engaged Carl Venth, a former concertmaster for the New York Metropolitan Opera Orchestra, as conductor. But he had to admit that "the work involved too much time, energy and responsibility for the few of us interested and we were reluctantly compelled to drop the matter" after two seasons.[48] When the orchestra was revived in 1914, Walter J. Fried, a young violinist who had studied conducting in Germany, was named conductor. In the ensuing years the Dallas Symphony survived several crises to become the civic adornment and cultural landmark that Dr. Greenburg, a man often ahead of his time, clearly envisioned.

While the rabbi actively pursued his role in the community, programs at the temple had come to a virtual standstill. Ultimately, the directors had to confront and wrestle with the unavoidable fact that Emanu-El's facilities were not large enough for any sustained expansion of religious life. As early as 1906 the directors had mulled over the prospect of enlarging the temple by building a gallery in the rear to accommodate the increasing membership. By 1909 the temple listed one hundred and sixty-five members, a gain of just forty-four in eight years but too many for the sanctuary to hold during the High Holidays. In 1910 the directors determined to look into the ways and means of building a new synagogue but waited until 1913 to sell the existing structure.

On January 19, 1913, the board of directors called a special meeting of the congregation to authorize the trustees to put the temple up for sale. At this meeting the secretary, David Eldridge, read a strongly worded letter from the Guild signed by its president, Mrs. Morris Liebman, promising the women's enthusiastic support toward building a new synagogue. She reminded the directors that the Guild had "been closely in touch with the work of the Temple for seven years and [found] at all times that the progress of the Temple [was] interfered with because the lack of modern facilities." Rosetta Liebman also informed the directors that, in her opinion a great many young people would "drift away from Judaism" unless they were given "at least as much encouragement as Jews as our Christian neighbors give their young." Moreover, in order to attract members from the large number of unaffiliated Jews in Dallas, she stressed socialization as an effective glue for Jewish community solidarity:

> Social life is the means of holding a congregation together in this great melting pot of America. This is impossible in our present quarters. On all sides we hear complaints from those who have been given no regular seats, and strangers are practically barred from our services, or when they come, meet with discourteous treatment because of the necessity of moving them from place to place in the Temple.[49]

With the approval of the congregation to sell the temple on Ervay and St. Louis streets, a special committee was appointed to find a buyer for the property. Shortly thereafter, the trustees accepted an offer of $35,000 from the Unitarian Church, which took possession of the building July 1, 1913, but allowed the congregation to use the facilities until a new temple could be built.

Rabbi Greenburg envisioned the new temple as an "institutional synagogue," a concept that was gaining credence among religious leaders. The idea of bringing non-religious activities under the auspices of the synagogue was conceived as a solution to the apparently peripheral role of the synagogue in the lives of its members. As early as 1901, The Temple in Cleveland built the first gymnasium in response to a petition by its young people. Later, Temple Sinai in Chicago built a gymnasium and a swimming pool. In New York, Rabbi Mordecai Kaplan expressed his belief that a reconstruction of the synagogue by the addition of new social and recreational activities would attract young people and create a pathway for them to identify with Judaism, perhaps leading them eventually to study their faith.[50] The "Jewish Center-Institutional Synagogue" hypothesis spread among Reform Jews and also found strong adherents within the Conservative movement.

According to a committee on social and religious activities appointed by the Central Conference of American Rabbis, this new institutional temple would "deepen the interest of the members in the synagogue and in each other:"[51]

> [The new temple would] bring to bear a system of institutional activities, social, educational and philanthropic, which would bring it into contact with its members' physical, mental and social nature as well. . . . Instruction in citizenship, immigrant classes for the study of the English language, Bible circles, athletic clubs, sewing clubs, dancing classes, a modern kindergarten, a music club, a literary club, a reading club, a dramatic and choral society, these are some of the regular activities of a modern institutional Temple, besides lectures, musicales, receptions and recitals.[52]

In Rabbi Greenburg's eyes, it would be "such a center of intelligent citizenship" that it would wield a powerful influence not only in the Jewish community but in the city of Dallas.[53] Such a democratic institution would be open to all Jews, whether rich or poor, whatever class or nationality.

The leaders of the temple enthusiastically supported Rabbi Greenburg. President Jules K. Hexter exhorted the membership to rally round:

> I feel that every one of you has given recognition to an obligation which we owe to Judaism at large, and especially to the Jews of the Dallas Community, and in the determination that we are to erect an Institutional Synagogue you have evidenced a sincere desire to put Congregation Emanu-El in the front rank of American Jewry, and to give to your Rabbi and the Board of Directors the facilities to work out their obligation, impossible of performance under existing circumstances.[54]

President Hexter felt quite sure that the "Dallas Spirit" would imbue the congregation with the will to lend its "support to this great enterprise."[55]

The "Dallas Spirit" to which Jules Hexter alluded in his report to the congregation was boosterism of a high order. The city, which had moved into the twentieth century with a population of 42,638, would reach 100,000 by 1913, a tremendous growth spurt that presaged even better times ahead. Dallas citizens swelled with pride when beer baron Adolphus Busch of St. Louis opened the twenty-one story Adolphus Hotel in 1912; when the city was awarded the 11th District Federal Reserve Bank in the newly created Federal Reserve System in 1914; when Ford Motor Company opened an assembly-line plant downtown between Commerce and Main streets in 1914. Dallas also campaigned to obtain a university. A donation of 133 acres of land for a campus by J. S. Armstrong, the original developer of Highland Park, and a gift of several thousand dollars by business leaders convinced the Methodist Episcopal Church South to open Southern Methodist University in 1915. Supposedly, when the first president of SMU and a visitor were touring Dallas Hall, the first campus building, the visitor commented on the pride the Methodists must feel knowing that their contributions erected the

71

first building of the university. Robert Stewart Hyer corrected his companion's assumption, observing, "The Methodists cannot take all the credit for this. Just as much Jewish money has gone into this building as Methodist. In fact, I believe almost all denominations have contributed to this edifice."[56] By their donations to establish the city's first university, which happened to be a Methodist school, Dallas Jews evinced their belief that their efforts benefited the entire city.

Inspired by the civic growth bursting all around them, the members of Temple Emanu-El unanimously approved payment of $14,500 for the purchase of a lot 150 by 150 feet located on the southeast corner of South Boulevard and Harwood Street.[57] Early in 1914 the directors engaged James P. Hubbell and Herbert M. Greene as architects for the new building. Hubbell and Greene had designed the Christian Science Church and the Scottish Rite Cathedral as well as the Fine Arts Building in Fair Park. Yet almost two years later Rabbi Greenburg, "who had confidently expected that the June 1915 annual meeting would be held in a commodious and beautiful assembly hall, had to confess, "I am weary of answering the question daily put to me by the non-Jew as much as by the Jew: When are you going to build—when are you going to build? 'Soon, I hope, has been the usual reply.'"[58] Apparently the disputes among congregants regarding the social features to be incorporated in the new temple had stifled progress, and the congregation was still sharing the old building with the Unitarians. Finally the directors instructed the architects to create the entire building as originally planned. On May 11, 1916, almost three years after the congregation sold the Ervay Street Temple, Rabbi Greenburg turned over the first spadeful of dirt to start construction on Emanu-El's third house of worship.

During the time that the South Boulevard temple was being built, Emanu-El's members primarily focused on their local expansion needs. Nevertheless, they could not help being concerned about the desperate situation of Jews elsewhere who were embroiled in the outbreak of the first World War. In 1917 President Woodrow Wilson committed the United States to the side of the British and French Allies against the Central Powers of Germany and Austria. The American Jewish Relief Committee had been raising money, however, for homeless and starving Jews since the start of the war in 1914. The plight of the Eastern European Jews was critical as most of them lived in the Russian Pale of Settlement, Poland, and the Ukraine, areas directly along the front of hostilities. Also, Jews in Palestine, cut off by Arab support of Germany and Austria, needed assistance. Spurred by a challenge grant of a million dollars from Sears Roebuck & Company president Julius Rosenwald, the Relief Committee attempted to raise ten million dollars to mitigate the suffering. To solicit funds from the Dallas Jewish community, Jules Hexter, president of the temple, headed the local American Jewish Relief Committee. In 1915 Hexter's committee raised $7,500, and in subsequent war years Dallas Jews raised more than $7,000 annually for suffering Jews in Europe and Palestine.[59] When President Wilson declared January 27, 1916, as national Jewish Relief Day, Rabbi Greenburg, secretary and treasurer of the Dallas Relief Committee, organized a mass meeting at the Municipal Building auditorium to recruit Christian Dallasites to subscribe to the relief effort. Dr. Greenburg was greatly disappointed by the amount, $3,582.95, contributed from all Dallas citizens, a sum which included Jewish donors. His discouragement over Dallas' meager response was given credence on January 31, by the *Dallas Morning News*:

> And the doctor is quite right to feel disappointed. The Jews of Dallas have always been liberal in their contributions to all causes that the town has considered worthy. They are now contributing heavily to the general charities of the city. The Jewish Relief fund is designed to take care of needs of an acute sort. The sufferings of the Jews in the countries of Central and Eastern Europe should attract sympathy if anything should. The people of Dallas did not distinguish themselves in their treatment of the relief fund. Dr. Greenburg does well to call attention to the poor record that was made.[60]

When war was officially declared in April 1917, young men belonging to Temple Emanu-El volunteered for the armed services. Herman

Philipson and Alfred Bromberg left almost immediately, followed by Lawrence Kahn, Charles Klein, Louis Tobian, William Tobian, and Clifton Linz. Before Philipson, the advertising manager at the *Dallas Times Herald*, enlisted in the Marine Corps, he had worked on the war bond drive. After training at Parris Island, North Carolina, the young gunnery sergeant sailed for France. On his homeward voyage in 1919, he was on the same ship as young Franklin Roosevelt, then assistant secretary of the Navy, and President Woodrow Wilson.[61] Lieutenant Clifton Linz was attached to the Quarter Master's Department transporting supplies across the Atlantic on the *Tippecanoe* when his vessel was sunk by a torpedo about 500 miles from the French coast. Fortunately, a few hours later a United States destroyer picked up the passengers who were paddling toward France in their life boats. In his next letter to his parents, Simon and Beccie Linz, Clifton jauntily described his adventure: "We had a fine trip in, and I am now waiting for orders as to what to do. I got sunburnt a little—and that's all. Never felt better in my life."[62]

While the country was engaged in "the war to end all wars," the congregation celebrated its first Sabbath service June 1, 1917, in its South Boulevard temple. Rabbi Greenburg had expressed his deep-seated sentiment that the burden of religious life was not only the rabbi's responsibility: "Though he work day and night, sapping his strength and using up his vitality to realize the goal he has set himself—spiritual success—the task is too stupendous for any one man, and the result is, consequently, failure." Unless everyone affiliated with the synagogue "contributes something of real value towards making your religious and cultural organization the success it ought to be," the rabbi predicted that the same "deadening conditions" that lay leaders all over the country were "wearily deploring" would descend once again upon Temple Emanu-El.[63] Dr. Greenburg was referring to the prevalent religious torpor during and after World War I when entertainment and worldly success, "automobiles, radio, the movies—not church or synagogue—captured popular attention."[64] America was developing into a non-religious, secular society.

Nevertheless, when Dr. Greenburg delivered his annual report to the congregation in 1917, he optimistically charted his far-reaching ideas for programs in the new temple. Of course, all the events which had taken place at the Columbian Club for the past four years while the congregation shared their old temple with the Unitarians—such as Hebrew classes, confirmation and post-confirmation classes, the study circle under the auspices of the Council of Jewish Women, the Temple Literary and Musical Society, and the children's Seder service—could now take place in the spacious quarters at the new building. The board of directors "heartily endorsed the inauguration of classes for instruction in citizenship, immigrant classes for the study of the English language, dramatic and choral societies and Bible study circles."[65] Rabbi Greenburg's long-held desire to sponsor a kindergarten class in religious instruction could not be immediately fulfilled as the kindergarten room, the kitchen, the gymnasium and the janitor's quarters would not be finished until a special committee could raise another $4,000.

The rabbi also advanced some innovative suggestions to enrich congregational life and the directors heartily endorsed these. He wanted to hold a dinner for the membership at the annual meeting and to change the date from a hot June day to an evening in early spring. Agreeing, the directors proposed to set the meeting for the first Sunday in April. In addition, the rabbi wished to have a reception in the parlors of the temple after Friday services once or twice a month, a suggestion which the directors agreed to inaugurate monthly. Moreover, he wanted to introduce congregational singing using the new hymnals recently issued by the Central Conference of American Rabbis so that congregants would have the opportunity to take a more active part in the service. The directors agreed, and to encourage further congregational participation in services, strongly urged "the speedy formation of a volunteer choir for Saturday morning services and ultimately to participate in the Friday evening services." The choir committee, chaired by Arthur Kramer, had provided a non-member double quartet to sing for services, but the directors thought that a volunteer choir could be organized under the direction of the women's Guild of Temple Emanu-El.[66] Now that the temple was almost completed, Rabbi Greenburg proposed, and the directors concurred, to launch a membership campaign immediately. Greenburg also suggested that the congregation be encouraged to celebrate events such as a birth or a marriage as well as the memory of a loved one by offering contributions to the temple. The directors acquiesed if the solicitation could be accomplished delicately; donors could be recognized by reading their names at the annual meeting.[67]

At the previous annual meeting the congregation insisted upon adopting a plan of free synagogue seating instead of continuing the traditional family pew sales which had raised the necessary funds for operating costs not covered by members' dues. This democratization was highly recommended by the Central Conference of American Rabbis and by Dr. Greenburg, but now that the customary avenue of revenue was closed, the directors were forced to raise dues to cover expenses as well as to solicit additional contributions to the building fund. Pew holders in the Ervay Street Temple accepted fifty cents on the dollar to release their pews, which they could apply to the payment of dues or to their building fund pledge. Most of the 207 members increased their monthly dues from the minimum $3 to $4, $5 or $6 while about twenty members paid $7.50, $10, or $12.50 per month, and three members paid $20 monthly.[68]

In his annual message Rabbi Greenburg also brought up his unhappiness with the specifications on the manner of electing a rabbi. He suggested that the congregation change the "antiquated" by-laws by which its rabbi could be elected for a term no longer than three years. He urged a by-law revision:

> The Rabbi [can] be elected at a meeting of the congregation for such a term as they may see fit to elect him. . . . According to this change of wording, a Rabbi need not necessarily be elected for a longer period than three years. But if the congregation manifests a desire to elect him for a longer term it seems to me as it must seem to every logical mind, nothing less than a flagrant injustice that it be prevented by a by-law such as we now have, from carrying out the will of the majority.[69]

The directors balked at this last recommendation, asserting their opinion that "it would be unwise to create a condition which would permit a congregation at any time to elect either its officers or its Rabbi for a term which would extend beyond the active participation in the affairs of the congregation of those conducting the election."[70]

Meanwhile, the directors changed the by-laws to read that the election of officers and the rabbi must be by secret ballot and that the rabbi should be elected at a special meeting of the congregation at the first Sunday in April prior to the end of his term. When Rabbi Greenburg's three-year term ended in June 1918, the board of directors voted for his reelection. At the meeting called to act upon the renewal of his contract, he was elected on the first ballot. But when, after the first vote of approval, more congregants rushed in to cast their votes, the crowd increased from seventy-four to ninety members, and Rabbi Greenburg failed to be reelected on the second ballot. In this uncertain situation, the rabbi and the directors decided to postpone the dedication of the temple because Dr. Greenburg "felt that the visiting rabbis might be embarrassed" even though invitations had already been extended to them, some press releases had already gone out to the Jewish press, and the printed program was ready for approval.

At the special meeting called on April 28, 1918, for the express purpose of reconsidering the election of the rabbi, 136 members elected Rabbi Greenburg for a term of eighteen months. Nevertheless, the directors held to their decision to defer the dedication until the temple could be completed, but they designated the Assembly Room in the Annex as the "Max J. Rosenfield Hall," in tribute to the building committee chairman's "invaluable and indefatigable services."[71] When Jules K. Hexter completed his six-year presidential term in June, Max Rosenfield was elected president of the temple.

After Rabbi Greenburg took his usual summer vacation of six to eight weeks, he returned to the pulpit of Temple Emanu-El. But after a few months back at work he sent a letter of resignation to the trustees in January 1919, setting his departure at the end of his term in February 1920. When the directors insisted upon once more casting a vote in March 1919 concerning his reelection, he wrote to the officers and members of Temple Emanu-El on April 5, 1919, expressing his frustrations:

Gentlemen:

The Board of Directors at its last meeting held March 25, saw fit to consider and vote upon my candidacy for reelection without consulting my wishes in this matter. Since my resignation had not been withdrawn, this action on their part was entirely unauthorized, and should therefore be expunged from the minutes.

Existing conditions have made absolutely impossible the realization of many constructive ideas I had planned. With no organization to work through, with no general secretary which had been promised me, and with a lack of cooperation, a deadlock has been brought about in the affairs of the Congregation. Hence permit me to say, that inasmuch as these same conditions, and other circumstances that prompted my resignation, remain absolutely unchanged and unrectified, I can not permit my name to be mentioned for reelection.

Yours respectfully,
William Greenburg

When the resignation of Dr. Greenburg was announced, a group of thirty-one prominent men headed by Alexander Garrett, Episcopal Bishop of Dallas, and M. M. Crane, the former attorney general of Texas, who had been associated with Dr. Greenburg in organizations such as the Critic Club, the symphony, and the United Charities, addressed a letter to the congregation. They conveyed their "deep regret" concerning his resignation and probable departure from the city:

We have been closely associated with him in many walks in life, and have learned to hold him in high esteem both as a man and a minister. His cultured, kindly, sympathetic and liberal minded character has won for him a place in the affections and manly regard of our citizens occupied by but few public men.

Furthermore, 168 members, well over half the approximately 275 congregants, signed petitions asking the board of directors to "submit to a meeting of the congregation the question of soliciting Dr. Greenburg to reconsider and withdraw his resignation, and of prevailing upon him to continue his connection with the congregation."

Once again, the board voted whether to recommend William Greenburg for reelection as rabbi of Temple Emanu-El. The vote was six for and seven against a recommendation. In the 1919 annual report president Max Rosenfield expressed his willingness to end the rabbi's tenure:

> I would be lacking in candor if I did not point out that these difficulties which have culminated at this time, have roots that go back into the past and their development sooner or later, was inevitable. This has manifested itself in a lack of unity and harmony in the Congregation that is too well known to need any elaboration from me.

Rosenfield attributed the absence of new members and the resultant precarious financial state of the congregation—in 1918 the deficit was $3,000—to the fractious situation. With few recruits, the burden of paying for the temple rested entirely on the current membership, particularly upon the directors, who had personally signed a loan for $18,000. With the hope of restoring harmony and attracting newcomers, since "our Temple contemplates a wider scope in its activities," Rosenfield and a bare majority of directors voted to change the rabbinic leadership of Temple Emanu-El.[72]

In the summer of 1919 the Greenburgs and their daughter Edith left the city for New York, where Rabbi Greenburg eventually entered the insurance business. At an evening reception at their home on Park Row in South Dallas, some 400 friends and acquaintances paid their respects and said their farewells. On their editorial pages both the *Dallas Morning News* and the *Times Herald* recognized Dr. Greenburg's contributions to the city and lamented the departure of a man who was so involved with civic betterment. The *News*, whose president George B. Dealey had been William Greenburg's friend for almost twenty years, paid tribute to the rabbi's accomplishments:

Dr. Greenburg has worked with so much energy, devotion and effectiveness for the moral and social welfare of Dallas, that his departure from the city must be regarded as a distinct misfortune. The announcement of his resignation as rabbi of Temple Emanu-El has brought forth expression of regret from people of all creeds and of none and from people of every station in life, and the regret is as sincere as the expressions of it have been fervent. His is a highly-cultivated social sense, and it has found expression in unremitting work in behalf of the people of Dallas. Almost every agency that has been created in Dallas during the last fifteen years for the social betterment of the community owes its existence no little to the energy and enthusiasm of Dr. Greenburg, while several of them are the result of his initiative.[73]

Certainly, Dr. Greenburg successfully promoted a great many idealistic concepts for the advancement of the Dallas community. But many of his ideas were more liberal than the thinking of his congregants. For instance, just before his resignation he suggested that the directors recommend that the whole congregation, not just the mourners, stand to recite the Kaddish, the prayer for the dead. At that time the directors would not hear of changing the age-old custom, a revision subsequently voted by the congregation.[74] In fact, every single one of his requests for an expanded social and cultural program at the temple—changing the annual meeting to a dinner in the spring, sponsoring a reception after services, forming a volunteer choir, and celebrating important life-cycle events by a contribution to the temple—have been adopted at some point over the years. Unfortunately, during his time as rabbi, William Greenburg was not able to gain broad-based support and bring to fruition all of the progressive programs he had envisioned. His replacement, David Lefkowitz, was destined to accomplish almost all of his predecessor's far-ranging goals. ♆

Felice Kahn (Sanger), on the left, played the violin at an early Symphony Club concert in 1900.

Blanche Cahn Greenburg and Rabbi William H. Greenburg
at the time of their marriage in 1905.

In 1908 the Linz "skyscraper" and the electric streetcar signaled progress.

Patriotic young girls sewed for the Red Cross at Sanger Brothers during World War I. Caroline Schinks and Fannie Koenigsberg (Kahn) are at the front table, Alice Roos (Ehrenfeld) and Frances Alexander at the back table, Dorothy Lorch (Schwab), Ines Munzesheimer Roth, Juanita Kramer (Bromberg) at the side table, and Fanchon Kahn standing.

While transporting supplies overseas during World War I, Lieutenant Clifton Linz's ship, the *Tippecanoe*, was sunk by a torpedo. He and his fellow passengers were rescued as they paddled toward France in their lifeboats.

CHAPTER 5

THERE WAS A MAN

Lefkowitz apparently made a hit in Dallas from the very moment he and his family arrived. . . .[He] was a leader; he was forthright, he was unafraid of critical and controversial issues and he spoke his mind.

Stanley Marcus

The sizzling summer in Dallas was traditionally vacation time for the rabbi and his congregation, so the president of the temple, Herbert Marcus, waited until the fall of 1919 to ask Vice-President Arthur Kramer to chair "the rabbi committee." The group included Alex Sanger, who had personally selected every one of the previous rabbis since the founding of the temple. A delegation of two or three men from the committee dispersed to different cities to investigate the suitability of the incumbent Reform rabbi for the position in Dallas. To the best of Stanley Marcus' recollection, his father, Herbert, along with Arthur Kramer and possibly another person, traveled to Dayton, Ohio, to interview David Lefkowitz.[1] Herbert Marcus later recalled, "We went unannounced to hear Dr. Lefkowitz, and he had not said two words when we decided we wanted him in Dallas."[2]

David Lefkowitz was born on April 11, 1875, in Eperies, Austria-Hungary, the sixth child of Benjamin and Lena Lefkowitz. His father died in 1879 from injuries sustained in a shipwreck while emigrating to the United States with two of the children. Two years later his mother took the three younger children to join their siblings in New York City, leaving behind David's oldest brother, who became a doctor and died in World War I fighting as a soldier for Austria-Hungary. As a lone woman in a patriarchal era Lena Lefkowitz could not care for all three young children, so she placed David, then seven, and his younger brother Herman in the Hebrew Orphan Asylum, where David remained during his public school and undergraduate college years. At nineteen he graduated from the College of the City of New York with a bachelor of science degree. For the last two years of his schooling he was governor of the orphan asylum under the direction of the superintendent, Dr. Herman Baar, a man who, in David Lefkowitz's fond words, "meant so much in my early life."[3]

While David Lefkowitz lived at the Hebrew Orphan Asylum, he discovered that one of his main interests was art. In fact, one summer he enrolled at the Art Students League. But his education at the orphanage in Jewish history, Hebrew grammar, the Bible, and the Talmud, as well as his relationship with the disciplined and learned Dr. Baar, also prepared him to consider the path of the rabbinate, and he entered Hebrew Union College in the fall of 1896. Coincidentally, Professor Gotthard Deutsch, the influential historian at Hebrew Union College who had motivated London-born Rabbi William Greenburg to occupy a Reform pulpit in America, was the man who persuaded David Lefkowitz to attend Hebrew Union College in Cincinnati instead of the more traditional Jewish Theological Seminary in New York.[4] While Lefkowitz was studying at Hebrew Union College, the major influence upon the character of his future life's work was the "reasoned religious outlook as opposed to the worship of tradition as such" of Dr. Isaac M. Wise. Wise's "humane attitude, opposing the stuffed-shirt and calling upon the young rabbi to live on the level of his people, certainly had great weight in the future years of service."[5] Like many of his fellow students at the college, Lefkowitz studied simultaneously at the University of Cincinnati, from which he graduated Phi Beta Kappa in 1899.

In June 1900, Isaac Wise "laid his hands in the traditional manner upon the head of David Lefkowitz and ordained him a rabbi, a teacher of God unto men." At the birth of the twentieth century "in an atmosphere of confidence and trust in the liberal progress of his generation," David

Lefkowitz, then twenty-five years old, embarked on his rabbinical career, departing for his first position as rabbi of Congregation Bene Jeshurun in Dayton, Ohio, a typical middle-size midwestern community.[6] During his first year in Dayton, Lefkowitz married Sadie Braham from Cincinnati, who had attended the Cincinnati College of Music. Their four children— Lewis, Harry, Helen, and David, Jr.—were born in Dayton. David, Jr., who was born in 1911, remembered "going everywhere with his father," especially to the Old Soldiers Home, where the veterans from the Civil War stood proudly to salute the flag. His mother, who also tried to interest the children in current events, took David to see his father's friend Orville Wright, who had been a Dayton bicycle mechanic before he perfected his flying machine, and to Wright Field to see the early World War I bombers.[7]

Besides ministering to his congregation of eighty-two families, which increased to 300 families by 1920, Rabbi Lefkowitz concerned himself with the human needs of his entire community. He organized the Playgrounds and Garden Association and served as president of the Humane Society and of the Associated Charities. At the beginning of World War I he established the Dayton Red Cross and served as its local chairman until he left the city. In 1913 Dayton suffered one of the worst floods on record. David Lefkowitz did yeoman service supervising relief efforts in one of the four sections of the city, heroically bearing the responsibility for the care and feeding of 28,000 refugees from the inundated district. In some instances he had, in his own words, "specific Rabbinical flood obligations, as for instance, taking the remains of a member of our Jewish community in a rough box, conveying it in a grocery wagon to the cemetery, digging the grave myself and saying the prayers."[8] Plainly, Rabbi Lefkowitz was a mainstay and pillar of strength in both the Jewish community and in larger Dayton.

Why, then, would a rabbi so vital to his congregation and to a community that fervidly petitioned him to remain in Dayton consider beginning all over again with unfamiliar people and with a whole new set of challenges and burdens? Rabbi Levi Olan, Rabbi Lefkowitz's successor, surmised that the time had come in Lefkowitz's ministry of twenty years to seek the opportunity to realize his vision for a "dynamic Jewish religious program" which could come alive only in an ample facility such as "the institutional Temple" just completed in Dallas.[9] The persuasive civic boosters from Dallas who recruited him must have not only ignited the imagination of the rabbi concerning the opportunities waiting for him at the temple but also painted a rosy portrait of a community with unlimited potential for growth, which already was the mercantile and financial center for the cattle ranching, cotton distribution, and oil industries in north Texas. Oil had just been discovered near the West Texas towns of Ranger and Eastland and the North Texas towns of Wichita Falls and Burkburnett. This new source of wealth would create a plethora of jobs and business opportunities in Dallas, especially when the massive, rich East Texas oil field was discovered by C. M. "Dad" Joiner and subsequently purchased and developed in 1930 by future oil magnate Haroldson Lafayette (H. L.) Hunt.

The two men who recruited Rabbi Lefkowitz were presidents of flourishing retail establishments, prominent in the mercantile and civic life of Dallas and active as officers and trustees of Temple Emanu-El. Herbert Marcus and Arthur Kramer were part of a group of competing Jewish retailers whose careers and lives intertwined and whose stores, which had generated a marketplace large enough to attract customers from around the state, were critical to the business climate of the city. Of course, these stores were located in the heart of downtown Dallas, for all business was conducted downtown. Neiman-Marcus had been founded in 1907 by Herbert Marcus, his sister Carrie Neiman, and her husband Abraham Lincoln "Al" Neiman. Herbert Marcus had begun his retail career in the women's shoe department at Sanger Brothers, where he caught the eye of Philip Sanger, who soon promoted him to buyer for the boys' department. Carrie Neiman had been the blouse buyer and top saleswoman at A. Harris & Company, another leading department store somewhat smaller than Sanger Brothers. While at Sanger Brothers, Herbert Marcus requested a raise because he and his wife Minnie Lichtenstein Marcus were starting a family. When Alex Sanger offered Marcus a mere $1.87 increase per month, Marcus elected to join Neiman in Atlanta where his brother-in-law had started to hustle a sales promotion business. After two successful years they decided to sell out, opting for cash instead of snapping up the offer of stock in the Missouri franchise for a new soft drink called "Coca-Cola." The Neimans and the Marcus family returned to Dallas to open their own specialty store featuring ready-to-wear apparel for ladies, a modern concept in the era of the private dressmaker and a venture that prospered from its inception.[10]

Unlike Herbert Marcus, Arthur Kramer did not have a retail background. He had graduated from the University of Texas with a law degree and had practiced law until 1912, when he joined his father-in-law's business, A. Harris & Company. Adolph Harris had journeyed from Galveston in 1886 to head a branch of his father-in-law's dry goods store, Fellman, Grumbach & Harris, eventually buying out his partners in 1897 and renaming the store after himself. When Harris died in 1913, Arthur Kramer assumed the presidency of the company. Just as committed as Herbert Marcus to civic and cultural projects, Kramer not only ran and promoted his business but also devoted his energies to the downtown business and arts organizations. President of the Chamber of Commerce in 1930, he would also serve as president of the Dallas Symphony Association from 1925 to 1939 and the Dallas Art Association from 1929 to 1941. Simultaneously, he played a major role in keeping the always underfunded symphony alive and assuring the erection of an art museum for the 1936 Texas Centennial in Dallas.[11]

Another retailer who was destined to become a partner in a major department store had also moved from Galveston to work for Fellman, Grumbach & Harris in 1887. Max Goettinger remained with Adolph Harris' firm until he met Edward Titche, who had come to Dallas from New Orleans to run a store owned by his uncle Aaron Titche. The elder Titche had been murdered in the course of a robbery at the store. In 1902 Edward Titche and Goettinger formed a partnership called Titche-Goettinger (usually shortened to "Titche's") and opened their successful Main Street store.[12] Titche's traffic was boosted when Neiman Marcus relocated nearby in 1914, for now both Titche's and Neiman's were situated several blocks uptown from Sanger Brothers' and E. M. Kahn's established trade. The Sanger Brothers and E. M. Kahn stores were the oldest Jewish firms in Dallas, dating from 1872 and 1873, and they still occupied the blocks on Elm and Lamar streets across from each other. Hurst & Dreyfuss, a men's store founded in 1879 by Gerard Dreyfuss and his brother-in-law Albert Hurst, had merged with E. M. Kahn in the early 1880s. Later Gerard Dreyfuss and his son Sol established their own business, Dreyfuss & Son, opening their store on Main and Murphy in 1910 and in time expanding to Main and Ervay.

Dallas' first skyscraper was built by the Linz brothers in 1898 on Main Street, where Simon, Ben, and Albert Linz occupied the first floor of their own six-story building. Proud, admiring Dallasites could gaze down on the city from a roof garden on top of the Linz Building. For years Linz Brothers Jewelry was reputed to sell more diamonds than any other jewelry store in Texas by dispatching their salesmen wherever Texans struck oil. Joseph Linz, riding horseback on trips to visit ranching customers in 1877, had started the firm in Paris, Texas, probably the first jewelry house in the state. After he moved the business to Dallas in 1891, Linz had an unfortunate falling out with his younger brothers concerning the installation of fans in the store. Long before air conditioning, Joseph's three brothers wanted to introduce ceiling fans to increase the customers' comfort, whereas Joseph did not want the obtrusive fans to ruin the beautiful decor of the new store. When he returned from a European buying trip, Joseph found the fans already oscillating from above. He was so enraged that he left the business.[13] Simon Linz then took over as president of Linz Brothers Jewelers. In 1924 Simon established the Linz Award, donating a large silver loving cup to the person making the greatest contribution to the welfare of Dallas during the past year. Almost sixty-five years later the annually selected Linz awardee continues to be honored at a luncheon, originally sponsored by the now defunct *Dallas Times Herald* and then promoted by the *News*.

The existence of this strong Jewish business community was an important factor in drawing David Lefkowitz to Dallas. When Rabbi Lefkowitz arrived in Dallas in February 1920 to tour the much-touted city of Dallas and look over Temple Emanu-El, Mrs. Victor Hexter, the president of the Women's Guild of Temple Emanu-El, remarked, "Fortunately for us, and we trust for him and his family, we found favor in his sight, and he accepted the call."[14] Even on his first trip to Dallas, Rabbi Lefkowitz demonstrated the leadership qualities that would increase congregational membership and firmly tie the temple to the national Reform movement. According to Minnie Hexter, the new rabbi was well aware of the powerful influence women exerted in bringing the "pulpit and home in unison" and wasted no time prompting the Guild of Temple Emanu-El to join the national organization of temple Sisterhoods formed in 1913. Thus, he formed a potent ally to help achieve his long-range goals for the temple: fostering the spirit of religion and encouraging social relations among the members and their families.

Minnie Hexter was not able to attend the first Sisterhood meeting with "the Doctor" as he was called, or the next meeting of the new board of directors, but she was their top choice for president. She later wrote of her trepidation upon assuming her new responsibilities:

Torn between conflicting emotions as to whether I should try to do my part, and by the more selfish one of sitting back and taking it easy, I attended the meeting on March 16th, one month later, with my mind still wavering. However I was won over tentatively; if proper cooperation were given and interest shown, I would serve, otherwise felt free to tender my resignation unreservedly.

I have minutely detailed this, to show how skeptical I myself was of results. So wonderful however has been the cooperation, so devoted and loyal the women in their service, due undoubtedly to the reverence and esteem in which both Dr. and Mrs. Lefkowitz are held, that what was undertaken with fear and misgiving, has come to be regarded by me as a real privilege and distinct honor.[15]

David Lefkowitz arrived to take up his duties at Temple Emanu-El on June 21, 1920, shuttling back and forth during the heat of the summer to the family's vacation home in Michigan. Then in September, Sadie

Lefkowitz and the children came to Dallas. Lewis was eighteen and ready for college. Sixteen-year-old Harry, fourteen-year-old Helen, and nine-year-old David, Jr., moved to their parents' rented house on Forest Avenue in South Dallas before they settled into the home the congregation built for them at 2415 South Boulevard.

Most of the Jewish community lived in this South Dallas neighborhood which, besides Temple Emanu-El, supported two Orthodox synagogues: Shearith Israel, on Park Avenue and Eakin Street, and Agudas Achim, on Forest and Wendelken. Temple members, mostly of German-speaking extraction, most often belonged to both Emanu-El and to the Columbian Club. With so much in common, they had forged a homogeneous and cohesive social group, generally clustering together in a neighborhood along streets intersecting and surrounding South Boulevard. Situated at South Boulevard and Harwood, the temple was in walking distance of most households, as were John Henry Brown Elementary School and newly built Forest Avenue High School, later called James Madison High School on renamed Martin Luther King Jr. Boulevard. The neighborhood children, who were related to or knew almost all of their neighbors, romped freely up and down South Boulevard, skating along the wide street or playing in the perennial baseball game. Life seemed much simpler in those days when "riding the streetcar downtown was a big event" and friends went to the nearby fairgrounds to enjoy the merry-go-round, while families could see the fireworks from their porches on the Fourth of July.[16]

Rabbi Lefkowitz immediately asserted his role as religious leader of the Jewish community by asking every Jewish place of business to close in observance of the Jewish New Year and the Day of Atonement "as an eloquent pronouncement of our faith to the City at large." Lefkowitz enunciated his rationale: "It is of course the only right thing to do, but many communities have become lax in this matter and have thereby caused a *Hillul Hashem*, a desecration of God's name, and have thus lessened the respect which the general community has felt toward Judaism and us. Let Us Continue To Have Reason For Pride In This Matter."[17] He received unanimous compliance from all businesses owned by Temple Emanu-El members.[18]

In his first few months at temple, comparable to a president's first hundred days, Dr. Lefkowitz set forth his program intended to involve every single member of the congregation. Moreover, before the first New Year service he had created the *Emanu-El Bulletin* to help "develop a congregational spirit" by publicizing the activities taking place at the temple and the opportunities for participation in temple life.[19] The four-page newsletter informed the congregation about the meetings of the newly formed Sisterhood, the well-attended Bible class conducted by Dr. Lefkowitz, the Music Club formed by Sadie Lefkowitz, the proposed Young People's Club, the fruitful results of the new membership committee headed by Lawrence Miller, and the successful efforts of Arthur Kramer to establish a temple library. Besides printing an account of each new club or class just getting under way, each monthly issue of the bulletin related activities of Jewish organizations such as the National Council of Jewish Women and B'nai B'rith, whose Dallas chapters met regularly at the temple.

Furthermore, the rabbi used the pages of his newsletter as a forum for his opinions. Aware that inclement weather drastically reduced religious school attendance, he asked, "Honestly, do you, dear fathers and mothers, keep your children from public school whenever the sky frowns?"[20] He did not hesitate to remind his congregants of their obligation as Jews not only to themselves and to their congregation but also to the Jews throughout the world. In order to help Jews faced with starvation in Europe after World War I, he exhorted his readers to contribute to the $14,000,000 campaign of the Jewish War Relief Fund. As chairman of the Dallas campaign (Jules K. Hexter and Alex Sanger were chairmen of the state campaign), he urged his congregation to "be ready to respond with great good will when the call comes, while we thank God that we can do it, and that is not we who must beg of our brothers. Above all, when a call for a special meeting for this purpose is called, Do Not Shirk."[21] The Dallas Jewish community responded to the campaign by exceeding its quota and contributing $42,000 to the Relief Fund, half of which was pledged after Friday night services at the temple.

When the temple was officially dedicated on December 10, 1920, the new rabbi had so successfully generated an audience for his ministry that 900 people flocked to the Friday evening service, even though David Lefkowitz concurred that "the Temple Board very wisely decided that the service of dedication should be as quiet as possible, in view of the fact that the man who helped build the Temple is not now occupying the pulpit."[22] The overflowing congregation was the first of many tributes to Sadie and David Lefkowitz. Dr. Lefkowitz appreciatively and solemnly observed in the bulletin that "the congregation was truly devout, and felt that they were dedicating themselves," but he could not resist editorializing, "May the pious impulses of the dedicatory service abide lastingly with the congregation."[23]

Even Rabbi Lefkowitz had to be pleased with the turnout at Friday night services, numbering about 400. Nathan Mittenthal, the membership chairman, credited the large crowd to the rabbi's magnetic personality (or what is now termed "charisma") and "interesting and instructive" sermons as well as to the "strenuous and effective membership campaign" under the initial leadership of Realtor Lawrence Miller. On the other hand, once the goal of 500 members was reached in 1922, the rabbi, who had "tried assiduously during the past two years to attend to his pastoral duties of visiting the membership," found that he had to limit his pastoral calls to the sick or to those who particularly needed him. Moreover, the temple board ruled that, because seating was only available for 1,200 people, reservations were essential for the High Holidays and admission tickets would have to be distributed.[24]

Sadie Lefkowitz was no stranger to organizational life. In Dayton she had been president of the Visiting Nurse Association and would found the Dallas Visiting Nurse Association in 1934 to provide adequate health care for the poor, especially for mothers delivering babies at home. The dynamic wife of the new rabbi immediately launched a Women's Exchange which met once a month to bake goods and sew decorative items for sale downtown during the Christmas holidays. Drawing on her earlier music studies, Sadie Lefkowitz also organized a Music Club and sponsored a Choral Club to sing at services and at concerts intended to raise money for the Sisterhood. The funds garnered by the women enabled the Sisterhood to buy a grand piano, discharge a portion of the $3,500 debt owed on the organ, equip the kitchen, supply flowers for the altar at services, and promote entertainments for the Sunday school. The Sisterhood also took charge of dinner arrangements for the annual meeting and the congregational Seder. Dr. Lefkowitz tried to revive the Seder dinner:

> It is replete with the most beautiful symbolism and with the finest poetry, and certainly does not deserve the summary manner with which it was banished from so many of our homes. Such disregard of a beautiful ceremonial is not Reform Judaism—it is deformed Judaism.[25]

In that same spirit of retaining some meaningful traditional Judaic rituals, the Sisterhood sponsored the Kaddish Memorial Fund and restored the "old time custom" of the rabbi's mentioning from the pulpit names of members on the anniversaries of their death.

Spurred by Dr. Lefkowitz, a group of men formed the Brotherhood in 1922, electing as president Lawrence Miller, who had chaired the successful membership campaign when Rabbi Lefkowitz first arrived; Herman Philipson, vice-president, Arthur Star, treasurer, and Edwin Sanger, secretary. The new organization invited interesting and informative speakers to their monthly meetings, supplied ushers to welcome visitors to services, and outfitted the temple basketball team for the Sunday School League. When the congregation decided to celebrate a Fiftieth Anniversary Jubilee in 1923, dating the inception of the temple from the beginning of the Hebrew Benevolent Association, the Brotherhood, with Clarence Linz as chairman of the banquet committee, supervised arrangements for the Congregational Jubilee Banquet held in the Junior Ballroom at the Adolphus Hotel.

While the temple was experiencing a renaissance of activity and celebrating fifty years of Jewish organizational life in Dallas, its members were well aware of the prominence in Dallas of the insidious fraternal order of the Ku Klux Klan. This hate group threatened to intimidate, exclude, and isolate the Jew as well as the African American and the Catholic. Originally formed in 1866 as a secret social club by a group of Tennessee Confederate veterans passionately opposed to Republican reconstruction policies, the Klan became a vehicle for continued white supremacy. Quiet for a few decades, the Klan was rejuvenated in the 1920s by a Spanish-American War veteran and former Methodist circuit rider, Joseph Simmons, who designed the white hoods and robes and formulated the "Masonically inspired ritual" of the Invisible Empire of the Knights of the Ku Klux Klan.[26]

The Klan's avowed aim—to preserve traditional moral and civic values seemingly disregarded by the Charleston-dancing, speakeasy-going generation coming of age in the 1920s—found a responsive audience in towns across America, particularly among fraternal organizations like the Masons. For many conventional people social mores were changing much too rapidly in the permissive era after World War I when women dared to bob their hair, shorten their skirts, and smoke and drink, while both sexes exploited the freedom and privacy of the automobile.

In 1921 Klansmen organizing new units or klaverns, as they were called, traveled across Texas. Dallas Klan Number 66 announced its existence on May 21, 1921, with an eerie torchlight parade in downtown Dallas:

> As if by prearranged signal, the street lights were extinguished over the route of the parade at 9 o'clock at the minute the first white-clad figure emerged from the old Majestic Theater building, bearing aloft the American flag. He was followed by a second carrying the burning cross of the Ku Klux. By single file and with ten feet distance between the marchers, the long, silent procession wended its way into the hurrying Saturday night crowds down Main Street to Murphy and across to Elm up Elm up to the theater. It wasn't a noisy demonstration. Not a word was spoken by the 789 shrouded figures in the line of march—and very few by the thousands on the sidewalks and in the streets who stopped to watch.[27]

96

Eight-year-old M. J. Mittenthal remembered how "scared to death" he was when he and his sister Blanche, with their parents Nathan and Emma Mittenthal, saw marchers carrying signs proclaiming "White Supremacy," "100% American," and "All Native Born."[28] After this grim spectacle a *Dallas Morning News* editorial on May 24 sounded the first alarm against the Klan, exclaiming that while "proclaiming themselves the conservators of law, the men who marched the streets of Dallas Saturday night made themselves the exemplars of lawlessness, in that they insolently exalt themselves over all constituted authority." David Lefkowitz wrote to George B. Dealey praising his "very courageous stand in both of your newspapers on the sinister Ku Klux Klan," an unpopular decision for the *Morning News* and *Dallas Journal* which cost them circulation.[29] In the resurgent Klan's heyday from 1921–1925 an estimated 13,000 Dallasites belonged to the organization, perhaps the highest ratio of Klansmen to the general population in the country.[30] Horace Landauer, the vice-president of Titche-Goettinger, came home from work one evening and told his family how horrified he was to hear that a number of his business acquaintances had joined the Klan.[31]

From 1920–1925, the Klan successfully pursued two agendas. First, they portrayed themselves as the guardians of morality with the near-vigilante right to punish "wrongdoers"; they intimidated their victims with threats and beatings without any check by law enforcement officials. Second, their members held positions of power in local and state governmental bodies and could change policy to conform to their exclusionary program of bigotry. In Dallas the Klan infiltrated city politics and was strong enough to demand the firing of Helman Rosenthal, a Jew, because the secret society wanted "one of their own kind in his position."[32] Rosenthal, an expert chemist, had come to Dallas in 1918 to head the water department. Even worse, hooded Klan members physically dragged Philip Rothblum, also Jewish, from his home and whipped him because he associated with an African American.[33]

In a small town the Klan could terrify people into leaving town. In Graham (between Dallas and Wichita Falls) Morris Zale had noticed that customers were starting to boycott the fledgling jewelry business he operated in leased space at the City Drugstore, even though he was a member of the Retail Merchants Association and the local Masonic lodge. Zale knew about the state-wide activities of the Klan and was aware that Graham had developed an active Klan membership. After viewing a downtown parade and a ceremonial cross burning, he decided to sell out and leave town. As "the only Jew in town . . . when I saw that cross burning, I was scared to death."[34] After being virtually run out of Graham in 1924, Morris Zale started all over again and founded the Zale Jewelry Company in nearby Wichita Falls, which had a small Jewish community and a less strident Klan membership than its neighboring city.

After reports of floggings and vandalism perpetrated on the homes of Dallas citizens by Klan members, a group of prominent citizens headed by Judge C. M. Smithdeal and former Texas Attorney General M. M. Crane issued a public call for a mass meeting to stifle the Klan:

> Recent events constitute our excuse for this call. Some of our citizens have been driven from the communities in which they live by threats of personal violence. Others have been seized in the presence of their wives and daughters and dragged away to some secluded spot and there brutally beaten and otherwise maltreated.

> In view of the situation, which we have not exaggerated, we call upon all citizens of Dallas county, who are not Klansmen to meet with us, the undersigned, at the City Hall in the city of Dallas, on Tuesday evening the 4th day of April 1922, at 8 o'clock for the purpose of considering what shall be done in the emergency that now confronts us. We must provide adequate protection to our people against mob violence.[35]

Rabbi David Lefkowitz was among the 400 Dallas citizens who signed the call for a mass meeting to demonstrate against the Klan, along with several members of Temple Emanu-El. The 5,000 citizens who answered the call, only 2,000 of whom could fit into the city hall, organized the Dallas County Citizens League, perhaps the first formal anti-Klan group in the country. In order to rid city and county government of Klan members, the Citizens League pledged to deny votes for any Klan member or "anyone who sympathizes with it or apologizes" for the organization or its acts. Klan candidates had already carried the 1922 election in Dallas county.[36]

The Klan's influence continued to burgeon in Texas, culminating in the celebration of Ku Klux Klan Day at the State Fair on October 24, 1923. The day began with the dedication of Hope Cottage, a home for unwanted babies, which had been built with Klan money. An ironic note to Alex Sanger's close connection to every single civic endeavor in the city was the fact that just as he was seated on the podium during the anti-Klan Citizens League meeting in 1922, he was again present on the platform at the Hope Cottage dedication to hear Mayor Louis Blaylock extol the efforts of the Klan. Later that day 7,000 Klan members, who had paraded to the fairgrounds, and 25,000 spectators assembled as Imperial Wizard Hiram W. Evans, a former Dallas dentist, addressed the crowd. Evans articulated one of the Klan's major objectives by underscoring the necessity of limiting immigration to Nordic types whose "highest allegiance" would be pledged to America. He flatly stated that Negroes, Jews, and Catholics could never assimilate into American society. Even though the Jews were "law abiding, family people" who were "mentally alert," "their homes are not American, but Jewish homes, into which we cannot go and from which they will never emerge for a real intermingling with Americans." Since the Jew "has been wandering upon the face of the earth . . . with no national attachment . . . patriotism [for him] as the Anglo-Saxon feels it is impossible."[37]

Rabbi Lefkowitz, who was positive he represented "all the Jewish people of Dallas" when he denounced the Klan, unhesitatingly refuted Evans' speech two days later in his Friday night sermon, which was printed in the Sunday edition of the *Dallas Morning News*. With cool clarity, the rabbi rebutted Evans' charges concerning the Jew's inability to intermingle in America, but he could not help vehemently and emotionally denying Evans' charge of the Jew's lack of patriotism: "He is a thousand times wrong. . . . [He] has wrongly flouted my people and I will not be silent."

99

Since the supreme act of patriotism was fighting and dying for one's country, how could the Jews who served valiantly side by side with their fellow Americans in World War I, men whose heroic deeds the rabbi detailed, be denied their rightful place as Americans? He eloquently defended "his people" in the forum offered by George Dealey, publisher of the *Dallas Morning News*, and he declared to an appreciative non-Jewish reader of his article, "I do hope with you that my words of warning and my appeals to patriotism, common sense, and love of God may break the hold of the Klan upon a great many well-meaning people who were lured into it at the very beginning."[38]

In the Masonic Lodge, Lefkowitz, who was a thirty-third degree Mason, minced no words as he grilled fellow Masons known to be Klan members, "Do you believe in God and brotherhood and care of the widow and orphan? How do you square that with your actions relative to discrimination as to race and creed?"[39] After this public stance against the Klan, the rabbi "was threatened with being ridden out of town on a rail and tarred and feathered," according to his son, Rabbi David Lefkowitz, Jr., who admitted that "things were sort of 'itchy' around the house for a few days."[40] Rabbi Lefkowitz's forthright stand, as well as the *News'* editorials against the Klan, plus the work of the Dallas County Citizens League, began to temper Dallas' responsiveness to the Klan. Then, Mrs. Miriam A. (Ma) Ferguson, whose husband had been governor of the state, won the 1924 Democratic primary for governor, beating Judge Felix Robertson, the Klan candidate from Dallas. Her victory, which was tantamount to winning the election in the Democratic state, indicated the decline of the Klan's power in Dallas.

In a very real sense, the Reform rabbi in America, often one of the most educated clergymen in his city, was the representative to the Gentile community not only for his congregation but also for all the Jews of the city. Noted Professor Jacob Marcus has stressed the importance of having "an eloquent, educated, cultured rabbi speak for them, defend them against calumnies, and emphasize the virtues of Judaism." Not surprisingly, an outstanding Reform rabbi attracted "Jews of means and social aspirations" who wished to be associated with a congregation led by just such a man.[41] The members of Temple Emanu-El felt, in the words of president of the congregation Arthur Kramer, that "both within the confines of the Temple and in his daily contact outside," their rabbi "reflect[ed] credit upon the name of the Jew, himself, and his congregation."[42]

Dr. Lefkowitz possessed a rare combination of mystical goodness, the willingness to speak up for his convictions, and the acumen to accomplish his objectives. For instance, he was a fervent exponent of and recognized authority on the principle of the separation of church and state, especially in the public schools, and wrote a definitive paper on the subject for the Central Conference of American Rabbis and the *Universal Jewish Encyclopedia.* On a different level, but adhering to the same tenets of freedom and fairness, he wrote Dr. Norman Crozier, the superintendent of the Dallas schools, on behalf of a well-qualified young Jewish woman who had been passed over for a position in the public schools "in favor of others less well prepared." Rabbi Lefkowitz remarked, "I have long felt that there must be something wrong in the situation that finds Jewish school teachers so little represented in the city of Dallas school system." His "suspicion" was that Jewish girls did not study to be teachers because of the anti-Semitic attitude of the school system. The rabbi went on unflinchingly: "A story of that kind gets noised about very soon, and I should prefer to have the matter cleared up in justice to all before unpleasant recriminations are made."[43]

Apparently, David Lefkowitz could write such a blunt letter about discrimination against a Jew to a school administrator—and expect his advice to be heard and followed—because he had earned respect as a recognized leader in the community. Besides his efforts against the Ku Klux Klan, he actively supported and became chairman of the Dallas County American Red Cross Chapter and participated in other community-at-large philanthropic efforts such as the Community Chest and the Humane Society. When the summons came for a mass meeting in 1930 to discuss a changeover from the commissioner form of city government to the council/city manager plan of government, David Lefkowitz was asked to lend his support to muster citizen approval. Every month he addressed ten or more civic or religious organizations in the community

101

ranging from the Highland Park Methodist Church Adult Bible Class, who heard him speak about "The Jewish Home," to an open forum at Southern Methodist University, where he spoke on "The Bible in the Public Schools," to the Auxiliary of the Dallas County Medical Society, whose members listened to "The Romance of Texas History."[44]

In addition to his speaking engagements and his sermons, the rabbi also broadcast a half-hour radio program every Sunday afternoon, during which he would conduct a brief service accompanied by the Sisterhood chorus led by Mrs. Lefkowitz or by the temple choir, deliver a short address, and perhaps answer some questions called in by his listeners. The Brotherhood, with Sol Dreyfuss in charge, originally arranged to air the High Holy Day services in 1925 for those housebound Jews who could not attend services. Then, after a few years of broadcasting monthly Friday night services, in 1929 Rabbi Lefkowitz started his weekly Sunday radio program to "feed" the "hungry Jewish souls" living in remote communities in Texas, Oklahoma, and Arkansas. He explained his purpose thus: "I conceive the service . . . as a religious service for all who desire to join . . .not only for the Gentiles who listen in, and not only for the Jews of Dallas, who can, if they desire have such services in the house of God very near to them, but also and in large measure for the Jews who have no such opportunities, the faithful, devoted Jews in the smaller towns and hamlets who would be without any Jewish services if it were not for the Sunday broadcast."[45]

Lefkowitz received heartfelt letters of thanks from the grateful Jews who tuned in to hear him. A Jewish woman in Big Spring wrote, "Every Sunday we listen to your wonderful radio services, and I cannot tell you how much it means to me out here in West Texas away from any Temple or Jewish services. It means so much to my boys who do not have the advantages I had as a child in being able to attend Sunday School and services in Chicago, and to have them hear these beautiful services means more than words can express." Interestingly, David Lefkowitz's fan mail, which was considerable, reveals a greater preponderance of non-Jewish listeners, people who had not had the opportunity to hear Jewish prayers and were interested in listening to the thoughts of a Jewish rabbi on topics relevant to them, such as, "What the Jews Think of Jesus" or "Americanism" or "Some Fictions About the Jews." Their letters, as well as the letters from Jews, expressed gratitude for the rabbi's spiritual guidance and succor during the time that the country was plunging into the Depression of the 1930s, but it was probably the response from the Gentile community, as well as the generous Brotherhood sponsorship, that kept Dr. Lefkowitz on the air for nineteen years until he became Rabbi Emeritus in 1949.[46]

During the 1920s as Dallas' population grew to 265,000, the leaders of Temple Emanu-El actively patronized and promoted cultural events and worked for civic betterment as participants on committees dedicated to improving the substance and quality of life in the city. Serving on the Ulrickson Committee on public works was Alex Weisberg, a lawyer with Thompson, Knight, Baker and Harris, who would become president of the temple in 1950. Chaired by C. E. Ulrickson, the committee drew up the most ambitious city planning project ever proposed for Dallas—the Ulrickson Committee Program of Public Improvements. Passed in a public election in 1927, the $23,900,000 bond issue insured the financial base for an orderly growth and expansion of Dallas' public facilities. With the rechanneling of the Trinity River, the city reclaimed the bottom lands between Dallas and Oak Cliff for industrial development and constructed an elaborate system of viaducts and underpasses to bind the city together, of which the triple underpass linking Commerce, Main, and Elm streets to the western part of the city was the most innovative. Moreover, the Ulrickson Plan also allocated money to woefully underfunded public schools, provided funds to widen and straighten streets for commercial traffic, and approved the construction of an art museum, public parks, and additions to Parkland Hospital. For Alex Weisberg's dedicated and conscientious work on the plan (he devoted several hours each day for two years to its preparation and gave up his summer vacation for its completion), the Linz Committee selected him as the 1927 Linz Awardee, the person making the greatest contribution to the welfare of Dallas during that year.[47]

Martin Weiss was another industrious temple member who pressed the city for improvements to benefit and improve the lot of all its citizens. Owner of a millinery supply business in downtown Dallas, Martin Weiss

103

lived across the Trinity River in Oak Cliff. As the founder and president for twenty years of the Associated Civic Leagues West of the Trinity River, the tireless Weiss promoted his home community of Oak Cliff, which he represented on the Ulrickson Plan Committee and the City Plan Commission, as well as on the committee that recommended the city manager form of government which Dallas adopted in 1930. A stalwart advocate of commercial aviation, Weiss was one of the dignitaries gathered at Love Field to welcome the American hero Charles Lindbergh as he taxied across the runway in *The Spirit of St. Louis*, the plane he had recently flown to Paris on his historic solo journey across the Atlantic. When Lindbergh stopped in Dallas in 1927 on his nation-wide tour to tout commercial aviation, 100,000 people turned out to see him dedicate Love Field. The 173-acre field used to train pilots during World War I had just been purchased by the city for development as a municipal airport.[48]

A successful man with little formal schooling, who was particularly interested in education, Weiss was an enthusiastic supporter of the religious school and chaired the religious school committee for several years. He awarded silver medals to pupils who maintained a record of ninety-five percent in studies, attendance, and deportment. Of the 460 pupils enrolled in the school in 1925, sixty met the requirements to earn the medals Weiss handed out. At the closing school assembly each May he also presented a book to the best boy and best girl in each room. When the congregation relocated to Northwest Highway and Hillcrest Road in 1957, the youth room was named for Martin and Charlotte Weiss to commemorate their commitment to the religious school.

Temple leaders also lent their vigorous backing to the city's struggling arts organizations. When the Chamber of Commerce selected Arthur Kramer as its president in 1930, the multi-faceted president of A. Harris & Company was already functioning as head of both the Dallas Art Association and the Dallas Symphony. The Art Association, which had been initiated by a group of women in 1903, displayed paintings and sculpture in the Fine Arts Building at Fair Park while trying to marshal support for a permanent museum. During the time Kramer was president of the organization, he enlisted Herbert Marcus to drum up funds for an arts facility. Business rivals Kramer and Marcus, who cooperated at the temple and for the museum, also competed to see who would be credited with bringing grand opera to Dallas annually. For years Marcus persistently raised much of the money to bring the Chicago Civic Opera to Dallas. Nevertheless, whenever Kramer went to New York on business, he kept prodding the more prestigious Metropolitan Opera Company to include Dallas in the itinerary for the spring tour. In 1939, when Kramer finally persuaded the Met to come to Dallas and turned to the Dallas Chamber of Commerce for financial assistance, the Chamber would not commit itself immediately. Undeterred, Kramer coolly signed the contract and raised the requisite underwriting himself.[49]

Eli Sanger, the son of Philip and Cornelia Sanger, founded the Civic Music Association in 1930 because he thought Dallas should have a series of concerts featuring outstanding artists. The series of six programs a year showcased such virtuosos as Lauritz Melchior, Marian Anderson, and Yehudi Menuhin performing in McFarlin Auditorium at Southern Methodist University and endured long after Sanger's death in 1952.[50]

For Temple Emanu-El, the 1920s concluded on a celebratory and convivial note. The congregation honored Dr. Lefkowitz' ten productive years of "service and leadership" in Dallas with a dinner at the Columbian Club. To express their love and appreciation to Rabbi and Mrs. Lefkowitz, the congregation presented them with the keys to a "classy Chrysler."[51] Rabbi Lefkowitz's peers also honored him in 1929 by electing him to the presidency of the Central Conference of American Rabbis, the rabbinic arm of the Reform movement. In his position as head of the Reform rabbinate, he undertook many more speaking engagements, addressing the graduation class of Hebrew Union College and delivering speeches at other temples' celebrations, as well as attending executive meetings of the Union of American Congregations. One of his main chores was securing a place for rabbis who were without a pulpit or who were unhappy in their present one. In 1927, just before he had taken on the conference role, he helped organize the Kallah of Texas Rabbis, an organization unique to Texas that recognized "all shades of Judaism." Orthodox, Conservative, and Reform rabbis convened once a year for "earnest discussion on academic Jewish subjects."[52] When the convention was held in Dallas in 1929 while David Lefkowitz was its second president, sixteen rabbis met at both Reform Temple Emanu-El and Conservative Shearith Israel. Along with encouraging communication between rabbis from around the state, the members of the organization acted in concert to fulfill certain objectives, such as purchasing the Judaica book collection of its first president, Houston's Abraham I. Schechter, in order to present it to the University of Texas as a nucleus for a Semitic library.

In a gesture which indicated how widely and warmly Rabbi Lefkowitz was respected in the community, SMU conferred an honorary Doctor of Laws Degree upon him in 1930, the first time any Methodist school bestowed an honorary degree on a rabbi.[53] Moreover, Rabbi Lefkowitz preached frequently in the university's chapel, and when he became Rabbi Emeritus in 1949, he lectured on contemporary Judaism as a visiting professor at SMU's Perkins School of Theology.

For a decade David Lefkowitz had fulfilled the role of rabbi as envisioned by the leaders of the temple who had welcomed him to Dallas in 1920. He readily enlisted the cooperation and affection of his congregation which had grown to 558 members during his ministry. An acknowledged civic force, he was highly esteemed and sought after in the Dallas community. He was a leader of his fellow rabbis in Texas and in the American Reform movement nationwide. Most pertinent of all, as Rabbi Gerald Klein said, "He in a certain sense gave a certain cohesiveness to the American Jewish community. There were people in this community who knew that there was a rabbi but they didn't [personally] know a rabbi, didn't see a rabbi, didn't listen to a rabbi, didn't sit and eat with a rabbi. He was a fellow who moved about the community whether it was on the basis of the rotary club or fellow pastors."[54] By his example and by his precepts the rabbi taught a new generation, heretofore unacquainted with the essence of Judaism, the Jews' fundamental ethical and intellectual outlook, their generosity, and their profound attachment to their own and to the larger community. By communicating to both Jews and non-Jews a notion of what it means to be a Jew, David Lefkowitz enhanced the image of his people to all of Dallas and heightened the cohesion and pride of his congregation. ☜

Rabbi David Lefkowitz

The congregation moved to South Boulevard and Harwood in 1917 but
the temple was not dedicated until Rabbi David Lefkowitz arrived in 1920.

Rabbi David Lefkowitz's first confirmation class, 1921. First row: Marie Herman, Frances Sanger (Mossiker), Anita Harris, Phyllis Pike (Cahn), Mildred Harris, Florence Levi, Olga Mandelstam. Middle row: Albert Kramer, Jr., unknown, Marguerite Rosenberg (Tobias), Dr. Lefkowitz, Bea Finneburgh (Fox), Marcella Lazarus (Iskowitz), Belle Friedman. Top row: Zellner Eldridge, Clarence Gradwohl, Ben Friedman, David Cahn, Mervin Weil, Morton Ullery, Lee Segal.

Sadie Braham Lefkowitz invigorated the temple Sisterhood and served a term as its president.

Minnie Werthheimer Hexter presided over the temple
Guild, the National Council of Jewish Women, and
the Sisterhood of Temple Emanu-El.

Children played up and down South Boulevard. Front row: Edward Bromberg,
Edna Kahn (Flaxman), Marie Levi (Bitterman), Jack Miller, Jean Miller (Garfield),
Lawrence Marcus, Clarence Agress, Herbert Marcus, Jr., Natalie Levin (Simon).
Back row: Henriette Fechenbach (Cline), Frances Levin (Singer), Helen Star (Flexner),
Frankie Kouza (Curry), Evelyn Wortsman (Eldridge), Zelman Brounoff, Henry Miller, Jr.

Beside presiding over Temple Emanu-El, Arthur Kramer also headed the Dallas Art Museum, the Dallas Symphony, and the Chamber of Commerce during the 1920s and 1930s.

Minnie Marcus, a president of Sisterhood, and Herbert Marcus, president of Neiman-Marcus and a president of Temple Emanu-El, with their sister-in-law Ophelia (Mrs. Theodore) Marcus.

CHAPTER 6

THE STORM CLOUDS LOOM

Please let me know if our dues cannot be lowered for 1933. We are not protesting that they are too high, but for the time being, we cannot afford to pay that sum. My mother is dependent now, to a certain extent upon me, and I'm just starting a new business having lost everything I had last year. If we have no more calamities, I'll be able to do better in 1934.

A Temple Member

When the stock market crashed in October 1929, its fall triggered the end of an era characterized by America's youthful exuberance. The burgeoning but fragile bubble of stock and commodities speculation and "fictitious prosperity with abnormal profits" had burst. Time had run out for those Americans who had gaily and heedlessly reveled in seemingly endless good times and indulged in the "reckless extravagance" of the "Roaring Twenties."[1] Even though Dallas seemed remote from Wall Street, the Depression was gradually but insidiously sapping prosperity across the land. By the end of 1930 unemployment began to reach ominous proportions. In order to "spread employment around," the city and county recommended certain expedients for business owners such as discharging married women from jobs and instituting a five-day week in retail stores as well as instructing state and county governments to use relatively cheap labor instead of costly modern machinery.[2] When the number of unemployed reached 18,500 out of a population of 260,475, an emergency relief committee appointed by Chamber of Commerce asked

111

the more fortunate citizens of Dallas to contribute $100,000 for the alleviation of hunger and destitution in the city. By 1932 the city had drafted a program of work-relief projects listed in a special bond issue in order to provide employment for the jobless.[3]

Late 1932 and early 1933, before President Franklin D. Roosevelt could implement his New Deal and start the national recovery program, marked the nadir of the Depression for Dallas. When federal funds became available for public works, the city filed an application in Washington requesting over two million dollars for civic improvements. The extensive public works program designed to put men back to work enabled the city to undertake massive projects such as the triple underpass at the foot of Elm, Main, and Commerce, later to be remembered as the site where in 1963 President John F. Kennedy was assassinated.

Understandably but regrettably, the Depression of the 1930s made life much harsher and even hopeless for many Americans. The scarcity of jobs exacerbated the anti-Semitism and xenophobia that had been on the upswing in the United States since the mass immigration of Jews, Poles, Slovaks, and Italians in the late nineteenth and early twentieth centuries, when severe economic dislocation and a wave of bloody pogroms had impelled "half of the Jewish population of Eastern Europe" to emigrate to the United States.[4] During 1912 and 1913, 101,330 Jewish immigrants flowed to the eastern ports of the United States, the largest number since the four-year span of 1904 through 1908.[5] In order to relieve the embarrassment of having his fellow coreligionists live in squalid and congested slum conditions on the lower East Side of New York, financier Jacob H. Schiff contributed half a million dollars for the purpose of piloting Russian immigrants through Galveston. For seven years, 1907–1914, until World War I brought an end to Russian immigration, the agents of the Galveston movement, directed by Rabbi Henry Cohen, greeted and sent 10,000 Jews on their way to jobs, most often menial, in towns in every state west of the Mississippi.[6] The Dallas Federated Jewish Charities agreed to accept three or four immigrants from each boat docking at the Gulf port and received an allowance from the Galveston Bureau for their care.[7] Meanwhile, in the United States an anti-immigrant attitude crystallized around the view that the poorly dressed and Yiddish-speaking newcomers from Eastern Europe, quite unlike the first wave of Jews from Western Europe who in dress and customs had resembled their fellow settlers, represented a dilution of American national identity and an economic threat because of their willingness to work cheaply.

In the 1930s many American Jews, particularly the children of the recent immigrants from Russia, Austria-Hungary, and Rumania who had concentrated in the eastern cities, often thought of themselves as outsiders. When Herbert Mallinson was president of the temple in 1939, he attended the National Council of Federations Meeting in Baltimore and "was amazed to learn of the wave of anti-Semitism that apparently exists in some sections of the East." Not only had Ivy League universities such as Harvard and Yale surreptitiously instituted a quota system that became universal in the nation's private schools, but access to certain professions such as medicine and law, journalism and teaching, as well as employment in certain large corporations, was tacitly restricted to but a few especially talented Jews. Yet Mallinson felt that a different climate existed in the Southwest, "especially in Dallas," where "we should be proud of our fine Jewish citizenship and the excellent good will between all creeds and faiths."[8]

The election of Franklin Delano Roosevelt to the presidency in 1932 heralded a "New Deal" for Americans buffeted by the worsening Depression. David Lefkowitz praised the president's inspirational inaugural speech, in which Roosevelt stated that "the only thing we have to fear is fear itself" as the "exceptionally courageous, forthright kind of an address that the American people have been waiting for."[9] Moreover, FDR welcomed Jews to positions in his administration, selecting Henry Morgenthau, Jr., his upstate New York neighbor, as secretary of the treasury and Felix Frankfurter, then a professor at Harvard Law School and a protege of Justice Louis Brandeis (who had been appointed to the Supreme Court by Woodrow Wilson in 1916), as one of his advisors.

In his effort to rally the country to the New Deal, Roosevelt also appointed Jews to positions of local authority. One of the most vital agencies was the National Recovery Administration (NRA), whose Blue Eagle emblem became the symbol of the New Deal. The NRA administered detailed mandatory codes for business and industry, such as a minimum wage law requiring an employer to pay $1.25 an hour and $60.00 for a forty-hour week. President Roosevelt appointed temple member Hyman Pearlstone, president of Higginbotham Pearlstone Hardware Company and a director of the First National Bank, as the chairman of the Dallas NRA Board. At this time Pearlstone also served as a member of the finance committee of Temple Emanu-El, which had elected his brother Julius as president of the congregation. Roosevelt also tapped Fred Florence, the president of the Republic National Bank who was then the treasurer of Temple Emanu-El, for the chairmanship of the Texas-Oklahoma District NRA Board. In a display of solidarity and patriotism, the Dallas banks strongly upheld the Roosevelt administration's plan for regulating business and industry with a Victory Jubilee featuring a downtown parade and a program at Fair Park.[10]

In order to enforce NRA codes, the government set up adjustment boards throughout the country. In April 1934 President Roosevelt appointed David Lefkowitz chairman of the National Recovery Administration State Adjustment Board for Texas. The local committee heard the grievances of employees and the counter arguments of employers and made decisions enforceable by law. When it arbitrated between the Dallas electrical firms and "their complaining employees who were ready to strike," Rabbi Lefkowitz was gratified that "practically all of the demands of the employees were sustained and the decision was accepted by the employers."[11] Just as Dallas Jewry had contributed to Dallas' earlier prosperity, so it united with the whole community to lift the city out of the financial quagmire that was synonymous with the thirties.

During the Depression practically every Jewish congregation in America struggled with building indebtedness and an inability to meet current expenses because of resignations and requests for dues reductions. Diminished income from dues made it necessary for Emanu-El's directors to take out a bank loan for operating expenses and to reduce all salaries, including the rabbi's. Dr. Lefkowitz' salary was cut from $12,000 to $10,000 and then to $8,400 in 1934. In order to conserve money and retain members, the board voted to pare down the temple bulletin from eight to four pages and decided to cancel back dues obligations of long standing, thereby allowing a member to retain his membership while paying on a monthly basis. The trustees also established a classification entitled "Contributors to the Religious School Budget" for those families who had children in the religious school but could not afford to join the temple.[12] Board member Jack Mann, who was co-chairman of the membership committee, undertook the task of soliciting the unaffiliated parents.[13]

By 1935, according to the Work Projects Administration history, "Dallas showed definite signs of recovery from the depression." Bank deposits rose as new businesses located in Dallas. A major factor in Dallas' recuperation was the upsurge of the oil business in Texas, Oklahoma, Louisiana, and Arkansas. Centrally located to service the entire oil-producing region, Dallas was just over a hundred miles away from the East Texas oil field, the largest pool of oil ever known until the discovery of the Saudi Arabian reserves. As Dallas became the financial and equipment supply hub of the oil industry for the region, oil replaced cotton as the generator of new jobs, businesses, and income for the city.[14]

Another forceful stimulus for economic recovery was Dallas' designation as host city for the Texas Centennial Exposition of 1936. Dallas, which did not even exist in 1836 when the Republic of Texas won its independence from Mexico, captured the prize over San Antonio, home of the Alamo, and Houston, an early state capital. The award was based on competitive bidding, and Dallas aggressively pledged the $4,000,000 plant of the State Fair and an additional $5,500,000 in cash for a new museum of art, a hall of state, and other facilities for the exposition. Supposedly the commission was also "influenced by the fact that Dallas was the population center of the state and had 46 years experience handling State Fair crowds."[15] In order to secure the Texas Centennial for Dallas, the presidents of the three largest banks in the city—Nathan Adams of First National Bank, Fred F. Florence of Republic National Bank, and Robert L. Thornton of Mercantile Bank and Trust—had joined forces to organize the Texas Centennial Central Exposition Corporation. Now Fred Florence became its president.

115

In an era when practically no Jews held executive positions in banks, Fred Florence was the exception. In 1920 William O. Conner, president of Guaranty Bank and Trust Company, and former credit manager at Sanger Brothers, recruited Florence, then president of the bank in Alto, Texas, and mayor of the town, as vice-president. Nine years later when Florence became president of the bank, whose name was changed to Republic National Bank, its deposits had made Republic the second largest bank in Dallas and by 1953 the largest in the Southwest.[16] Just before he became president of the bank, Florence married Helen Lefkowitz, only daughter of the rabbi. Before their marriage the banker had taken an active interest in the temple, becoming its treasurer in 1927, a position he would hold for over thirty years.

United States Secretary of Commerce Daniel C. Roper formally opened the Centennial Exposition on June 6, 1936. Shortly afterward, President and Mrs. Franklin D. Roosevelt and Vice-President John Nance Garner, a Texan who had formerly been Speaker of the House of Representatives, also visited the art deco buildings depicting the splendor of Texas' romantic history and economic progress. Along with a Hall of State, the exposition boasted a Civic Center that included the Dallas Museum of Fine Arts, Hall of Domestic Arts, Hall of Horticulture, Hall of Natural History, Aquarium, and Open Air Theater. Among the exhibition buildings, of which the largest was the Ford Motor Company's, Lone Star Gas Company erected a Hall of Religions to be used for exhibits of different religious groups in Texas, as well as for its own company exhibit.

As chairman of the Committee on Jewish Participation in the Texas Centennial, Dr. Lefkowitz presented several worthwhile ideas designed to illuminate the role of Judaism in Texas. First, he planned an exhibit similar to those of other religious groups. He also wanted to publish a booklet about the Jewish pioneers of Texas written by Rabbi Henry Cohen of Galveston. Lastly, he suggested a program of important Jewish speakers. Fortunately, Rabbi Lefkowitz was able to obtain the Jewish Exhibit displayed at Chicago's "A Century of Progress" Fair, and he also enlisted Rabbi Stanley R. Brav, his new assistant, to install it in a booth alongside other religious exhibits. Furthermore, funds for the projected speakers program seemed assured when the National Council of Jewish Women offered to sponsor and sell Dr. Cohen's booklet, "One Hundred Years of Jewry in Texas."[17]

For the principal speaker at Jewish Day at the exposition, Dr. Lefkowitz tried to induce Rabbi Stephen S. Wise, the political activist and Zionist who was "easily the best known Jewish figure of his time," to come to Dallas.[18] Because both Hadassah and other Zionist organizations were holding conventions in Dallas during the week of November 1, 1936, David Lefkowitz asked Rabbi Wise to talk on the general topic of "Jewish life, Jewish belief and Jewish hope" since "the Zionist point of view is going to be stressed quite positively."[19] A proven speaker, Dr. Wise had visited Dallas in 1928 to present the case for the Jewish Institute of Religion, a new rabbinical school which he had founded. At that time he addressed the largest crowd, about 1,500, "that ever squeezed its way into the Temple," and attracted such a large audience to the open forum of the Civic Federation of Dallas that guests had to be turned away.[20]

When Dr. Wise regretfully wrote that he could not appear in Dallas and the expected sale of the small historical booklet proved to be "disappointing in the extreme," Dr. Lefkowitz dropped all plans to have a special program during the Centennial.[21] That decision seemed prudent, especially when he learned that attendance was minimal at services programmed by other religious groups. Perhaps not from a religious standpoint, but in all other ways, the Texas Centennial from June through November 1936 was a resounding success, enticing millions of visitors to Dallas. It was so popular that the exposition committee repeated it from June to October the next year under the name of the Greater Texas and Pan American Exposition.

Rabbi Stanley B. Brav, who set up and sometimes manned the Jewish exhibit at the exposition, was Temple Emanu-El's first assistant rabbi. He came to Dallas with his wife Ruth after graduating from Hebrew Union College in June 1934. With the country still in the midst of the Depression, Brav's salary was set at a bare minimum. Rabbi Lefkowitz realized that "it will be a little difficult for a married man to live on $1800 a year in the way he should as a representative of the congregation," though he did not believe it was impossible as "a furnished apartment in a good section of the city can be easily had for fifty or sixty dollars a month, leaving over a thousand dollars for food, clothing and insurance."[22] Five days after his arrival in June, Brav's "chief" left for a month's vacation, though probably not without a detailed letter listing the duties of the new rabbi.

In order to lighten Rabbi Lefkowitz' schedule, Rabbi Brav became as busy as his mentor. He supervised the intermediate department of the religious school while Ruth Brav supervised the primary department. He taught prospective confirmands, preached periodically, and addressed Jewish and civic audiences. In addition, he traveled each month to nearby Sherman to conduct services there and served as advisor to Jewish students on the campus of SMU. He and Rabbi Lefkowitz developed a strong and affectionate relationship during the three years Rabbi Brav remained in Dallas. They continued corresponding long after Stanley Brav accepted an invitation in 1937 to become rabbi at Congregation Anshe Chesed in Vicksburg, Mississippi, succeeding Rabbi Sol Kory, David Lefkowitz' brother-in-law. Much later, Stanley Brav related how, before he left, "Aunt Sadie in her affectionate way said, 'Now, Stanley, if you decide not to take the pulpit, be sure to put in a good word for David, Jr.' [who was a senior at Hebrew Union College in Cincinnati]. If you knew Aunt Sadie, that was translatable into 'Stanley, be sure to accept the new pulpit. You know how much Uncle Dave and I want the joy of having David, Jr., with us, when he graduates.' Of course, our little family moved to Vicksburg."[23]

David Lefkowitz, Jr., did indeed join the temple as assistant rabbi in April 1937, during a very trying period for his father, who was recuperating from an eye problem that impaired his vision. David, who was nine when he moved to Dallas, had grown up on South Boulevard, where he perpetrated more than his share of pranks. When he entered Hebrew Union College, David's best friend, Henri L. Bromberg, Jr., wrote a letter telling him that he understood his motivation for becoming a rabbi (part of which was the love he had for his father) but that knowing David's mischievous ways, he thought David was making a mistake. The aspiring rabbi kept that letter and showed it when he preached his first sermon, "Building our Temple."[24] That same year David Shor, whose multi-generational family were mainstays of the temple (his grandfather William Waldstein was caretaker for fifty-two years) also graduated in the 1937 class from Hebrew Union College. After a stint in the service and intervals in London and at Marshall, Texas, and Helena, Arkansas, Shor commenced his long and distinguished career in New Mexico as rabbi of Temple Albert in Albuquerque.

While at Emanu-El, Rabbi Lefkowitz, Jr., took charge of the religious school and filled in for his father while the older rabbi was on vacation, traveling, or speaking at meetings of both Jewish and civic organizations. David, Jr., and his wife, Leona, welcomed their first child, also named David. The assistant rabbi described his time at temple as a "tough but loving apprenticeship." After all, it was his father's temple, and "he wanted to make sure I wasn't lousing things up." Notwithstanding, father and son had a very strong and warm relationship. After delivering a "chewing out," David Lefkowitz would then put his arm around his son and say "Tomorrow will be better."[25] When David Lefkowitz, Jr., accepted the position of associate rabbi at B'nai Zion Temple in Shreveport, Louisiana, in September 1940, David Lefkowitz, Sr., wrote his brother Herman Lefkowitz that although the position will be a "very definite advancement for David, I am trying not to think of the terrible personal and professional loss it will be to Sadie and myself. He has been tremendously helpful a thousand fold and has relieved me more than I can say."[26] Once again, Dr. Lefkowitz, whom the congregation had elected "rabbi for life" in 1935, would have to look for a new assistant rabbi.

During the 1930s, in spite of economic adversity, the congregation managed to keep its financial affairs in order and even initiate some new programs. In the fall of 1934 it invited the community to the temple auditorium on South Boulevard for a newly developed lecture series called the Lyceum Course. For just $2 a subscriber for the 1935–1936 season could hear interesting speakers hold forth on the crucial events of the day: author Dorothy Thompson, the wife of Sinclair Lewis; foreign correspondent Marvin Lowenthal; political observer Prince Hubertus Loewenstein,

119

the leader of the Catholic Youth Group in Germany; and historian Dr. Abram Sachar, the national director of Hillel Foundations and future Brandeis University president. Benjamin Lewis was chairman of the Lyceum Committee in 1937. He was followed by Eugene Solow, who chaired the committee that met with SMU President Umphrey Lee in his office to discuss joint sponsorship of the series with the university. University leaders had long recognized the need for a lecture-concert series both for the benefit of the students and as a "public relations medium to bring interested Dallas citizens to the campus" but had been wary of the financial drain if ticket sales did not meet the cost of importing name speakers.[27] Agreeable to a joint venture, SMU and Temple Emanu-El collaborated to underwrite the financing and to assume any losses on a fifty-fifty basis. For its initial 1939-1940 venture in McFarlin Auditorium at the university, the newly named "Community Course" presented noted author, critic, and actor Alexander Woolcott; blind pianist Alec Templeton; British statesman The Right Honorable Alfred Duff Cooper; drama critic John Mason Brown; author and Nobel Prize winner Thomas Mann; the Martha Graham Dancers; and the Curtis String Quartet. A ticket for all seven stellar evenings cost $3.50.

The temple hosted the first Union of American Hebrew Congregations convention held in Dallas, notable for the establishment of the Southwest District of the UAHC in 1936. Eli Wiener, later president of the temple, chaired the assembly in which the temple Brotherhood, Sisterhood, and the newly formed Junior Congregation heard leading Jewish Reform educator Dr. Emanuel Gamoran, head of the Union's Department of Education, deliver a series of addresses. The Junior Congregation acted in "little theater" productions under the direction of Barnett Shaw and sponsored a basketball team that played, among others, the Baylor Medical Team in a city league. Over sixty young people met for social activities such as "tea dances" and joined in discussion groups at the temple, whose members now enjoyed an air-conditioned auditorium and religious school.

During the 1930s while the world was preoccupied with efforts to pull itself out of the mire of the Depression, events in Germany were taking a sinister turn. Paradoxically, on March 5, 1933, the day after Franklin Delano Roosevelt was inaugurated as a harbinger of hope for America, Adolph Hitler also won an election enabling his installation as the iron-fisted dictator of the German people. Fearing that anti-Semites in Germany would find fertile ground for their venom in the United States, some Jews wanted to keep the extent of the problem quiet. At the request of Richard E. Gutstadt of the Anti-Defamation League, David Lefkowitz was able to prevent Hitler's book, *Mein Kampf* (*My Struggle*) from appearing on Dallas Public Library shelves.[28] However, in retrospect, it might have been wiser for thinking people to pay attention to Hitler's intended scenario for Germany and for the Jews. Immediately after taking power, Hitler threatened to boycott Jewish stores in retaliation for American threats to boycott German goods in the United States. Rabbi Stephen S. Wise had proposed a boycott of German goods by stores such as Saks Fifth Avenue, Lord & Taylor, and Gimbel's in New York, but it did not take place until the fall of 1933. Meanwhile, on behalf of the pro-Zionist American Jewish Congress, Rabbi Wise had announced plans for a mass rally in New York's Madison Square Garden in New York to protest the policy of keeping a low profile advocated by the American Jewish Committee and B'nai B'rith.[29]

On March 27, 1933, former New York Governor Al Smith, Senator Robert Wagner, Stephen Wise, and Bishops William Manning and Francis McConnell addressed a crowd at Madison Square Garden, which was "jammed with twenty-two thousand participants, with thirty thousand others gathered outside" to protest the increasingly vituperative German rhetoric against Jews.[30] A few days after the rally, on April 1, 1933, Hitler followed through with his threat to boycott Jewish stores. Identifying the shops with signs saying "Danger—Jew Store" and "Attention—Beware of the Jew," the Nazis baldly stated that they were avenging the Jews' responsibility for World War I.[31] Temple member Gerda Hollander (Yaffe), then a thirteen-year-old in Unna, a small town thirty miles from Cologne, vividly remembered the day a clerk bolted from one of the Jewish stores to warn her religious school class, which was meeting at the synagogue, to run home immediately—the Nazis were starting the boycott. She dashed for home and found a mob standing in front of her family's tailoring and clothing store. Trying to hide her terror, Gerda stood as straight as she could, walked slowly through the mob, and rang the bell at a side door to be let in to the Hollanders' upstairs apartment. She escaped harm that day and five years later caught the last legal boat from Germany to the United States.[32]

A few days before the boycott, the Nazi government discharged all Jews holding government and municipal offices, and Nazi storm troopers ousted Chief Justice Kurt Spelling and other Jewish members of the bar. In the Nazi state, where only Aryans were allowed to govern, a Jew was any person with one Jewish grandparent. Jews also had to turn in their passports and were forbidden to flee the country. The Nazis wanted to eliminate the Jews from their midst, but they also wanted the Jews to pay for the privilege of exodus. If Jews wanted to emigrate, they would have to pay a "flight tax" of twenty-five percent of their capital; by end of 1938 Germany prohibited removal of any money from the country.[33]

Dallas citizens protested against the German government's anti-Semitic restrictions, which were emblazoned every day on the front page of the *Dallas Morning News*. The Civic Federation, a social research and community education organization, sponsored a mass meeting at Rabbi Lefkowitz' suggestion. Representatives from all faiths drew up a set of resolutions decrying the policies of the Nazis and sent their written complaints to Secretary of State Cordell Hull. Twelve hundred Christian clergymen, including Dr. Charles Selecman, president of SMU, and Dr. Umphrey Lee, minister of Highland Park Methodist Church who followed Selecman as president of SMU in 1939, signed a letter of protest published in the *New York Times*. Dr. George Truett, pastor of the First Baptist Church and president of the Baptist World Alliance, also sent a telegram to Secretary Hull expressing his horror at the persecution of the Jews.[34] One Dallasite who acted to allay the plight of the refugees from Nazi Germany, both Jewish and Christian, was Karl Hoblitzelle, who was president of the Interstate and Consolidated Theaters and chairman of the board of Republic Bank. When Rabbi Jonah B. Wise wrote Rabbi Lefkowitz about a German refugee benefit he had attended, David

Lefkowitz went to see Karl Hoblitzelle about the possibility of producing a similar affair in Dallas. Instead of simply underwriting a benefit, Hoblitzelle pledged the entire receipts of his 137 movie houses in Texas and New Mexico on December 7, 1938 (approximately $80,000 to $100,000) to the Joint Distribution Committee, the United Palestine Appeal, the Committee for Catholic Refugees from Germany, and the American Committee for Christian German Refugees.[35]

Unfortunately, most Jews in Germany "couldn't or wouldn't believe" what was happening to them.[36] Only a small number realized the danger of inaction and judiciously left soon after Hitler became dictator or, like scientist Albert Einstein, never returned to Germany from traveling abroad after Der Führer came to power. But the remaining Jews were "caught in a net that dragged on for a long time and they adjusted to each phase." The older German Jews, in particular, felt that "Hitler couldn't last long."[37] The ugly discrimination was especially hard on men who had loyally served in the German army in World War I.

Irmgard and Fred Brooksaler, who emigrated from Germany in 1938, knew people were taken to concentration camps, but they were kept ignorant of what happened to the deportees who never returned. The Brooksalers decided to leave Mannheim in 1937, when their neighbors not only started picketing Dr. Brooksaler's pediatric office with placards saying "Don't go to the Jewish doctor" but also stopped people to determine whether they were his patients. A second cousin of Irmgard Brooksaler's mother signed an affidavit, the first step in the process of emigration for the Brooksalers, attesting financial responsibility for them upon arrival in the United States. Once the Brooksalers had that prized document in hand, their next step was to get a number that would permit them to go to the American Consulate at Stuttgart for an interview and a physical before receiving a visa for embarkation. They were allowed to take $100 and their household furniture out of the country as long as they paid in German marks.[38] The Brooksalers left Germany in January 1938 and headed to Texas because Fred Brooksaler had a cousin, Leo, in Dallas. Texas was also appealing because supposedly it was one of the few states that allowed foreign graduates to take state medical boards.

On the crossing to America, people felt sorry for the Brooksalers because they were going to the "wild West," a fact corroborated by a friend in Hot Springs who in a fit of hyperbole told them that Dallas had only three paved streets. When they arrived in the city, Dr. Brooksaler met Dr. Emil Aronson who suggested he contact Dr. H. Leslie Moore, the leading pediatrician in Dallas. Fortunately, Dr. Moore offered Dr. Brooksaler an internship at Bradford Hospital on Maple Avenue. The internship, forfeited by a student who had taken ill, paid only $25 a month, but it was a job. Irmgard Brooksaler went to work at the Jewish Federation for Social Services. She had studied social work in Germany and could help German refugees in Dallas as well as translate the pleading letters deluging the federation offices from Jews desperate to emigrate.[39]

The Jewish Federation, representing the entire Jewish community, did not really become involved in the Jewish refugee problem until 1939. A committee appointed in November of 1937 to study the issue of Dallas' role in the immigration of German refugees recommended further study, suggesting that any emigrants who should come to Dallas be handled only through the local Social Service Bureau and that they should be limited to tradesmen needed by the community.[40] Then the Nazis staged the horrific raid during the night of November 9, 1938, and the following day, dubbed *Kristallnacht*, after the shards of broken glass that lined the streets. Nazi storm troopers systematically destroyed hundreds of synagogues and other Jewish communal institutions, plundered thousands of private Jewish businesses and houses in Germany and Austria, and sent Jewish men to concentration camps. That catastrophic day wrecked any hope for the Jews in Nazi-occupied countries; it was obvious that American Jews must respond to the European Jews' frantic pleas for help.

Even though the United States' quota, only 27,370, was filled for 1939, the Jewish people of Germany and Austria persisted in writing letters by the thousands pleading for affidavits. To take care of the requests for help coming into the federation, its president, Jake Landau, a member of Temple Emanu-El, appointed Herbert Mallinson, a former federation president who was then the current president of the temple, to head a newly formed Federation Co-ordinating Committee for Refugees that would function within the Social Service Bureau of the federation. Until then the National Council of Jewish Women had been supplying affidavits, locating relatives, and helping to resettle the refugees who arrived in Dallas. At the time there were sixty-three known "newcomers," as they were called, in the city.[41]

Under the auspices of the federation, temple member Stephen Kahn took charge of furnishing affidavits to anyone who wanted to bring relatives from Germany, Austria, Czechoslovakia, and Poland to America, England, Palestine, Cuba, and Central and South America. The federation guaranteed the signers (who had to verify possession of $5,000 in the bank or in property) that they would never have to sustain a loss.[42] For the year 1939 Jewish communities in Texas took 225 refugees. Houston accepted the most, committing its Jewish people to fifty-two newcomers. Dallas took in the next largest number, pledging to settle twenty-six refugees in Dallas or nearby communities. Morris I. Freedman, as chairman of the sub-committee for the placement of refugees in nearby communities, and George Levy, director of the Jewish Federation for Social Services, persuaded the small Jewish community in Corsicana to shepherd two refugees.[43]

The German Jews who came to Dallas were welcomed by the Jewish community.[44] Various committees assumed responsibility for finding employment for the newcomers. Council of Jewish Women members also "adopted" families to help them adjust to the community. Fannie and Stephen Kahn adopted Greta and Paul Wolff and their two children, and Reba and Ernest Wadel mentored the Fulda family. Fannie Kahn remembers that the Dallas families and their foster German families interacted on an intimate basis and formed lifetime friendships."[45] Irmgard Brooksaler also recalled that "the Sisterhood invited us to everything and didn't charge any dues." Nor did the temple. When called from the federation office for High Holy Day tickets for the German emigres, Rabbi Lefkowitz invariably responded with complimentary tickets for Rosh Hashanah and Yom Kippur.[46]

During the crucial months from early 1938 though mid-1941, approximately 150,000 refugees from Nazism entered the United States.

Possibly 55,000 were able to reach Palestine in that period. From 1933, the beginning of the war against the Jews in Germany, until the end of World War II in 1945, about 250,000 refugees managed to enter the United States and around 150,000 reached Palestine.[47] The rigidity of the quota system and the absence of any expectation of liberalizing immigration legislation in Congress left very little hope for an expansion of the quotas. When President Roosevelt refused in late 1938 to expel 15,000 refugees who were in the United States on visitors' visas, he was "treading the outer limits of Congressional toleration."[48] Yet Roosevelt also left refugee policy "almost entirely up to the State Department . . . [which] discouraged or actively opposed virtually all efforts for a more generous American policy."[49] In every area—visa approval by American consuls, resettlement plans for refugees, granting children special entrance—the State Department prevented Jews from entering the United States.

Endeavoring to rescue a cantor from a concentration camp in Germany, the temple board of directors attempted to engage the services of Reuben Moses Eschwege of Wurzburg as assistant rabbi for 1940. Supposedly, religious functionaries were exempt from the quota. But the American Consul in Stuttgart would not issue him a visa because he was not ordained as a rabbi through graduation from a recognized seminary, even though Rabbi Lefkowitz wrote United States Senator Tom Connally to try to expedite Eschwege's exit visa.[50] As in the cases of all the other desperate Jews under German rule, such as Moses Fink from Cologne, who wrote Rabbi Lefkowitz in 1939 that his exit number was 20,192, any anticipation of Eschwege's rescue was pathetically unrealistic.

In the midst of the grim news in Europe as Germany first annexed Czechoslovakia and then invaded Poland, Temple Emanu-El planned to commemorate a triple anniversary. On April 11, 1940, the congregation celebrated David Lefkowitz's twentieth year in Dallas, his fortieth year as a rabbi, and his sixty-fifth birthday at a banquet in the Crystal Ballroom of the Baker Hotel. The *Dallas Morning News* accorded the occasion a full page spread complete with photographs, and its columns quoted the participating dignitaries in an effort to describe how "not only his congregation but friends and neighbors of Dr. David Lefkowitz, gentiles as well as

Jews, paid tribute to him for his services to his community and his fellow men."[51]

David Lefkowitz described the adulation with tongue in cheek, writing to a colleague: "It may have been boring to the rest of the diners, but my wife and I ate it up. Of course, I mean, not the banquet, but the attendant ceremonies . . . even though all of us have to take these things with some grain of salt."[52] Nevertheless, he was human enough to be "greatly pleased" by the community's recognition of his ministry in Dallas.[53] By lauding the efforts of Temple Emanu-El's rabbi, who was one of the most influential Jews in the power structure of Dallas, the community was perhaps also expressing its appreciation to its Jewish citizens at a bleak time for Jewish people all over the world. 🕎

Bank president Fred Florence (on the right) was president of the Texas Centennial in 1936. Secretary of Commerce Daniel C. Roper (left) and Governor James V. Allred opened Texas' centennial celebration of its independence from Mexico. *Courtesy Dallas Historical Society.*

CHAPTER 7

WAR AND REASSESSMENT

The Jewish question exists: it would be foolish to deny it.

Theodore Herzl

By November of 1941 the German war machine had handily over-run Europe. Britain stood alone as a deterrent to the German juggernaut, partly because the English Channel served as a natural barrier to Nazi forces in France. But no one knew how long England would be able to withstand the incessant bombing by the Nazi Luftwaffe. In America, public sentiment was isolationist, "strong against entering the war in any way."[1] Then, without warning, on December 7, 1941, Japanese warplanes bombed the American naval base at Pearl Harbor, and the surprise attack sealed the entry of the United States into the Second World War.

As soon as President Roosevelt began to muster the nation's full capacity to wage war, members of Temple Emanu-El, like patriotic Americans everywhere, became fervently involved in the war effort. By October 1942 over 130 temple members had joined the armed services, and by 1945, 271 men were represented by stars on the service flag proudly displayed at the temple. Private Joseph Sanger Linz wrote Rabbi Lefkowitz from Kelly Field in San Antonio that he was "prouder of his uniform than anything else he ever had."[2] As the war widened and the number of casualties increased, gold stars appeared among the blue service stars on the temple flag. The first gold stars commemorated Captain Emmett Blakemore, Jr., a pilot instructor whose plane crashed, killing him and his student pilot, and Joseph Warren Weyl, who went down with the cruiser *Houston* in a Pacific battle. Jack Miller, son of a former president of the temple, Realtor Henry S. Miller, was one of the first temple members to enlist, becoming a Marine a month before Pearl Harbor. First Lieutenant Miller joined a special Marine raider battalion that fought Japanese forces at Guadalcanal in December 1942; he died there from wounds suffered while leading his platoon in an attack on the enemy. Major Arthur Berwald, who had been company leader of the ROTC at Forest Avenue High School, was a casualty of friendly fire on the beach at Kiska in the Aleutians when Canadian pilots, thinking they had spotted Japanese soldiers, mistakenly strafed American landing troops. Another temple president's son, Sergeant Robert J. Solow, was one of the last members of Temple Emanu-El to lose his life in World War II. Determined to go overseas to fight, he was only twenty when he was killed in 1944 in the blood-soaked Battle of the Bulge. At the war's end, seventeen men from the temple family had died in the service of their country.

Back home, individuals in the congregation devoted themselves to volunteer jobs helping members of the armed forces. Henry Jacobus became head of the Dallas United Service Organizations (USO), then located in a large building on Main Street between Ervay and St. Paul, where volunteers entertained and counseled service men and women. He felt that "he got more out of it than any job he ever had" because the boys were so appreciative of Dallas hospitality and of the people committed to making the Dallas USO Club a "home away from home." In the patriotic spirit of the time, one morning Henry Jacobus went to the Baker Hotel, picked up three soldiers, and invited them home for dinner. He remembered that "one never came back [for dinner] but the other two came every Sunday for nearly a year."[3]

Other temple members signed up for the Red Cross. Valerie Aronoff worked in the Red Cross news office, and Louise Mittenthal drove for the Red Cross Motor Corps Unit. Dorothy Lewis had started working for the Red Cross in 1931 as its only home service volunteer, responsible for social case work with World War I veterans and their families. Now she took charge of knitting and sewing production, the preparation of surgical dressings, and the assembling of service kits.[4] Blossom Myers, trained to be a "cutter," operated a machine that turned out flannel pieces later sewn into bathrobes for the wounded, just as she had done in World War I.[5] As a group, Sisterhood women made articles of clothing for the Red Cross in their sewing circle chaired by Seline Roos. Edward Titche, who was a charter member of the Red Cross in 1905 and a worker during World War I, purchased the red brick mansion on McKinney which housed the Dallas County chapter and presented it to the Red Cross in memory of his sister, Rose Titche Spencer.[6]

Carlyn R. Hohenberg, head of the Red Cross Canteen, organized the patriotic women who met every troop train and plane arriving at Union Station and Love Field. Helen Loeb spent "many the night" from midnight to seven in the morning serving soldiers who came through Love Field. Despite fatigue, she enjoyed her work at the canteen because "although you'd see some sad and heart-rending sights you felt as if you were really doing something" of value.[7] Adlene Nathanson quit her retail job at Volk's to join the Red Cross Motor Corps. Later she recalled, "I liked feeling a part of the war effort. I liked wearing the uniform. I liked driving. I liked getting to know people. I liked the sense of adventure—not knowing what would happen next."[8] Driving with Olga Mae Schepps, Adlene transported soldiers disembarking in Dallas with orders to proceed to the veterans hospital at McKinney or to camps around Dallas—Camp Wolters near Mineral Wells, Camp Maxey at Paris, and Camp Howze close by Gainesville. When the young women stayed for lunch at Camp Howze, they were served by German war prisoners, men who also performed other tasks on the base.

Americans at home tried to make life easier and more pleasant for men and women preparing to fight overseas. The congregation invited Jewish soldiers at area camps to attend services as honored guests, especially welcoming them to High Holy Day services and Passover Seder. In 1945 the temple hosted army and navy servicemen, WACS, and WAVES at a community Seder that had to be held at the spacious Masonic Temple in a room large enough to accommodate 600 people.

131

Sisterhood "regulars" cooked the dinner. Years later, Sisterhood member Frances Bernstein remembered five dedicated women who were invariably in the kitchen for every temple dinner, every Sisterhood luncheon, and every Brotherhood affair: her grandmother Josephine Waldstein; her mother Jeanette Waldstein Shor; her aunt Dora Waldstein; Seline Roos; and Sara Jacobs. Since the kitchen was downstairs, Frances Bernstein and the other "servers" ran up and down the stairs from the kitchen to the dining room carrying two plates at a time in a seemingly endless marathon. But Frances recalled, "We were speedy."[9] A servicemen who attended Seder wrote Dr. Lefkowitz, "You folks in Dallas really turn out a wonderful job of entertaining us people in the services."[10] Besides offering holiday hospitality, many temple members, such as Frank and Mildred Bettin, opened their homes for meals and overnight lodging to service men and women who were billeted near Dallas.

During the war the Federation sponsored dances at the Jewish Community Center, then located on Park Avenue near Pocahontas. When servicemen on furlough came to Dallas, they could spend the night on cots set up at the center. On Saturdays, Rosalee Cohn (Cohen) and her sister Bernice picked up lox, bagels, and cream cheese to prepare breakfast for the boys at the center. Then they hospitably piled some of the young men in their Oldsmobile convertible to take them home for lunch. In the evening Rosalee and Bernice again returned to the center, preparing dinner for the whole group before the dancing began. Eugene Solow, 1943 Jewish Welfare Federation campaign chairman and subsequent Temple Emanu-El president, was so impressed with the women's preparation of food in the kitchen under the tutelage of Julia Aronoff, that he bought a commercial stove for the Community Center.[11]

For many men and women stationed far from home, being part of some group activity with religious content, such as a Jewish service, became integral to their lives. Lieutenant Charles A. Levi, Jr., was not the only confirmand who wrote his rabbi that he had "got religion" in the service. Rabbi Lefkowitz replied that "we have to wait sometime for a shattering event in our life to get to the real substance of our existence; and that's when you get religion."[12] One question which temple member Alvin

L. Goodstein, stationed in Seattle, asked Dr. Lefkowitz was, "Where are all the Jewish chaplains?" as services on Lieutenant Goodstein's base were conducted by volunteers.[13] In the absence of a Jewish chaplain on his base, Private First Class Carol Miller held services for his fellow recruits at Wendover Army Air Base in Utah. The chaplain on his base, who often listened to the Jewish service, was so impressed by Miller's sermons that he later suggested to Miller's parents that their son should consider the rabbinate. Chaplain Mansen was not aware that Miller was reading copies of Dr. Lefkowitz's radio sermons sent to him by the rabbi.[14] Of course, the problem was one of numbers. Jewish servicemen were dispatched to posts all over the world, and only about one hundred rabbis, mostly Reform, had been trained as chaplains. Cognizant of an obligation to fill the void, David Lefkowitz, Jr., joined the army in 1943. If he didn't enlist, he told his congregational board in Shreveport, "When the boys came back from their military service in the Army and Navy, they will ask, 'Where the hell were the rabbis?'"[15]

Tragically, even before the United States joined Britain to fight against Germany, the optimal chance had passed to save not only German Jews but also Jews in occupied countries. When Germany prepared to invade Russia in the spring of 1941, the Nazis made the fateful decision to annihilate Jews living in territories captured by the German army. Special mobile units barreled behind the German infantry with orders to track down Jews and shoot them in mass killings. Meanwhile Hitler secretly ordered the systematic roundup of Jews in the European countries of Poland, France, Belgium, and Holland, which were occupied by the Nazis, in preparation for their transport to Auschwitz and the other exter-mination camps in Poland.[16] When the Nazis first invaded Poland in 1939, they ordered all men between the ages of sixteen and thirty-five to build dikes on the Vistula River. One of those boys on the work brigade, Sam Milstein, later recounted how the Jewish Federation in his town of Szydlowietv ransomed him and other Jewish boys from the Nazis, but then the Germans sent them to a concentration camp. At Skarciska, Milstein saw individual Poles rewarded with four and one-half pounds of bread and two pounds of sugar for turning in a "hidden" Jew to the camp

133

commandant. That Jew was immediately shot.

Throughout the war Milstein was shunted from camp to camp. In Hasag Wirk C he made picrate, an explosive powder that pervaded his system and turned his body "yellow like a pigeon." Only two "canaries," Milstein and another man in his section, escaped being shot in cold blood by the Ukrainians firing as the inmates stood in open graves. A Jewish policeman from his home town yanked them out of line and managed to put them on a train traveling to another camp. After working in a steel factory building rails, Milstein was transferred to Dora, where inmates toiled underground making V-1 and V-2 rockets deployed to bomb Britain. In Milstein's four months at Dora he "saw so many people hanging" while the loud speaker surrealistically played Chopin. Toward the end of the war he was taken to Bergen-Belsen in a cattle car with "no food, no water, nothing" and was reduced to eating grass and roots. By then, he was down to fifty-two pounds and "the mind was not working any more. We were zombies lying in ditches, in the mud" until the British liberated the camp on April 15, 1945.[17]

As early as the summer of 1941 reports from Poland and the Soviet Union confirmed the ongoing massacre of European Jewry. Although British military intelligence had kept secret reports of the killing that they intercepted between Belarus or Ukraine and Nazi headquarters in Berlin, within a few months, "anyone who had a radio or read a newspaper knew that Europe's Jews in colossal numbers were being murdered."[18] The full magnitude of the horror was revealed in 1945 when victorious American troops actually entered the concentration camps. Lieutenant Lee H. Berg wrote Dr. Lefkowitz how shocked and grieved he was upon entering the concentration camp in Dachau which his infantry division had liberated. In his reply, the rabbi tried to offer solace, but his words could not begin to assuage the pain of an American Jew upon seeing the emaciated, disease-ridden survivors of a world of terror ironically sequestered in the bucolic German countryside just eleven miles north of Munich.[19] Rudy Baum, who had emigrated to America from Frankfurt in 1936, reentered Germany as a propaganda and psychological warfare officer assigned to interrogate German prisoners of war. "The crematory ovens were still

134

burning and bodies were stacked like cordwood in front of the ovens" when he first saw Buchenwald in 1945. "Worst of all, was the sight of the remaining survivors, those human beings whom we came to call 'the walking dead.'"[20] To make the German citizens of nearby Weimar confront the existence of the atrocities perpetrated against the Jews, General George S. Patton ordered the townspeople taken to Buchenwald where they were forced to look at the piles of dead, the instruments of torture, and the lamp shades and book covers made from tanned human skin.

Because of the catastrophe suffered by European Jewry, more and more Jews in the United States began to accept the goal of the Zionist movement for a national Jewish homeland in Palestine. American Jewry realized that, even if thousands of Jews could be rescued, no country was willing to accept the deluge of immigrants. In the late nineteenth century, a time of high nationalist fervor, Theodor Herzl, an Austro-Hungarian newspaper correspondent reporting from Paris, had first penned the political concept of an autonomous state for the Jews in Palestine, *The Jewish State: An Attempt at a Modern Solution of the Jewish Question.* Herzl was struck by the eruption of deep anti-Semitism harbored by the French people, as manifested during his coverage of the trial of Alfred Dreyfus, a Jewish captain on duty with the French General Staff falsely accused of spying for Germany. This outburst of hatred convinced Herzl that the establishment of a Jewish nation constituted the only answer to centuries of alienation and persecution of the Jewish people in their home countries.[21] In 1897 more than 200 delegates from around the world answered Herzl's call to come to Basel, Switzerland, to found a World Zionist Organization committed to establishing a Jewish national home in Palestine.

After having been ruled by the Ottoman Turks for four centuries, Palestine came under control of British forces who entered Jerusalem in 1917 during World War I and terminated the Muslim rule of the German-allied Turks. That same year British Foreign Secretary Lord Balfour, a friend of chemist Chaim Weitzman whose work with explosives had immensely helped the British war effort, declared his "sympathy with Jewish Zionist aspirations," thereby giving British sanction to Jewish immigration to Palestine.[22] In 1922 the League of Nations entrusted

Great Britain with the mandate for Palestine and called upon the English to facilitate the establishment of a Jewish national home.

At first the Reform Jewish movement in America seemed unalterably opposed to political Zionism. In 1897, a few weeks before the first Zionist Congress in Basel, the Central Conference of American Rabbis declared unanimously, "We totally disapprove of any attempt for the establishment of a Jewish state." The Union of American Hebrew Congregations at their convention the following year reaffirmed the rabbis' viewpoint, "The Jews are not a nation but a religious community . . . . America is our Zion."[23] Nevertheless, some individual Reform Jewish rabbis and lay people were early Zionists, and most Reform rabbis, including Isaac Mayer Wise, accepted Jewish colonization in Palestine. During World War I, Supreme Court Justice Louis Brandeis lent his prestigious leadership to the Zionist cause when New York became the provisional headquarters of the Zionist movement, formerly based in Berlin.

Reform rabbis and laymen who were not Zionists but who still believed in the reclamation and rebuilding of Palestine to make the land habitable for Jewish settlement supported and contributed to the Jewish Agency for Palestine, whose working extensions included Keren Hayesod (Palestine Foundation Fund), Hadassah, and the Jewish National Fund. In 1929 Fred Florence was state treasurer of the United Palestine Appeal while Arthur Kramer was chairman of the Dallas United Palestine Appeal. Rabbi David Lefkowitz, along with forty other American non-Zionists, took his seat on the Council of the Jewish Agency of Palestine. Lefkowitz considered his election "a high compliment to be thus chosen" because not only did he support "great constructive results in Palestine" but, more important, he was gratified by "a unified and harmonious Jewry" as both Zionists and non-Zionists were represented on the Jewish Agency Board. Nonetheless, his view concerning the restoration of the Jewish people in Palestine did not embrace statehood:

> I do not believe in a political Zionist program, though I am wholeheartedly in favor of the rehabilitation of Palestine with a Jewish community of the size that is economically possible residing in the

land. Toward this purpose, namely, the eventual establishment of between 350,000 to 500,000 Jews in Palestine, I have given my service and my financial support.[24]

The split between those who favored Zionist objectives and those who opposed a political state of Israel came to a head when the Central Conference of American Rabbis voted to uphold a resolution demanding that the Jewish population of Palestine "be given the privilege of establishing a military force which will fight under its own banner." With this decision the conference sanctioned one of the prime prerogatives of a sovereign state, the legitimate use of force, virtually approving the formation of such a state. The dissenting rabbis saw no course but "public dissociation" from their Zionist-minded peers.[25]

The resolution by the Central Conference outraged not only the non-Zionist rabbis in attendance, but it also aroused congregational lay leaders. A member of Temple Emanu-El in New York, Lewis L. Straus, persuaded his rabbi, Samuel Goldenson, to "take action." Goldenson, a former conference president, met with two of Philadelphia's rabbis, Louis Wolsey of Rodeph Shalom, also a former conference president, and William H. Fineshriber of Keneseth Israel. The three rabbis contacted twenty colleagues to convene "a meeting of non-Zionist Reform rabbis to discuss the problems that confront Judaism and Jews in the world emergency."[26] The thirty-five men who attended the 1942 conference in Atlantic City issued a statement asserting their readiness "to render unstinted aid to our brethren in their economic, cultural, and spiritual endeavors" in Palestine. However, the group's members spelled out their unwillingness to support the "political emphasis now paramount in the Zionistic program." Moreover, they added, "We cannot but believe that Jewish nationalism tends to confuse our fellow men about our place and function in society and also diverts our own attention from our historic role to live as a religious community wherever we may dwell."[27]

The anti-Zionist rabbis and like-minded lay leaders formed The American Council for Judaism, which quickly branched out and multiplied in chapters across the country. The organization's most ardent

137

support reposed in the "highly acculturated Reform Jews who rejected Jewish nationalism and defined themselves as a purely religious group."[28] Lessing Rosenwald, the retired chairman of Sears Roebuck & Company, accepted the presidency of the organization. Some Temple Emanu-El members lent substantive support to the American Council. Fred Florence became a national vice-president, and I. Edward Tonkon served as regional vice-president from the South. From the organization's inception Rabbi David Lefkowitz supported it by serving on the national board of directors. He actively solicited members, encouraging the council to mail literature to every congregant of Dallas' Temple Emanu-El, and also collected the membership dues for Dallas. Initially, twenty-three temple members joined the council.[29] At its peak in 1944, the American Council for Judaism membership across the country numbered 15,000.[30]

During the early 1940s, while the American Council for Judaism tried to influence American Jewry to reject the Zionist cause, Zionists succeeded in winning over the vast majority of Jewish organizations in America. During the American Jewish Conference in 1943, at which every American Jewish organization was represented, Rabbi Abba Hillel Silver electrified the audience with his impassioned plea for a bold declaration in favor of a Jewish state in Palestine. Still, American Council members protested that not all Jews wanted a Jewish homeland in the Middle East, even testifying before Congress to that effect. Ultimately, the horror of the Holocaust and the inability to save the Jews and to find a refuge for them after the war fueled American support for the establishment of a Jewish state in 1948. Chaplain David Lefkowitz, Jr., who was attached to the European Army of Occupation with the Ninth Air Force, spoke for a great many American Jews when he said, "I could never be an American Council for Judaism member after being in Dachau."[31] With the same kind of conviction, Mrs. Henry S. Miller also declined to be associated with the American Council for Judaism. Rarely disagreeing with a husband who was perfect in her eyes, she told him, "I don't want my name on there," asking him to remove her name, joined with his, from the council roster. Carmen Miller then joined Hadassah, underscoring her support for aid to Israel.[32]

Nevertheless, the American Council for Judaism remained strong in the South and the West, where the Jewish population of German descent, small and generally integrated into the community, was hostile to Zionism. In Houston, Beth Israel's trustees deliberately selected Hyman Schachtel, an anti-Zionist rabbi who was a member of the council, to fill the pulpit and tried to limit the input and influence of the more traditional pro-Zionist members of East European ancestry who had recently joined the congregation.[33] Adherence to a set of basic principles binding Beth Israel's members to classical Reform Judaism, as well as disavowing any prayer for the return to Palestine or the need of the Jews for a national home, seemed to be a prerequisite for full congregational membership. Those unwilling to commit to Beth Israel's stipulations could worship only as non-voting members. Associate Rabbi Robert I. Kahn, who was serving as chaplain in the army, described the nonadherents as "second class citizens."[34] Kahn was so shocked by the notion that any set of principles could supplant the monotheistic faith in one God as criterion for membership in a Reform congregation that he resigned from Beth Israel. About 142 members also left Beth Israel "more or less through unwillingness to conform to [its] Basic Principles" and formed the Houston Temple Emanu-El.[35] After his army service Robert Kahn became rabbi of the new congregation.

Fortunately, the dramatic confrontation that polarized and ultimately split the oldest Jewish congregation in Houston did not erupt in Dallas. Individual members of Temple Emanu-El, however, worried about the potentially divisive issue, and small groups of friends met to debate, sometimes acrimoniously, the opposing viewpoints actively advocated by divergent members of the congregation. Although a few temple members eventually withdrew over the controversy and the Reform temple was perceived by the Dallas Jewish community as being outside the Zionist camp, in the long run, healthy dialogue, rationality, and compassion for uprooted, decimated European Jewry won out and preserved the congregation. As former temple President Irving Goldberg stated in an address to the 1966 annual meeting of the Jewish Welfare Federation, "Our Dallas Jewish community survived the wrenching process of the issue of Israel

139

because our leaders remained sane and sensible."

First, David Lefkowitz may have agreed with the anti-Zionist beliefs of the American Council for Judaism, but he did not believe a political view should supersede the basic tenets of Judaism. He wrote to his son-in-law Fred Florence, "A Jewish congregation, it seems to me, should neither come out for or against Zionism, but rather for Judaism, which is the uniting principle of all congregations."[36] In other words, David Lefkowitz would never maintain that a Reform Jew could not be a Zionist.[37] Second, many of the most prominent and civic-minded members of Temple Emanu-El had continuously served as president of the federation since its founding in 1911 and were actively raising funds for the United Jewish Appeal. For instance, Lawrence S. Pollock and Julius Schepps co-chaired the Emergency Jewish Appeal Drive, a vital part of the 1946 federation campaign.

Henry Jacobus, later president of Emanu-El, was president of the Dallas Jewish Federation in 1948, just after Israel declared her independence and was beleaguered on all sides by heavily armed Arab states. Jacobus attended a Council of Federations meeting in Chicago with temple member and federation Vice-President Joseph Ross, an executive with Neiman-Marcus, and Fannie Schaenen, Shearith Israel member and leader of the women's campaign. All three were so galvanized by Golda Meir's dynamic appeal for American money to buy tanks and guns critical for the defense of the young state that they rushed to Jacobus' room to call Fannie's brother, staunch Zionist Jacob Feldman, to elicit his guarantee to collaterize the immediate borrowing of a million dollars to help arm Israel. They knew that Israel required money instantly and that Dallas Jews could solicit pledges to repay the debt later.[38]

The fighting chance to save Jewish lives also propelled Dr. Lefkowitz into the Zionist camp. At a Jewish Welfare Federation board meeting on June 10, 1948, when a member articulated the wish of some Jews to keep their money in Dallas, Lefkowitz spoke strongly in favor of carrying on the combined United Jewish Appeal and Jewish Federation Drive in order to maintain the campaign's momentum for Israel's benefit.[39] And when federation executive director Jack Kravitz asked

Lefkowitz to talk to an important visiting rabbi about toning down his anti-Zionist views when he spoke in Dallas, just three days before the opening federation drive kickoff, Dr. Lefkowitz gladly complied.[40]

Many other temple members were industriously raising funds for Israel both locally and nationally. Herbert Mallinson, a former president of Temple Emanu-El, was co-chairman of the southwestern area for the Joint Distribution Committee, which aided distressed Jews everywhere, and also served as the Texas State Chairman of the National Refugee Service. In fact, Mallinson was fatally stricken by a heart attack in 1941 while attending a rancorous federation meeting concerning the distribution of funds.[41] Taking up the torch, Reba Mallinson Wadel, who like her late brother was involved in local philanthropic matters as a board member of the Dallas Community Chest (renamed the United Way), became the national chairman of the Women's Division of the United Jewish Appeal. In a way Wadel was a casualty of the massive fight to secure Israel's autonomy. Coming home from a United Jewish Appeal conference in Atlantic City after her term of office ended in 1947, she was killed when her plane crashed at Love Field. In turn, her tragic death inspired women such as Hortense Sanger, whose husband Morton was president of the Jewish Welfare Federation in 1953, to become more involved in the Women's Division as it solicited money for Jews overseas and at home.[42] The very first Women's Division fundraiser in 1946 was a $100-per-plate banquet at the Columbian Club hosted by Mrs. Herbert (Minnie) Marcus and Mrs. Carrie Neiman, civically prominent women who were always responsive to Jews in need.

Predictably, working for the Jewish Welfare Federation became a recognizably cohesive social force for interaction among Dallas Jews. Previously, the Reform Jews of German and Western European descent who had founded Temple Emanu-El and the Russian and Eastern European Jews who felt more at home at Orthodox (later Conservative) Shearith Israel had formed two separate social communities. However, helping to raise money for Israel's survival drew together long-established Dallas residents of both synagogues as Jack Kravitz brought members of the Conservative community to sit at the table with the Reform leader-

141

ship. Bess Feldman Nathan, sister of Fannie Feldman Schaenen, whose family was a mainstay of Shearith Israel, and Fannie Koenigsberg Kahn, whose roots reached back to Emanu-El's beginnings, were best friends at SMU, but their parents had little contact socially. In later years when federation leaders Fannie and Bernard Schaenen were invited to fellow federation leader Leslie Jacobs and his wife Helen's house for dinner, Bess Nathan commented, "That never would have happened when I was growing up."[43] Once the social barriers were dissolved between Russian-Conservative and German-Reform Jews, Temple Emanu-El affiliation also ceased to be a benchmark for acceptance in the Columbian Club.

After the end of the war in Europe in the spring of 1945 and the final Japanese surrender three months later, servicemen and women streamed home in overwhelming numbers. The temple membership, which was preparing for the Seventy-fifth Anniversary Jubilee, welcomed them warmly. The 1947 anniversary was an occasion that struck more resonant emotional chords than the simple commemoration of a historical reckoning. First, the congregation, as were all Americans, was still rejoicing in the return of their members who had served in World War II. The temple's special anniversary booklet honored those men and women who had been part of the war effort and commemorated the congregants who had sacrificed their lives for their country. Next, the temple was celebrating one of the last anniversaries when its members could still relish an occasion attended by some of the founders of the congregation. Just a few of the original pioneers, including Rudolph Liebman and Victor Hexter, as well as one of the first members of the confirmation class of 1877, Hattie Mittenthal Lichtenstein, were still alive and able to participate in the congregation's observance of its history. Third, and most important, David Lefkowitz was now seventy-two years old. His congregation, his fellow rabbis, and his community wanted to pay him and his wife, Sadie, heartfelt tribute for their lengthy contributions to the temple, to the Reform movement, and to Dallas.

Rabbis whose lives David Lefkowitz had touched in his long career gladly journeyed to Dallas for the celebration. Addressing the congregation at Friday night and Saturday Sabbath services were his former assistant rabbis Stanley R. Brav, David Lefkowitz, Jr., and Lou H. Silberman, who were joined by the current assistant rabbi, Joseph Ginsberg. Born in Louisville, Kentucky, Joe Ginsberg had joined Temple Emanu-El after graduating from Hebrew Union College, where he excelled scholastically and at the same time held down a teaching fellowship for three years. Rabbi Ginsberg briskly took charge of the religious school and generally assisted Rabbi Lefkowitz. Ginsberg was vitally needed by the congregation after David Lefkowitz suffered a heart attack before the High Holy Days in 1941, and although he wanted to enlist as a chaplain, he felt duty-bound to postpone his service until the fall of 1943.[44]

After Rabbi Ginsberg entered the army chaplains' school at Harvard University, Rabbi Lou H. Silberman, who had just earned a doctoral degree from Hebrew Union College, assumed the duties of assistant rabbi. Silberman remained in Dallas for a little over a year until, as Dr. Lefkowitz realized, "a real opportunity came to him in the offer of the pulpit at Omaha, and we [Lefkowitz and the congregation] can't blame him for accepting it."[45] Clearly, his departure left Rabbi Lefkowitz in the lurch, making it necessary for the temple to rely on Hebrew Union College students to assist in the religious school and to try to lighten the senior rabbi's pastoral and community obligations. First came Rabbi Solomon Kaplan in the summer and Rabbi Joseph Buchler in the fall of 1945 and then Rabbi Moshe P. Machenbaum in the spring of 1946. After the war ended, both Dr. Lefkowitz and Winfield Myers, congregation president, wrote to the Chief Chaplain in Washington, D. C., for assistance in hopes of accelerating Captain Ginsberg's return to the temple to relieve Dr. Lefkowitz.[46] Since Ginsberg was still needed at Camp Kilmer in New Jersey, where he ministered to returning troops on their way to hospitals or back to civilian life, he was not discharged until August 1946 and arrived in Dallas just in time to help Dr. Lefkowitz prepare for the High Holy Days and for Emanu-El's seventy-fifth anniversary.

To ensure the attendance of rabbis that Dr. Lefkowitz invited from Texas and around the country, the congregation graciously paid their travel expenses. Rabbi Harvey Wessel from Tyler, who paid $7 for a double room at the Baker Hotel and $5 for gasoline for the trip, said that he was "most reluctant to accept a return of this outlay because of the very great pleasure we had in attending the several functions . . . at the same time, if rabbis receive this special consideration, I am no exception to the willing takers of this additional courtesy."[47] Dr. Lefkowitz also invited his predecessor, Dr. William Greenburg, to take part in the festivities. Dr. Greenburg, who had been an agent for Mutual Life Insurance Company of New York since his departure from Dallas in 1919, sent his regrets and did not come to Dallas.

The weekend celebration, which Dr. Lefkowitz and co-chairmen Eugene Solow and Arthur Star had started planning a year in advance, stirred the entire congregation. Sisterhood and Brotherhood, led by their presidents Mrs. Joseph Koch and Sig H. Badt, directed the Sabbath reception on Friday evening. In addition, on Saturday morning the pupils of the religious school presented a pageant "Through 75 Years—Till Now" depicting the history of the congregation. The Youth League, a post-college group formed after the war as part of the National Federation of Temple Youth, joined in the celebration.

On Saturday evening, March 8, at the Diamond Jubilee banquet in the Crystal Ballroom of the Baker Hotel (now razed), the officers of the congregation along with the assembled well-wishers listened as Mayor J. Woodall Rodgers and the Very Reverend Gerald Moore, president of the Dallas Pastors Association, proclaimed their esteem for Temple Emanu-El's contribution to the growth and spiritual welfare of Dallas. Next, the congregation heard two leaders of Reform Judaism whose careers seemed to represent the past and the future of the Reform movement, Dr. Julian Morgenstern, president of Hebrew Union College, and Dr. Maurice N. Eisendrath, president of the Union of American Hebrew Congregations. Dr. Morgenstern, who had been the president of Hebrew Union College since 1922, was a member of David Lefkowitz's "classical Reform" generation, and, in fact, the two were very close friends. Rabbi Eisendrath, a contemporary of Glueck's, had been a congregational rabbi in Toronto until he became executive director of the Union of American Hebrew Congregations and then in 1946 assumed its presidency, a position which until that time been filled by a lay person. Over much objection, Maurice

Eisendrath moved the union from Cincinnati, the symbolic center of Reform Judaism, to New York, the city where the largest concentration of Reform, Orthodox, and Conservative Jewish people resided and where all the major Jewish and Christian organizations were headquartered.[48]

The move had symbolic as well as logistical implications. Eisendrath wanted to expand the Reform movement by broadening its appeal to the mass of unaffiliated American Jews and by having the union offer monetary support to newly formed congregations. To stimulate interest in the Reform movement, the union sponsored "The American Jewish Cavalcade," which showcased one or more rabbis on visits to communities where they lectured inspiringly on Reform Judaism. Leo Baeck, "the most valued participant in these Jewish revival meetings," was a revered German rabbi who in 1926 founded and later served as president of the World Union of Progressive Judaism, an organization that tried to promote and sustain Reform Judaism around the world.[49] Rabbi Lefkowitz not only served on its board as a vice-president but delivered a sermon at the West London Synagogue in 1930, when he was chairman of the American delegation to the World Union Conference in London. Despite many offers to leave Nazi Germany, Leo Baeck, as the elected head of the Reich Union of German Jews, remained in Berlin in order to help his fellow Jews until he was taken to Theresienstadt concentration camp in 1943. Having survived his internment, Baeck emigrated to England after the war. Although quite feeble by this time, he made the supreme effort to come to Dallas to plead the case for the college and the Union of American Hebrew Congregations at the regional meeting of officers and rabbis of the southwest Reform congregations in 1948. His halting, heavily-accented English may have been difficult to understand, but "as a symbol of personal courage and devotion to his people, he succeeded in winning their full-hearted applause" and securing pledges on behalf of the UAHC at the meeting in Dallas.[50]

At this time the congregation also welcomed a new assistant rabbi, J. Aaron (Jack) Levy, after Joseph Ginsberg accepted a position in 1947 at Anshai Emeth Congregation in Peoria, Illinois. Rabbi Levy had served as an army chaplain and as rabbi at Temple Israel in Stockton, California.

145

Both Rabbi Lefkowitz and his family appreciatively welcomed Rabbi Levy to the congregation, whose membership now numbered over 900 families and whose elderly rabbi had more duties than the sometimes fragile state of his health could bear. Meanwhile, Dr. Lefkowitz had informed the board of trustees that he wanted to retire and become rabbi emeritus after conducting his last confirmation service for the class of 1948.[51] For years afterward, when his confirmands fondly remembered this saintly looking, handsome, cleft-chinned gentleman rapping his imposing signet ring on the podium to quiet, in one small motion, a noisy bunch of teenagers, they were fully aware that this small gesture epitomized the power of a man both commanding and benevolent, wise in the ways of the human heart. As the end of a twenty-five-year era was drawing to a close, the *Dallas Morning News* paid David Lefkowitz tribute:

> If not the greatest greatness, at least that greatness which savors most of goodness is the kind that comes to a man who, through years of work, faith and sympathy, builds for himself a reservoir of confidence and affection in the minds and hearts of a widening circle of fellow men.[52]

Quietly, but actively, a committee on the rabbinate began to search for a successor to Dr. Lefkowitz. ♆

146

Lieutenant Colonel A. J. Beck, (later General) was stationed in the Philippines
during World War II. He named "Little Beverly" after his
great niece, Beverly Gremm (Fetterman).

Infantry Staff Sergeant George Golman was captured in the Ardennes Forest during
the Battle of the Bulge and later liberated from a German prison camp. His parents Anna
and Abe Golman greeted him at Love Field in 1944.

Chaplain David Lefkowitz, Jr., of the Ninth Air Force
rededicated the synagogue at Bad Neustadt, Germany.

Leo Fields, Edna Zale, and Marvin Zale found their cousin Mike Korman
(second from right) in Eschwege, a camp for displaced persons in Germany,
and brought him to America in 1948.

"For God and Country." Servicemen of Temple Emanu-El who died fighting in World War II.

Henry Jacobus, chairman of the Jewish Welfare Board Fourth Army Area Armed Services and past chairman of the Dallas USO during World War II, greeted Leonard Bernstein in 1947 when he conducted the Israeli Symphony Orchestra in Dallas. Dorothy Jacobus is third from the right.

The Seventy-fifth Anniversary Celebration Diamond Jubilee Banquet at the Crystal Ballroom, Baker Hotel, March 8, 1947. Listening to Dr. David Lefkowitz are Winfield S. Myers, immediate past president, Blossom Myers, Dr. Maurice N. Eisendrath, president of the Union of American Hebrew Congregations, Eugene M. Solow, president of Temple Emanu-El, Mrs. Solow, Arthur Star, Helen Star, Dr. Julian Morgenstern, president of Hebrew Union College, Helen Florence, Fred Florence, vice-president and perennial treasurer of Temple Emanu-El.

Joan Lynn lit the Hanukkah candles as Barbara Ravkind (Friedman),
Dr. Lefkowitz, and an unidentified boy looked on.

Dr. David Lefkowitz and Leo Baeck, a renowned German rabbi, in Dallas when Rabbi Baeck
spoke for the Union of American Hebrew Congregations in 1948.

CHAPTER 8

THIS HALLOWED GROUND

Religion is an art, and like all art, one can only appreciate it by doing something about it.

Levi A. Olan

When Rabbi Levi A. Olan arrived in Dallas on January 1, 1949, he celebrated the fine sunny day by doffing his winter coat and accompanying temple president Eugene Solow to the Cotton Bowl football classic. Olan was a long way from Massachusetts, where the respected and well-loved rabbi was in his element as an integral part of the large and progressive New England academic community that included Harvard University, Brown University, Clark University, and the Worcester Biological Foundation. Besides the obvious change in weather, the rabbi was aware that the Dallas intellectual climate differed from the atmosphere to which he had become accustomed in Worcester.

Louis Tobian, a former president of the temple serving at the time as treasurer, was the first temple member to meet Rabbi Olan. Eugene Solow had asked his fellow officer "to go over to Worcester and see a rabbi there named Olan" while Tobian was in Massachusetts to attend his daughter Jean's graduation from Wellesley College, only a short distance away. Solow had already made prudent inquiries and had received extremely positive responses about Levi Olan's abilities. Joshua Loth Liebman, rabbi of Temple Israel in Boston and author of the enormously popular book *Peace of Mind*, had answered Solow's request for information about Levi Olan by replying that he was "one of the outstanding minds in American Reform Judaism. He has done magnificent work in Worcester as preacher and teacher and representative of the best in liberal Judaism in this whole area."[1] Although the temple was interested in talking to Levi Olan, Louis Tobian "doubted, several of us did," that Olan "would think much of Dallas," especially when the rabbi "came to Dallas to look it over" in August of 1948 "and it was about 110 degrees here.... But he was looking for wider fields and he decided he would be associated with us."[2] Rabbi Olan later recalled that when he visited Dallas he was impressed by the lay leadership dedicated to the temple and felt they would be receptive to innovative programs.[3]

Levi Arthur Olan was born Levi Olanovsky on March 22, 1903, near the city of Kiev in the Russian Ukraine. At the age of three he emigrated with his parents to the United States, where his father shortened the family name to Olan at the suggestion of an immigration officer at Ellis Island. The family settled in Rochester, New York, where the elder Olan became a peddler and later opened a clothing store. Levi grew up in a Yiddish-speaking home in which American culture was distinctly subsidiary to the tradition of *shtetl* life as his parents had lived it in Russia. Clearly, his parents' lives revolved around their Orthodox *shul*, subject, of course, to the overriding necessity of making a living. Rabbi Olan later recalled, "Between immigrant parents and their children there was always a gap—the parents never really understood American life, their children became part of it." After attending Rochester High School, Levi enrolled at the University of Rochester where he was guided by Lawrence Packard, "one of the greatest teachers [he] ever came across," to become a history teacher. As the young student learned about the universe by studying Darwin and the theory of evolution, his thinking so evolved that the Orthodox beliefs of his home were "no longer meaningful" in the way they had been.[4]

At the same time Levi Olan was expanding his intellectual horizons, he was also influenced by his boyhood friends, Milton Steinberg and Sidney Regner, fellow Hebrew students at the Talmud Torah. Together the three boys participated in extracurricular activities, such as the Boys

Literary Club, offered at the nearby settlement house. After high school Levi lived at home while attending the University of Rochester. His friends, meanwhile, had decided to prepare for the rabbinate: Milton was leaving for New York to study, and Sidney planned to enroll at Hebrew Union College. One day when Levi was practicing basketball at the Unitarian Church gymnasium, the minister, William Gannett, concerned about Levi's direction in life, persuaded the teenager to talk to Rabbi Horace J. Wolf of the Rochester Reform Temple. Rabbi Wolf steered the adolescent Olan toward Hebrew Union College, an institution appealing to a young, penniless student because the school offered free tuition and scholarships for room and board. "Fed up with staying at home" and happy to be near Sidney Regner, who became a lifelong friend, Levi left for Cincinnati in 1923 to enroll in Hebrew Union College and the University of Cincinnati.[5] After he completed his courses in six years, he accepted an offer in 1929 as rabbi at Temple Emanu-El in Worcester, Massachusetts, where he remained until he moved to Dallas.

Besides being active in the civic life of Worcester, Rabbi Olan also exchanged pulpits with various Christian ministers, preaching on Sunday morning at the Methodist Church or the Unitarian Church, even taking over for his best friend Thomas Roy and occupying the pulpit when the Baptist minister was out of town. In contrast to his experience in Worcester, almost a year after Rabbi Olan came to Dallas, he wrote Roy, "The religious atmosphere here is, in the main, much more fundamentalist and, therefore, exclusive of my point of view. While it is too early to estimate the situation, there is the probability that I shall never be able to make the cooperative relationship with other religious leaders as I did in Worcester."[6] For the most part, Dallas in the 1950s had a conservative bias, and religious leaders in the so-called "Bible-belt" did not enjoy the same easy camaraderie found in the Pastor's Association in Worcester.

Nevertheless, at this crucial time in its history when Temple Emanu-El was searching for a rabbi with the intellectual brilliance and personal integrity of Levi Olan, he was receptive to the idea of moving to another pulpit. He later reminisced, "I knew in the back of my mind that a man ought not to spend his entire rabbinic career in one pulpit where he comes as a young man just out of college, where he has always been the young man just out of college. He ought to have somewhere in his career a beginning as an adult rabbi, if you can call it that."[7] When he was trying to decide whether or not to come to Dallas, he discussed with his colleagues, the president of Hebrew Union College Nelson Glueck and Jewish historian Jacob Marcus, the pros and cons of accepting the Dallas offer. The two Reform leaders indicated that should Rabbi Olan accept the new pulpit, he could introduce into the southwestern part of the United States—a rapidly growing part of the country—a Reform program that could also inspire other congregations in the region. Marcus and Glueck also felt that Dallas exhibited the kind of lay leadership that would respond to these "adventures" in religious life.[8] On his part, Rabbi Olan felt that because his social and political outlook was liberal—he was a socialist—he might be able to make a difference in a part of the country where liberalism was not as acceptable as it was in New England. Even though a friend of his said, "You won't last a day. If you get up and spout some of your things you'll be out on your ear," the rabbi was willing to take the risk of serving as gadfly to the community. In short, becoming the rabbi of Temple Emanu-El posed numerous challenges which Levi Olan was prepared, even eager, to confront.[9]

Rabbi Olan's first few years at the temple were a time of transition. The board engaged a new assistant rabbi, Herbert M. Yarrish, who arrived at Love Field in August 1949 to begin his duties as director of education. For a few weeks Rabbi Yarrish lived with the Olan family, cementing a relationship as close friends. He and Rabbi Olan found time to go together to the YMCA gym several times a week, and they often lunched with each other. Before selecting Yarrish, Rabbi Olan and Sam R. Bloom, the president of the temple, had interviewed several about-to-be ordained seniors at Hebrew Union College in Cincinnati. The three men met again in New York for working sessions to lay plans for an enlarged youth and religious school program. Then Bloom, Olan, and the religious school committee decided to bring a nationally recognized expert, educator Irving Levitas, from Kansas City to Dallas to perfect the curriculum, interview possible faculty members, and guide Rabbi Yarrish in his new role.[10]

Seeking the best professional advice was a characteristic of Sam Bloom, who at the time was business manager of the *Dallas Times Herald*. For instance, he encouraged the board to hire a male secretary with executive abilities since Aline Rutland, who had been Rabbi Lefkowitz's secretary for twenty-five years was contemplating retirement. The daughter of former temple president Max Rosenfield, Aline Rutland with her years of congregational experience could not be replaced. She not only knew the temple members "exceedingly well" but also knew precisely how the Jewish community functioned.[11] Rabbi Gerald J. Klein, who became associate rabbi in 1952, recalled that when he joined the temple as a young rabbi, her perspicacity was very helpful to him, especially when he was called in an emergency.

The newly created post of executive secretary was filled by Sidney Friedman, a young man just twenty-five years old who had been the assistant secretary at a Reform temple in New Orleans. In 1951 Ernest Stark, who moved from Washington, D. C., where he was involved with social and religious agencies, took Sidney Friedman's place. When he left in 1953, the board engaged Hyman Kantor. Then thirty-eight years old, Kantor had served for eleven years as controller of the National Federation of Brotherhoods and Sisterhoods at the Union of American Hebrew Congregations in both Cincinnati and New York City. He would spend the bulk of his career at Temple Emanu-El, heading the administrative office for twenty-seven years until his retirement and replacement by Joe Abrams in 1981. Richard J. Rosenberg, Jr., succeeded Joe Abrams in 1995.

After two years at Emanu-El, Rabbi Yarrish left in 1951 to serve as a chaplain in the air force during the Korean War. Before his departure, Rabbi Olan described to him the kind of person he would like as his replacement. Herbert Yarrish recollects that "the man I recommended most highly was my friend and former roommate at Hebrew Union College, Rabbi Gerald J. Klein. A most fortunate and enduring choice for all parties."[12] Taking Yarrish's recommendation and the concurring advice of Professor Jacob Marcus, Rabbi Olan telephoned Rabbi Klein concerning a move to Dallas. Gerald Klein, at the time, was the rabbi of Congregation Gates of Heaven in Schenectady, New York, having deliberately chosen a small congregation after his ordination in 1948 "because he wanted to be on his own."[13]

A native of Canonsburg, Pennsylvania, Klein had graduated from Washington and Jefferson College before attending Hebrew Union College. When contacted, he did not know whether he wanted to come to Dallas, but he agreed to talk to Rabbi Olan. Deciding to consider the Dallas offer, Gerald and Dorothy Klein came to Dallas on July 4th weekend in 1952. Before the Kleins' meeting with the trustees at Morris and Edna Zale's house in Greenway Parks, Louis and Isabelle Tobian and Ben and Dorothy Lewis took the young couple to dinner at Mario's restaurant on Ross Avenue. In a "dry" town like Dallas, the diners at fine restaurants customarily brought a bottle wrapped in a discreet but still telltale paper bag so they could enjoy cocktails before dinner. Rabbi Klein later remembered that Louis Tobian toted an entire suitcase fitted with bourbon, Scotch, and gin, which he handed to Mario Vaccaro so the owner could take it and then fill the table's orders for drinks without violating the law.[14]

At a luncheon meeting the next day, Rabbi Klein met with Rabbi Olan, Lawrence S. Pollock, Sr., and Henry S. Miller, Sr., who made reference to another man, Sam Bloom, unavailable to join them that day. The Kleins returned to Schenectady with the encouraging words "You'll hear from us" echoing in their ears. Several weeks passed by with no word, until one day Gerald Klein received a call from the aforementioned Sam Bloom who "was in Schenectady for a little while." After he met with the rabbi, Bloom checked Klein's credit, investigated Klein's role in the general community, and then flew back to Dallas. Shortly thereafter, Gerald Klein received and accepted Temple Emanu-El's invitation to come to Dallas by November 1. On a beautiful warm day somewhat reminiscent of the sunny January day when he himself had arrived, Levi Olan met the northeasterners at Love Field. Dressed for a frigid New York winter, Gerald Klein and his five-year-old son Alan could barely wait to shed their overcoats and hats and Dorothy her fur coat in the eighty-seven degree weather of their new city.[15]

For years before Rabbi Olan and Rabbi Klein arrived in Dallas, the leaders of the temple had been weighing the idea of relocating the building from South Dallas to North Dallas. Since the late 1920s it was evident that the general shift of the population was toward the northern part of the city. The decline of the South Boulevard area partly resulted from the development of industry along the Houston and Texas Central tracks coupled with the lack of zoning restrictions which allowed for the commercialization of Forest Avenue. Moreover, as families began to move away from the area to more fashionable residential homesites developed in North Dallas, African Americans began to move into South Dallas, accelerating the abandonment of the neighborhood by the white population in a typical case of white flight.[16]

Of course, quite a few Jewish families had always lived outside the South Boulevard neighborhood. For years temple members had established homes in Old East Dallas, on Swiss Avenue, and on Bryan Parkway. Others had moved to the Lakewood community around the Lakewood Country Club. In the late 1930s and early 1940s many temple members moved to what was then deemed "far north," the independent municipalities of Highland Park and University Park, whose well-regarded school system and city services functioned separately from those in the city of Dallas. Some young families moved even farther north to Preston Hollow. The reality was that by 1951 over sixty percent of the congregation was clustered in North Dallas.

The congregation, which had more than tripled to over a thousand families since Dr. Lefkowitz arrived at the newly built temple on South Boulevard in 1920, obviously had outgrown its building. In order to provide a facility large enough to accommodate the 1949 High Holy Day Services, the trustees settled on Fair Park Auditorium (now called the State Fair Music Hall) for Rosh Hashanah and Yom Kippur Services, which fortunately fell on the calendar just before the State Fair began. Religious school classes were scattered in classrooms from South Dallas to North Dallas. Part of the religious school's 700 children gathered in classrooms on the SMU campus, whereas others met in private homes. Rabbi Klein remembered "one Hanukkah celebration that we held at the Village Theater in Highland Park Shopping Center. See, we were just all over the place in order to keep things going" for the 1,300 families who made up the growing membership of Temple Emanu-El in the early 1950s.[17]

The difficult selection of an affordable site seemed to be solved by the generosity of temple member Sylvan T. Baer. He offered the congregation a beautiful, secluded, wooded tract of eleven acres located just south of the Park Cities between Blackburn Street and Lemmon Avenue adjacent to Turtle Creek Boulevard. President Sam Bloom appointed Louis Tobian chairman of a building committee, and the board invested it with the responsibility of commissioning an architect, preparing a survey, and generating a report on the temple's needs. Bloom asked to be relieved of serving the last year of the usual presidential two-year term so that he could devote his time to fund raising as chairman of the campaign committee for a new building. At the time, he was also serving with Jerome Crossman as co-chairman of the 1950 Jewish Welfare Federation Campaign.[18]

Alex Weisberg, who assumed the presidency of the temple, had just stepped down as president of the Dallas Museum of Fine Arts. Since he was particularly interested in the aesthetic quality of the new building, he immediately began inquiries about the credentials of qualified architects to be considered for the project. He called the deans of the Harvard School of Architecture and the Massachusetts Institute of Technology, both of whom recommended Eric Mendelsohn, Eero Saarinen, and Max Abramovitz, all internationally esteemed architects. Wasting no time, Weisberg immediately invited all three men to come to Dallas at the temple's expense and meet individually with the building committee. Analyzing the interviews, the committee agreed that it was most favorably impressed with Eric Mendelsohn, a famous German refugee architect living in California, who was the premier post-World War II designer of synagogues. After Bloom, Tobian, and Weisberg visited the St. Louis and Cleveland temples Mendelsohn had designed, Louis Tobian remembered that "we kind of fell in love" with Mendelsohn's modern temple in Cleveland and "wanted one just like it in Dallas." By November 1950, on the recommendation of the building committee, the board agreed to engage Eric Mendelsohn to draw up preliminary plans and construct a model for the new building.[19]

Even though Louis Tobian and Sam Bloom were pleased with

Mendelsohn's Cleveland temple, the committee as a whole was not entirely happy with the model he designed for the Turtle Creek site. One member asked "whether or not the structure as planned gives the appearance of a religious structure and has the basic awesomeness and dignity which must be inherent in the Temple."[20] On a more practical note, the committee disagreed with Mendelsohn's premise that air conditioning was not a matter of course, an "absolute necessity" in the Texas heat.[21] Then the committee reviewed the "impossible" parking problem inherent in the site and mulled over its inconvenience for the majority of the membership, who did not live in close proximity to Lemmon Avenue and Turtle Creek. The most troubling contingency was donor Sylvan Baer's demand that no mortgage be attached to a new building. After much deliberation, the temple returned the Turtle Creek property to Sylvan Baer and discharged its responsibility to Eric Mendelsohn.[22] Sylvan Baer later donated the land to the Dallas Theater Center, which commissioned Frank Lloyd Wright to design its building, at that time the only theater created by the illustrious architect.

In May of 1952, Louis Hexter, Victor Hexter's son who owned a title company, brought what Louis Tobian considered a "magnificent offer from the Caruth family,"[23] who at one time held the largest contiguous parcel of land in North Texas. William Caruth offered to sell the temple 17.7 acres on the northeast corner of Hillcrest and Northwest Highway for $5,000 an acre, property that was "worth many, many times that amount for commercial purposes."[24] (Later the temple bought two additional acres on the north side at twice the price but also far below the commercial rate.) However, before Caruth would sell Temple Emanu-El the property, he wanted to know something about the leaders of the congregation. Irving Goldberg recalled going with fellow lawyer Henri L. Bromberg, Jr., one Sunday afternoon to explain "in great detail the whole history of the congregation. The price was not really a very important factor with him. [Caruth] was interested in the temple, what kind of building it would be, and who would be there."[25]

Fred Florence, the temple's treasurer for over twenty-five years, bought the initial acreage for the temple. In order to develop the land,

161

Emanu-El had to meet certain stipulations set forth by William Caruth. The original owner specified that the land could be used only for religious or educational purposes and that all structures must be brick or stone. Furthermore, the congregation could not hold the property for an indeterminate time but must break ground and spend a sum of $500,000 on new construction by January 1, 1956. The negotiating committee headed by Henry S. Miller, Sr., completed arrangements for the acreage with William Caruth's widow, Earle Clark Caruth, in June 1952, with all parties signing the contract deeding Temple Emanu-El the choice property.[26]

Meanwhile, the search for a suitable architect continued. There was no dearth of candidates. Eric Mendelsohn expressed his desire to draft a plan for the new site, Eero Saarinen flew down to meet with the building committee for another interview, and Percival Goodman, professor of architecture at Columbia University who had designed over fifty synagogues since World War II, appeared in Dallas to discuss the project. Yet when the time came to make a decision, the building committee decided not to hire an internationally known architect but instead to engage Howard Meyer and Max Sandfield, two local architects well respected for the homes and civic buildings they had designed in Dallas. Because of their personal connection to the temple—Howard Meyer was a member of the board of trustees and Max Sandfield's father-in-law, Eli Wiener, was a former president—both men displayed a special empathy for the needs of the temple and the desires of its rabbis and its board of trustees.

For this project alone, the two architects became associated and proved to be what Rabbi Gerald Klein called "an excellent team and an inspired choice. . . . Howard was the dreamer and exceedingly stubborn. Once he got an idea he would never change."[27] Howard Meyer was a native New Yorker, a graduate of Columbia University, who had worked in an architectural firm where Frank Lloyd Wright officed when in Manhattan. Meyer admired modern, trailblazing architects such as Mies van Der Rohe and Le Corbusier, whose works he visited while traveling in Europe, and he appreciated Frank Lloyd Wright's singularly American style.[28] In Dallas, where he lived after marrying Waco native Schon Landman, Howard Meyer designed Dallas' first high-rise apartment house, 3525 Turtle Creek. Rabbi Klein volunteered his impression that "Max was approachable and knew materials and workmen and how things were implemented."[29] He was also a sculptor and later designed an outdoor Hanukkah menorah for the temple. Max Sandfield was born in San Antonio and graduated from Massachusetts Institute of Technology with a degree in architecture. After working for different firms in Boston and New York, he returned home to San Antonio to open his own office. During World War II he was stationed with the Corps of Engineers in Dallas, where he married Carol Wiener. Among other projects, he had designed the new Columbian Country Club building in nearby Carrollton.[30]

Much to their credit, Max Sandfield and Howard Meyer engaged an outstanding consulting architect, William W. Wurster, professor of architecture and dean of the School of Architecture of the University of California at Berkeley, as well as a partner in his own architectural firm, Wurster, Bernardi and Emmons. Writing to a colleague in 1958, Rabbi Olan called him "a man of great architectural knowledge, imaginative, and enough of a human being to work with lay people." His professional stature added considerable weight to the local architects' suggestions; on his part, William Wurster found a "generous and constructive attitude" in his work with the temple committees.[31]

Now that the building program was on target, the scope of the whole religious and educational agenda also began to emerge. In the spring of 1951 the board invited Rabbi Olan to express his ideas about the contributions the temple should make to its members' lives and to share his views in a series of meetings with the congregation. In response, Rabbi Olan created guidelines and challenges for the rabbis and for the congregation. First, he felt that the temple "should teach Judaism and its religious values—in the pulpit, in adult classes, in the religious school for children, in the meetings of the Brotherhood and Sisterhood—at every possible time and place." Second, in Olan's words, "the Temple through its rabbis, must be a counselor and a guide to you in time of sorrow and of joy . . . a pastor in the profound meaning of the word." Third, the temple "must express in art forms and in symbols, the religious ideas of our faith

163

. . . a religious service must be a moving emotional experience . . . encompassing art, music and liturgical expression . . . which will send the worshipper out exalted, courageous, and confident." Finally, the temple "must join our neighbors of other denominations in a unified effort to strengthen the religious faith of the community." Of all the goals to be met, Levi Olan thought that in the past the temple had come closest to fulfilling the goal of conveying a religious view to the community. And that accomplishment was the fruit of Dr. Lefkowitz's efforts, especially his weekly radio program.[32]

In order to elevate Emanu-El's programs to a level commensurate with those of other progressive temples in the United States, the board began to search for personnel to implement an amplified religious and educational program. In 1951 the trustees hired Raymond Israel as director of education. He was then thirty-five years old and serving as both the principal of a public school in Washington, D. C., and as principal and director of the Washington Hebrew Congregation Religious School. Israel held a master's degree from George Washington University, had done graduate work at Columbia and the University of Maryland, and had attended seminar courses at Hebrew Union College. At the time he became director of the religious school, no standard comprehensive curriculum guide for a Reform religious school was serviceable. The Union of American Hebrew Congregations had compiled a list of textbooks applicable for each grade level and suggested topics for discussion, but teachers could not rely upon a complete lesson plan for an entire semester. To enrich a child's experience and make the child aware of the Jewish way of life, Israel, who had been part of a public school curriculum revision committee in Washington, D. C., fashioned a basic curriculum for all grades with specific suggestions on scheduling projects involving music, art, and dramatics. The new school director also sent information home in hopes of involving the parents in the school.

Ray Israel has said that he was a product and disciple of the late John Dewey, the foremost American educator of the twentieth century, who believed that "for education to be meaningful it has to be relevant."[33] In that vein, the task of the Reform Jewish religious school was not inconsiderable. In only two and one-half hours on Sunday morning an instructor attempted to impart to his students the basic Jewish concepts of justice and compassion and to enlighten them about the Jews' substantive contributions to civilization. Furthermore, the religious school teacher was expected to stimulate an appreciation of Jewish ritual and holiday celebrations.

In his comprehensive plan for improving programs, Rabbi Olan had included the position of music director. The man he sought was Sam Adler, the son of the cantor at Olan's temple in Worcester, who had just finished a stint in the army. After graduating from Boston University College of Music and earning a master's degree in music from Harvard University, Adler had conducted the Seventh Army Symphony Orchestra during the Korean War. Sam and his father, Hugo Chaim Adler, had been very close to Olan from the day the Adler family arrived in Worcester. The new cantor was particularly charmed by Olan's propensity to crack jokes, considering that in Germany the rabbi hardly ever smiled.

Hugo Adler, previously cantor at one of the main temples in Mannheim, was counted among the leading composers of Jewish music. When the Nazis first seized power, Adler felt it his duty to stay with his fellow Jews as long as possible. But after the systematic devastation of syn-agogues and homes during *Kristallnacht* in 1938, he decided it was the better part of valor to flee with his family to America. Since the German quota for 28,000 available American visas had been filled, the family's exodus was possible in part because a rich uncle in America helped them and in part because of a technicality: Hugo Adler had been born in Belgium, and he and his family fell under the Belgian quota. When Sam Adler recounted his harrowing experiences, he stated, "I tell you very frankly, the big Nazis [actually] were the people at the American Consulate who tried everything to put stumbling blocks in the way."[34] Hugo Adler was able to leave immediately, but Sam's mother had caught a cinder in her eye while traveling by train to the American consulate in Stuttgart, and the American consul made the rest of the family wait until Selma Adler's slightly red eye cleared up.

The very day that Sam Adler was discharged from the army, he received a phone call from Levi Olan asking him to come down and discuss what a music director should do. However, Adler "had been offered Leonard Bernstein's job as music director at Brandeis University [Bernstein was going to New York] doing the choral work, the band, and the orchestra."[35] But because of his close relationship to Rabbi Olan, Adler flew down to meet with the music committee. By the end of a lunch at the Lorch Manufacturing plant on Ervay Street—with Magda Lorch Folz, Louis Tobian, Louise Lipps, and Dorothy Jacobus—he was hired. Adler arrived in Dallas in February 1953 and immediately captured attention by originating a children's choir to sing on Saturday mornings with the Sisterhood Choir directed by Sadie Lefkowitz. At that time Edward Boettcher led a choir of eight professional singers for Friday night services. Adler organized a volunteer adult choir. Among those invited to join was the newly confirmed Rosalie Cinnamon, who was the first confirmand to sing at a confirmation service. In 1972 she became soloist with the temple choir, a position she still held twenty-five years later.

When the choir grew to about fifty members, it began singing on a regular basis during Friday night services.[36] Sam Adler felt that Temple Emanu-El, "more than any other temple, contributed to the growth of Jewish music in America by performing every new piece that came out. [During the 1960s] we were the only large Jewish choir in this country."[37] If the choir did not perform a new piece, then Transcontinental, the only Jewish publisher in America, could not afford to publish that particular piece of music because the temple's disregard was tantamount to the work's gathering dust on the shelf. Some of the highlights of Sam Adler's tenure were the choir's performances of Handel's *Judas Maccabaeus* and *Samson*, Mendelssohn's *Elijah*, and Mozart's *Judith*, as well as works by contemporary composers Ernest Bloch, Franz Waxman, and Darius Milhaud. Elizabeth Olan, Rabbi Olan's older daughter, found singing in the choir exciting because Sam Adler not only explained each piece of music but discussed the history of a piece of music in relation to the whole Jewish musical tradition.[38]

While Rabbi Olan was marshaling the professionals he wanted to employ, the architects were progressing with blueprints for the new building.

They had come to the juncture in the planning when the crucial decision had to be made about the design of the sanctuary, about the sacred objects that are most important to the worshiper in the temple: the Ark of the Covenant, the Eternal Light, the menorah, and the Ten Commandments tablets. Howard Meyer, Max Sandfield, and William Wurster felt that they needed a fresh approach, perhaps even an art coordinator. At about this time Sam Bloom had become chairman of the art committee. According to Howard Meyer's recollection, Bloom suggested a man who had been a professor at North Texas State College in Denton in 1943. When Bloom mentioned Gyorgy Kepes' name at a meeting one day, William Wurster was in complete accord, spontaneously pronouncing, "That's the very man we ought to have."[39] For it had been Wurster, when he was dean of the School of Architecture at the Massachusetts Institute of Technology, who had recruited Kepes as professor of visual design.

Gyorgy Kepes, who still taught the theory of art at MIT, agreed to mull over the problems of design for the main brick wall in the sanctuary where the Torahs were held in the ark of the covenant. To the architects' delight, he arrived at a "brilliant solution . . . a weaving of mosaics in the very fabric of the brick wall itself" in the design of a menorah.[40] After the Art Committee members saw the mock-up of the mosaic wall that Gyorgy Kepes had brought to their first meeting, they commissioned him to create the furniture for the pulpit and all the art work for the sanctuary and the chapel. Rabbi Klein remembered going with Kepes after Friday night services to Rabbi Olan's home on Edmondson in Highland Park, where Kepes "asked questions about the history of the *Ner Tamid* (Eternal Light) and the menorah and wanted to know about other aspects of the Jewish religion. He absorbed everything."[41] Vividly recalled by Howard Meyer was Kepes' second visit, when he brought "a lovely sketch of the eternal light that is in the sanctuary. And the committee took one look and said 'Yes, that's right.' And that's the way it went working with him."[42]

Kepes based his grand scheme for the sanctuary on the premise that "not the various individual liturgical symbols but only their absolute conveyance into visual harmony could give a true expression to the high purpose of the space."[43] He envisioned the stunning abstract glass windows whose colors increase in intensity as they draw closer to the ark, and he commissioned artist Anni Albers, wife of noted painter Josef Albers, to weave the fabric for the doors of the ark to echo the vibrant blues and greens in the glass windows. Kepes designed the menorah in the chapel, but he delegated to Richard Philipowski, professor of architecture at MIT, the design and execution of the menorah in the sanctuary. In concert, the architects and the building committee decided that the eternal light should contain real oil and that the menorah should burn real candles.[44] Dallas artists Velma Dozier and John Szymak designed and executed the silver and blue and green enamel *kiddush* cup and Sabbath candlesticks, whose colors repeated those in Albers' ark doors.

One of the knottiest problems revolved around the illumination of the sanctuary. Originally the architects recommended six great hanging chandeliers, an idea which was greeted with "stony silence" by the committee.[45] Kepes then worked with lighting expert Richard Kelley, who suggested hanging cylinders of different sizes to focus the viewer's eyes on the pulpit. These hanging lamps were fashioned to beam the same intensity of light both day and night and to illuminate each worshiper's prayer book.[46] Unfortunately, lighting alone could not solve the problem of the unexpectedly dull appearance of the completed mosaic on the ark wall. When sculptors Octavio Medellin of Dallas, who had fabricated the shining silver, gold, blue, and green mosaics in his studio, and Charles Williams of Fort Worth painstakingly placed the mosaics on the ark wall to form the candelabra, some of the glass pieces did not catch and reflect the light. Aspiring to perfection, the artists removed each piece and patiently reset them at the proper angle in the wall.[47]

As construction of the building progressed, Rabbi Gerald Klein maintained that "we really had the feeling, because of our main cheerleader, Louis Tobian, that we were building a cathedral. . . . [H]e always asked for the best first."[48] Initially, the fund-raising chairmen and their committees procured $1,000,000 to finance the project. Sam Bloom's committee obtained substantial pledges in the opening phase of the campaign, and Henry Jacobus, the treasurer of Pollock Paper Company, and Irving Goldberg, law partner in Goldberg, Fonville, Gump and Strauss, then headed a committee to solicit the general membership. Using pledges of $1,000,000 as collateral, the board authorized borrowing the remaining $500,000 essential for completion of the new building. Milton Tobian, Louis Tobian's son, assumed the chairmanship of the second fund raising phase targeted to reach the campaign goal of $1,500,000. Louis Tobian later related that when construction estimates appeared a little over budget, the architects accommodatingly suggested cuts, such as substituting a galvanized roof for a copper one and pine floors for maple. But with "faith in our ability to do what we had to in order to get financial assistance for what we needed, we decided to go first class," Tobian insisted, although Irving Goldberg later remembered that "there was a battle over everything."[49]

Finally, on a warm but windy and then rainy day, June 5, 1955, members of the congregation gathered for the groundbreaking ceremony at the Hillcrest site. Sadly, on the very day that Louis Tobian turned over the symbolic first clod of earth for the new temple the assembled throng learned that Dr. Lefkowitz had died. Sadie Lefkowitz, five years younger than her husband, had died at age seventy-five just the previous February. At the end of one era and the beginning of another, the speakers at the site dedication ceremony voiced their sentiments about the role of a Reform Jewish community in Texas and its responsibility to build for the future. Jews, like other Americans, were experiencing a religious revival. Reform congregations more than doubled, from 300 in 1943 to 656 in 1964, as congregational leaders erected new houses of worship for existing congregations in need of expansion as well as for those which were newly formed. It was a time in which belonging to a church or synagogue became a hallmark of the American way of life, the era when Congress made "In God We Trust" the official motto of the United States and added "under God" to the Pledge of Allegiance.[50]

In the years after World War II the most important demographic trend for American society was the migration to the suburbs. In the course of leaving a predominantly Jewish neighborhood, where being Jewish was taken for granted, for a more desirable suburban locale, many parents realized that if they wanted their children to remain Jewish in a multi-faith environment, they would have to provide a sound religious education for them. But parents of children at Temple Emanu-El in South Dallas had to cope with inadequate classrooms for the growing religious school while planning for relocation in North Dallas. Attending religious school meant dealing with logistical problems as classes spread from South Boulevard to rooms at SMU to homes in North Dallas. In one parent's opinion, busing back and forth during this period of flux left some young students feeling uprooted and may have contributed to a feeling of alienation that weakened their attachment to Judaism and the temple. Rabbi Olan recognized the problems of fragmentation when he remarked at the groundbreaking ceremonies, "It is unwise and unsound for us to keep on postponing the day when we can teach our children—properly—their religious heritage."[51]

Many synagogues built to accommodate the influx of Jews to suburban communities were architecturally beautiful and imposingly large—buildings in keeping with the Jews' sense of accomplishment in American society. Lewis Lefkowitz, Rabbi Lefkowitz's son who was president of the temple, believed that "the new temple and religious school buildings must reflect the stature, dignity and eminence attained by Emanu-El in the general community through the years"[52] Louis Tobian spoke frankly of the temple's responsibility to the community: "A great congregation like ours is, and rightfully should be, a powerful influence for good in our city. We've lived too long and achieved too much in Dallas, and through radio we are too well known over the state, to go borrowing rooms and halls for our meetings."[53] Clearly, Temple Emanu-El's lay leaders and rabbis were representative Jews as they enacted their civic roles in the community. How the temple leadership conducted themselves imprinted the image of the Jews as perceived by the larger Dallas society. To illustrate, after the temple moved to North Dallas, a Jewish newcomer to an old Preston Hollow neighborhood was asked by her new neighbor to what church she belonged. Upon hearing that her place of worship was Temple Emanu-El, the inquirer said, "I know Louis Tobian and he's a fine man," accepting her as a neighbor simply on the basis of her co-religionist's stature.[54] As the builders expected, the monumental new modern temple symbolized to everyone the Dallas Jewish community's civic pride, rectitude, and pursuit of excellence.

In an impressive and moving ceremony, members of Temple Emanu-El assembled on November 27, 1955, to lay the cornerstone of the new building at Northwest Highway and Hillcrest Road. Julius Schepps, a vice-president of the congregation, presided over the program, which highlighted leaders of the congregation preserving for posterity memorabilia relevant to the history of the temple and the Dallas community. Julius Schepps, himself, was an exemplar of Jewish prominence in the community. Born in St. Louis, Schepps moved to Dallas in 1901 when he was six years old and, at twelve, started his business career as a delivery boy for his parents' bakery. With his brother George, Julius eventually ran the bakery. Tall and lanky Julius was an excellent baseball player. After he was recruited in 1914 to play baseball for Texas A&M University, the school discovered seventeen days into the term that Julius lacked a high school diploma and dismissed him. Undaunted, Schepps became an Aggie booster, and twelve years later the A&M Former Students Association elected him president. In 1938 he founded the Schepps Wholesale Liquor Company, which became the keystone of his varied business activities. A tireless civic worker and unparalleled fund raiser, Schepps received the prestigious Linz Award in 1954 for his unstinting effort to establish the Jewish Home for the Aged and for his work with the Dallas Salesmanship Club boys' camps, the Boys Ranch project of the Variety Club, the Park Board, and the United Way, whose headquarters in downtown Dallas he donated. He served as president of the Jewish Welfare Federation and Golden Acres Home for the Aged, and when the new Community Center on Northaven Road was built in 1958, its board justifiably named it the Julius Schepps Community Center, later changed to the Jewish Community Center.[55]

The vice-president of the temple who had the privilege of sealing the cornerstone, Lawrence S. Pollock, Sr., had been a member of the building committee since its inception in 1950 and a trustee of Temple Emanu-El in alternating terms since 1931. Born in Dallas in 1892, he founded a paper jobbing business after returning from service in World War I as a first lieutenant in the infantry. As the Pollock Paper and Box Company expanded its manufacturing business, Lawrence Pollock also

171

stepped up his activities in the community, serving as president and financial supporter of the Dallas Symphony Orchestra, director of the Dallas Chamber of Commerce, campaign co-chairman of the Jewish Welfare Federation, director and vice-president of the Dallas United Fund, and member of the Master Plan Committee of SMU. In 1965 Hortense and Lawrence Pollock donated the art galleries at SMU, which are part of the Owen Fine Arts Center.

Another leader in the Jewish community, Irving Goldberg, had just been installed as the president of the temple. He had taken the office of leadership, which his friend Levi Olan urged him to accept. The rabbi wrote to him, "You and I see eye to eye about the importance of our Jewish community life and the place of the Temple within it."[56] A native of Port Arthur, Irving Goldberg was a prominent attorney who moved to Dallas in 1932. As a young man his leadership abilities had been spotted by Dr. David Lefkowitz, who wrote to Eli Wiener, president of the temple in 1941, asking that Goldberg be considered for a Brotherhood position since "he represents the younger element and has been faithful in his attendance at the Temple."[57] Goldberg also served as president of the Jewish Welfare Federation and Golden Acres, the home for the Jewish aged which was established in 1953 on Centerville Road in southeast Dallas. In 1966 President Lyndon Johnson named him a judge of the United States Court of Appeals, Fifth Judicial Circuit, located in New Orleans.

With the buildings under construction, the architects, who envisioned the temple situated in a grove of trees, engaged Marie and Arthur Berger to formulate a landscape design. William Wurster expressed his feeling that "a grove of trees on the great plains always evokes a feeling of pause and refreshment. The weary traveler finds this true the world over. His spirit is refreshed as well as his body."[58] Stephen Kahn, who, along with his brother Edmund, was a vice-president of the temple, had been involved in planning the new building and became chairman of the landscape committee. Hortense Sanger, who succeeded Morris Zale as secretary of the temple, chaired the furnishings and decorations committee, whose members were guided by Beth Armstrong, an interior designer from San Francisco chosen by the architects. One of the main chores of the committee was sitting on what seemed to be an infinite number of chairs to test which were the most comfortable before ordering 750 permanent seats for the sanctuary and enough portable chairs to accommodate an additional 250 worshipers.[59] Including the adjoining auditorium, where 1,000 more chairs could be set up, the temple could hold 2,000 people at one service during the High Holy Days. The smaller chapel named in memory of Rabbi David Lefkowitz was planned for a gathering of 250 people.

The board hoped that the problems of overcrowding in the religious school would be permanently erased by providing forty-seven classrooms. The trustees named the youth room in honor of Charlotte and Martin Weiss, the dedicated former chairman of the religious school and his wife. They designated the new library in memory of Alex F. Weisberg, who had died before he could finish his term as president during the initial phase of planning the building. Upon recommendation of the permanent memorial committee, the board named the auditorium in honor of Louis Tobian, the man "more nearly responsible for the building of the Temple than any one individual in the congregation."[60] Louis Tobian later joked that he spent so much time at the temple that his grandchildren thought he owned it, but the reverse was closer to the truth. Through the generosity of Blanche Linz, the social hall was named in memory of Clifton Linz. The completed building, budgeted for $1,500,000, eventually cost $2,000,000.[61]

The final gathering in the South Boulevard Temple, which had been the religious home of the congregation for fifty years, was the Sukkot Sabbath service on September 21, 1956. Rabbis Olan and Klein solemnly removed the Torah scrolls and the ark of the covenant on Friday night along with the pulpit Bible. These sacred objects were carried out of the temple by a procession of past presidents of the congregation and transported to the David Lefkowitz Chapel in the new temple for services on Saturday morning. Coincidentally, the first Friday evening Sabbath services in the new building, held in the Louis Tobian auditorium as the sanctuary was not yet finished, fell on Sabbath B'reshit, the Sabbath on which the first book of the Torah is started anew. Rabbi Klein preached

173

the first sermon, "More than Gratitude," in the new building. Fittingly, Sam Adler selected music from Joseph Haydn's masterful oratorio *The Creation* for the choir to perform.

The new temple was dedicated the weekend of February 1–3. On Friday evening the congregation participated in the dedication of the sanctuary to the "temple family" as various officers stepped up to the pulpit to light the candles on the menorah for the first time. Saturday morning, after the dedication of the children's classrooms, parents and religious school children proceeded from their classrooms to the sanctuary for the Children's Dedication Service. Saturday evening, members of the Texas rabbinate and lay leaders of other Reform congregations in Texas were special guests at the temple's dedication to Judaism ceremony. Guest speaker Nelson Glueck, president of the Hebrew Union College-Jewish Institute of Religion, who had installed Rabbi Olan at Temple Emanu-El in January 1949, chose the apropos topic "The Role of Judaism in the World" for his sermon. On Sunday afternoon, the congregation invited Dallas religious, civic, educational, and cultural leaders to join in a service of dedication to the community. Because of the close ties between the rabbis and congregation of Temple Emanu-El and SMU, Rabbi Olan had invited Umphrey Lee, chancellor of the university, to speak for the community.

The contemporary building evoked a spiritual response in people of all faiths. Dallas architect William Parker McFadden wrote Howard Meyer that he was "quite overwhelmed as [he] first walked into the sanctuary. It seemed to soar and my own inner spirit somehow surged."[62]

Life magazine featured a full page color spread photographed during the dedication and declared:

> In the towering spaciousness of their new temple the congregation of Temple Emanu-El of Dallas, Texas dedicated one of the most remarkable synagogues in the U. S. The edifice has a 90-foot-high dome supported by curved walls of acoustical fins and hung with 47 tubular lights. On the brick ark wall, inlaid with flecks of gold that form a giant candelabrum, hang the Ten Commandments

marked in gold on marble plaques, and a curtain of metallic cloth is drawn over the ark.[63]

San Antonian O'Neil Ford, possibly Texas's foremost architect, wrote to Irving Goldberg in praise of the building's artistry:

> I saw the building just last week and it has been in my mind much of the time since. When I first approached it I was constantly asking myself, "how?" How, in this day of vulgar automobile design, of ostentatious and exhibitionist architecture and self-conscious decoration, could a group of people and the artists they engaged hold these influences in check throughout the long process of discussion, drawing and studying, and final detailing?[64]

The Dallas chapter of the American Institute of Architects selected Temple Emanu-El in 1957 for an Award of Merit with special commendation for the sanctuary; in 1959 the American Institute of Architects also presented the structure an Award of Merit. The Dallas Chapter again recognized Temple Emanu-El in 1966 for excellence in architectural design and gave its Twenty-Five Year Award to the temple in 1991.

To many people the new temple seemed to epitomize Rabbi Olan's feeling that "it must be the kind of a religious house in which a person entering would have the experience of the holy." His daughter, Elizabeth Olan Hirsch, remembers that her father felt that "when you go into a service you should be able to leave the ordinary world." The sanctuary should be a "physical place where this could happen . . . this included the architecture of the building, the music that you heard, the words, of course, that you heard, and the art on the walls."[65] The leadership of Temple Emanu-El had succeeded in building a house of worship of great beauty, dignity, and strength, which expressed silently, but more eloquently than any words could convey, the pride they felt in their faith and their place in the community. ☥

President Sam Bloom, left, and Rabbi Levi A. Olan, right, conversed with
new Assistant Rabbi Herbert Yarrish, 1949.

Ida Lou Rosenthal, Rabbi Levi A. Olan, Selma Ross, and Rabbi Gerald J. Klein
discussed Sisterhood's American Institute on Judaism.

Temple Presidents Henry S. Miller and Irving Goldberg walked with Cemetery Chairman
Morris I. Freedman (in center) at the Hebrew Benevolent Association Cemetery on Akard Street
before the graves were moved in 1956 to the Temple Emanu-El Cemetery on
Lemmon and Howell streets to make way for the Civic Center.

Louis Tobian broke ground for the new temple building at
Hillcrest and Northwest Highway as Rabbi Gerald J. Klein, Rabbi Levi A. Olan,
Irving Goldberg and Henri L. Bromberg, Jr., looked on.

Sam Adler, at the piano, Ray Israel, behind him, and Seymour Hootkins, at left, celebrated ground breaking for the new temple.

Rabbi Levi A. Olan addressed the crowd gathered on November 22, 1955, for the cornerstone-laying ceremony. On the platform are architect Howard Meyer (hidden by the flag), architect Max Sandfield, contractor Leo Morgan, building committee Chairman Louis Tobian, Treasurer Fred Florence, Vice-President Lawrence S. Pollock, Vice-President Julius Schepps, President Irving Goldberg, and religious school supporters Martin and Charlotte Weiss.

The temple at Northwest Highway and Hillcrest Road was situated,
as the architects had imagined, in a grove of trees.

Dr. Umphrey Lee, chancellor of Southern Methodist University, spoke for the community
at the dedication weekend for Temple Emanu-El in February 1957.

Sisterhood Presidents Shirley Tobolowsky,
Ida Papert, and Josephine Goldman prepared for
Sisterhood's County Fair, 1960.

CHAPTER 9

REACHING OUTWARD

Unless from these fluted and mosaic walls—from the slate and cork floors—there goes forth a community dedicated congregation, our mission will have failed.

Irving Goldberg

From 1949 until 1957, while the congregation had been planning and then constructing a new temple, vast sociological changes took place all over America that, in retrospect, helped shape the entire second half of the twentieth century. In his book, *The Jews in America*, Arthur Hertzberg observed that religious and ethnic groups that had formerly been outside the dominant white Protestant society—Catholics, Jews, and African Americans—returned from World War II determined to stake their claim in the American Dream and partake of the democratic ideal of equality. During the war, men and women of all religions and nationalities (except for the still segregated African Americans) lived, fought, and died together. Moreover, the war propelled the different groups "out of their urban ghettos and gave them, for the first time, a sense of the larger society and of the possibilities that might be open to them."[1] After the war, men and women from divergent parts of the United States who had been stationed in the Southwest for part of their military training chose thriving southwestern cities such as Dallas to establish their professional and business careers and start their families. Successful entrepreneurs from small towns in Texas moved to Dallas to take advantage of its financial services, transportation network, and cultural and educational opportunities.

181

At Temple Emanu-El Irving Goldberg, president, expressed the feeling of the growing membership when he said, "One of the mandates of Reform Judaism is to demonstrate not only in Cincinnati but here in Dallas that we can refurbish and enrich our faith in the context of contemporary society."[2] For the congregation of 1,500 families the time seemed propitious to evaluate current congregational activities with a view toward making the overall program more relevant.

American Reform rabbis had usually approached the teaching of the Jewish religion and history through adult education programs. Rabbi Olan wrote to the membership in 1957:

It is almost futile for me to urge upon you the value or the importance of learning something about our faith and our history. A desire to know is not created by a word from me. But this much seems clear—we, as Jews, are the heirs to a great religious faith and philosophy, which can help us live our lives more fully. The courses are planned to make that faith more meaningful for you.

Accordingly, lecture series continued to play a prominent role in temple programming. The rabbis resumed the Fall Institute, which traditionally included four meetings focusing on some aspect of Jewish study, and the Spring Institute featuring four consecutive lectures that emphasized the importance of religion to contemporary society. Topics ranged from Jewish history to business ethics. Jacob Marcus, Olan's and Klein's friend from Hebrew Union College, discussed "The Dawn of American Jewish History—The Beginnings of American Jewish Institutions," and Erik Jonsson, president of the Dallas Chamber of Commerce and chairman of the board of Texas Instruments, later mayor of Dallas, related "Aspects of the Good Society" to business. In addition, Rabbi Olan continued his weekly Bible class, sponsored by the Sisterhood. Moreover, in 1963 the rabbis, Music Director Sam Adler, and Religious School Director Ray Israel presented a series of lectures on twenty-one consecutive Wednesday evenings, entitled "Interpreting our Faith," offering courses in modern Jewish philosophers, parent education, music, Torah, prophets, and writings and rabbis.

In many instances the adult education program began to embrace the Dallas community. The Rabbi David Lefkowitz Memorial Lectureship, formally established in 1961, evolved from Rabbi Olan's yearly invitation to a rabbinical colleague to deliver a lecture on the anniversary of Lefkowitz's death. Cognizant of Dr. Lefkowitz's involvement in the Dallas community, the committee presented rabbinical speakers of scholarly interest to both the Jewish and the Christian communities. The first lecturer, Maurice Samuel, a noted author, Biblical scholar, and historian, drew a crowd of 800 people to hear a discussion of "When Jew and Christian Parted."

Undoubtedly, the most widely attended lecture course was the Significant Book Series launched by Shirley Polluck and Patsy Nasher for the Sisterhood in 1957. Rabbi Olan's criterion for the books he discussed was their "significance for our time." Initially, he reviewed *The Nun's Story* by Kathryn Hulme, *The Menninger Story* by Walker Winslow, *War and Peace* by Leo Tolstoy, and *The Dead Sea Scriptures* by Theodore H. Gaster. Over 900 attended the first review. The following year 1,900 people bought series tickets, and 700 more bought single tickets. Significant Books had become a sought-after North Dallas social and intellectual event which its devotees "would not miss for anything."[3] With the sizable proceeds from the reviews, Sisterhood was able to purchase a series of eighteen Old Testament lithographs by Marc Chagall and to commission Ben Shahn to design a tapestry for Linz Hall. The piece was woven by Pinton Freres at the Aubusson Factory in France.

Rabbi Olan later related how he went to see Ben Shahn at his home in Roosevelt, New York, had lunch, and spent five hours "with one of the great storytellers and one of the great people of our time . . . four hours and fifty minutes telling each other Yiddish stories that we already knew and ten minutes talking about the commission."[4] According to Olan, both he and Shahn conceived the idea of using the triumphant 150th psalm to express the "Hallelujah spirit." The artist decided to use musical symbols and flowers in a pastel palette with Hebrew lettering in gold to express the line "Let everything that hath breath praise the Lord." When Rabbi Olan retired in 1970, Sisterhood carried on the Significant Books Series,

183

inviting the temple's rabbis and different guest speakers to give the reviews.

In amplifying the scope of its agenda, Sisterhood also advanced interfaith outreach programs. One of its most successful seminars was the Interfaith Committee's Institute on Judaism in 1957 for public school teachers. Dr. W. T. White, superintendent of the Dallas public schools, and several hundred public school teachers learned about the Jewish faith as they listened to Rabbi Klein and Samuel Adler explain the symbols and liturgy of the synagogue. After a dinner prepared and served by Sisterhood members, the educators also toured the new temple.

Also carrying on special projects was the other programming arm of the temple, Brotherhood, which in 1962 received an award from the National Federation of Temple Brotherhoods as one of the outstanding large brotherhoods in the nation. The Brotherhood's sponsorship of Rabbi Olan's widely disseminated radio program, broadcast over WFAA on Sunday mornings at 8:30 a.m., represented an important service to the entire community. One listener asked his Baptist Sunday School teacher "if he could guess the radio program I listened to on the way to church. The teacher replied, 'I have an idea it is the same one I listen to—Rabbi Olan. He is the best preacher in Dallas.'"[5]

One of the Brotherhood's best attended programs was its 1962 "Ask the Rabbis" panel featuring Rabbis Levi Olan, Gerald Klein, and Saul Besser on the "witness stand." Moderator Joseph Rosenstein entertained questions such as "Is the temple too large?" or "Is our house of worship too impersonal?" Other inquiries included, "Should there be a second Reform congregation in Dallas?" as well as "Need the temple involve itself in civic affairs, such as the low-cost housing controversy, or race relations?" These topics would occupy the attention of the rabbis and the temple leadership even beyond the decade of the 1960s. Rabbi Besser, the new assistant rabbi, was born in Colorado and had obtained his Master of Hebrew Letters and Doctor of Divinity from Hebrew Union College before joining the congregation in the fall of 1962. At twenty-eight, just the age of the many newly married couples now associating with the temple, Besser became advisor to the Interested Couples Group. Even though the temple already sponsored the Livaleers for its single members, the new group was purposely molded to draw young couples who up until then had no activity especially devised for them.

Like the Sisterhood, whose programs it often backed, the Brotherhood leadership wanted to interest its membership in a large project that would attract people from the community as well as appeal to the congregation. In 1963 the organization decided to present an art festival at the temple. Harold Kuhne and Edward Stern chaired the first event, an exhibition of 207 pieces of art displayed gallery-style in Tobian Auditorium. About 134 artists, mostly members of the congregation, contributed their work to the successful affair. Individuals bought scrip in advance of the sales, boosting the total gross income to approximately $3,700. Even more significant, the exhibit invigorated and engaged the Brotherhood membership of over 500 men, as sixty-seven men worked on various committees which solicited the art, checked in the artists' work, set up Tobian Auditorium, and planned the preview for benefactors held the night before the festival. Eventually the art festival mushroomed into a week-long community-wide show including over 450 artists and donors and grew to be the main fund-raising event for Brotherhood projects until 1983, the last year it was held. Competition with other organizations such as the Knights of Columbus, who produced their own exhibits, as well as thinning crowds, dwindling income, and a diminishing pool of volunteers dictated its end.[6]

Even though Temple Emanu-El welcomed the community to special events, some of its members agreed with Rabbi Olan that the collective congregation needed to become involved at a deeper, more caring level in a project that would have genuine impact upon a critical social problem. No problem loomed larger than integration of the public schools. In 1954 desegregation of public schools had become the law of the land when the Supreme Court in *Brown v. Topeka Board of Education* unanimously outlawed segregation in public schools on the basis of race. Rabbi Olan spoke forcefully on the racial issue proclaiming the ethical rectitude of the court's landmark decision:

Segregation is immoral. It is immoral to say to any person, regardless of the color of his skin or the church of his faith, that he cannot sit where I sit, eat at my table, study in the same school as my children, apply for the job of work as I do. The question is not whether segregation shall continue but whether we shall voluntarily do what is right or be forced by experiences painful and damaging.[7]

In the late 1950s, racial integration, not just of the schools but of all areas of society covered by Jim Crow laws, became extremely controversial. During the 1955–1957 term of Irving Goldberg as temple president, N. Anthony Jones, an African American professor of international relations and government at Bishop College, took classes with Rabbi Olan and, with Olan's unconditional support, applied for membership in the temple. Judge Goldberg later summarized the dispute over Jones' joining the congregation:

Some meetings were held with respect to this. There were some problems, some, I must say opposition. And there was genuine fear because at that time synagogues all over the country were being bombed. I know one in Atlanta was, that I can recall, and there were others in the East. And I remember great discussions about this and it was my position and the position of the majority, by far the majority, and I think in the end unanimously that we accept this man as a member of the congregation.[8]

Elizabeth Olan marched with her father in demonstrations for civil rights, a concept that Levi Olan wholeheartedly embraced. She never forgot how "people would call the house and say awful things" and "tossed eggs at our door." In his daughter's opinion, her father was an "unrepentant liberal, never hedged, never said 'yes, but.'" He also made a point of emphasizing his Jewish origins—talking about his mother's *latkes,* or his going to Hebrew school. In essence, she felt that even those people in the city who disagreed with her father's politics and social liberalism respected Levi Olan because "he lived his faith for all to see."[9]

186

After President Dwight D. Eisenhower ordered the National Guard into Little Rock to face down Arkansas Governor Orval Faubus' defiant attempt to block nine African American students from enrolling in Central High School, it became apparent that the federal government would back desegregation of the public schools in the South. In hopeful expectation of avoiding the riots that savaged the Little Rock and New Orleans communities, the Dallas Citizens Council, an organization of powerful businessmen who virtually ran the city, asked one of their members, advertising and public relations expert Sam Bloom, to handle the complex problem of public acceptance of desegregation. Bloom put the Bloom Agency's resources at the disposal of the council.

In 1960 the Bloom Agency filmed the persuasive *Dallas at the Crossroads*, which stressed the necessity for integration without coercion or violence, and showed it across the city "before many hundreds of neighborhood PTAs, luncheon clubs, religious groups, and business associations." Stanley Marcus, a former president of the Citizen's Council, recalled that "Sam made the recommendation that the drive for acceptance of integration should be based on the idea that it was not fair to ask children to shoulder the burden of integration. Therefore, the adult population should lead the way, by accepting integration graciously and in good spirit."[10] Small homogeneous groups watched the movie, listening to the avuncular, resonating voice of CBS anchor Walter Cronkite, who donated his services. The film portrayed the traumatic events which paralyzed Little Rock and New Orleans when those cities resisted integration of their public school systems. Bloom Agency staff advised the Citizens Council "how to hold the meetings, how to conduct [them], how to get somebody to speak favorably, how to make sure that they were homogeneous." The purpose of this public relations blitz was to create an atmosphere in which citizens could "get up and advocate for [desegregation] without being shot down, politically shot down or ostracized in the community."[11]

During the 1960s Dallas "reluctantly accepted the necessity of a desegregation plan"[12] for its public schools because civil rights bills passed by the federal government and upheld by federal courts made it difficult

187

to receive federal funds for segregated facilities. As the city in the early 1970s began to dismantle its segregated school system, Judge William Mack Taylor, the presiding judge for the desegregation case, strongly called to task members of the business community for their lack of participation in the educational process. Taylor knew that the backing of the city's traditional leaders was essential for the success of any desegregation plan. Goaded by the judge, the Dallas Alliance, a group working within the Chamber of Commerce, formed a representative task force of Anglo, Mexican American, and African American leaders. To achieve racial balance, the task force recommended busing students in grades 4–8, building new high schools to help mix students of different races, and establishing ethnic ratios for top administrators. Most people were relieved by Taylor's concurrence with the proposal.

On the day Judge Taylor handed down his decision, March 10, 1976, Mayor Adlene Harrison, a temple member, stood ready with an important statement urging full support of the United States District Court Order. Determined to keep the peace, Harrison, the assertive mayor pro-tem who had ascended to Wes Wise's seat when he resigned to run for Congress, assured all Dallas citizens that "any act of civil disobedience will be dealt with promptly and firmly."[13] No violence marred that day or the opening of the new school term in August 1976.

During these troublesome times several temple members became enmeshed in the city's attempt to alleviate incendiary interracial problems which exploded when African American families who lived on the fringes of areas inhabited by whites began to move across heretofore tacitly observed lines of demarcation into areas that were all Caucasian, mainly in South Dallas: "As each family moved in, they were greeted by a bomb. From the spring of 1950 until the summer of 1951 there were more than 15 bombings of black homes in South Dallas."[14] An interracial committee, sponsored by the Dallas Chamber of Commerce and chaired by its president, John W. Carpenter, called for a special grand jury to investigate the attempted intimidation. The grand jury, of which Julius Schepps was a member, was convened, but no perpetrator of the violence was ever indicted. The committee's assertion that "most of the racial friction in

Dallas in the last decade was caused by a critical housing shortage" sparked the city's development of 1,100 public housing projects for African Americans in South Dallas and Oak Cliff as well as a 3,500-unit housing project in West Dallas.[15] At that time Louis Tobian, as chairman of the Dallas Housing Authority, oversaw the building of public utilities and streets specified for all new projects designated for lower income families, including those for African Americans.

With the expansion of Love Field in 1951 and the consequent displacement of black homeowners in the area, the city leadership felt it must find a suitable site to relocate these families. Consequently, the Dallas Citizens Inter-Racial Association, Inc., was created to find appropriate locations for single-family development. Chaired by Jerome Crossman, a temple member who headed the Chamber of Commerce Inter-Racial Housing Committee, its members included Fred Florence and Louis Tobian. With funds from the Hoblitzelle Foundation, the association purchased 170 acres in North Dallas for a housing addition located within the Richardson School District. The development of 750 houses in Hamilton Park created an island of middle-class African American families in North Dallas that, although segregated, was a point of pride for the black community. Furthermore, earmarking Hamilton Park Elementary School as a magnet elementary school created a superior educational facility which attracted children of all races.[16]

The question not just of individual members' participation but of the entire congregation's involvement in social action issues such as public housing and school desegregation was a grave one that Reform congregations across the United States grappled with and pondered. After attending the 1958 Union of American Hebrew Congregations Biennial in Washington, D. C., Bernard Hirsh presented the problem to the temple board: "Should Jews speak out on social issues?" and "Should the directive come from a central body in Washington, D. C.?" The UAHC had just received $100,000 from philanthropic activists Emily and Kivie Kaplan of Boston, later president of the National Association for the Advancement of Colored People (NAACP), for the establishment of a social action center in Washington, D.C.[17]

189

Temple Emanu-El had already been exposed to the union's stand on social action. In 1958 Emanu-El sponsored a Fall Institute on the theme "Aspects of the Good Society" and invited four speakers to address the role of education, labor, religion, and business in the good society. Among then was Albert Vorspan, director of the Commission on Social Action of the Union of American Hebrew Congregations and the co-author of *Justice and Judaism*, a guide to Jewish social ethics. During the course of his visit, Vorspan met with a few members of the board and other interested congregants to discuss the formation of a social action committee at Temple Emanu-El. The union's avowed position was that "a synagogue cannot isolate itself from the fundamental issues of social justice which confront the community and the nation, that to do so would be false to the deepest tradition and values of the Jewish heritage."[18] Adhering to that principle, the union's Commission on Social Action was "attempting to stimulate the formation of local congregational committees to undertake the study of important local and national problems from the standpoint of the moral principles of Judaism."[19]

No real consensus emerged among the leadership regarding a community project until the officers and board of Temple Emanu-El met in a day-long retreat with Rabbis Olan and Klein "to explore together the progress and direction of the Temple program in order to define our goals and purposes." At this meeting, the participants decided to "undertake, as part of its 90th anniversary observance [in 1962] the establishment of some community service project, perhaps in a slum area, to meet a particularly glaring need."[20] The attendees also suggested that a new committee, community affairs, be added to the table of organization. The board began to wrestle with the practical application of a social action program, keeping in mind Rabbi Olan's admonition that a religious congregation "should have a concern for the welfare of human beings." Instead of theorizing about the problems of youth, welfare, and integration, Olan was ready for the congregation to decide whether or not it wanted to act on a project specifically tailored to aid the Dallas community. Irving Goldberg proposed that the board appoint a community affairs committee.[21]

The first leaders of the new committee, long-time community volunteer Hortense Sanger and Sisterhood President Billie Stern (Frauman), began to familiarize themselves with the programs of similar committees throughout the country. Consulting with Rabbi Klein, they selected committee members of different ages and from diverse fields of interest and professional backgrounds.[22]

Once the Community Affairs Committee decided upon its course of action, it formally recommended in January 10, 1965, that "Temple Emanu-El develop a pre-school center for disadvantaged children, providing skilled professional leadership and adequate equipment, in a neighborhood suitable for such program." At the time Dallas was the largest city in the United States without public kindergartens.

Temple Emanu-El was not the only visionary religious institution planning a pre-school to help the underprivileged in South Dallas. The First Presbyterian Church also announced plans for a pre-school on Harwood Street. Both religious institutions echoed the Johnson administration's pledge to forge a Great Society to ameliorate the plight of the disadvantaged.

Shortly thereafter, Rabbi Olan wrote a letter of appeal to the congregation requesting donations to establish a pre-school in the Rhoads Terrace Housing Project on Pilgrim Street. The members responded immediately and enthusiastically, funding sixty percent of the two-year budget of $25,000. The rest of the Rhoads Terrace budget was supplied by a charitable foundation and a budget allocation from the board. The temple also established a tribute fund for contributions, and past president Henri L. Bromberg, Jr., became the temple advisor for financial matters at the school.[23] The physical facilities of the pre-school were readied for the school year by individual temple members. Edward Bromberg lent his carpentry skills to build and paint the shelves, cabinets, and cubbies and the Temple Boy Scout troup, led by scoutmaster Dan Levy, and the Temple Teens Social Action Committee collected and renovated playground equipment, toys, usable books, and records.

Temple Emanu-El's Rhoads Terrace Pre-School opened in September 1965 with twenty-nine children—seventeen five-year-olds and twelve four-year-olds—occupying space provided by the Dallas Housing Authority. Sue Lichten headed the temple advisory committee and professional teachers staffed the school. The director, Mrs. Richard Scher, assisted by Elsa Callier, depended upon Rhea Wolfram and Linny Yollick's group of about 100 women from the congregation to prepare and serve lunches, drive the children on field trips almost every week, assist in the classroom as teacher-aides, and help with clerical work. Hermine Sallinger and Edie Kuhne fixed and froze lunches once a month so that each school day two volunteers could bring lunch from the Temple Emanu-El kitchen to the children. Blanche Lefkowitz and Carolyn Horchow planned the children's field trips, taking them to ordinary places like a pet store, a supermarket, the library, or the zoo, which almost none of them had seen before. As chairman of youth activities, Florence Winer coordinated special projects planned by temple volunteers, and Robert Bloom and Shirley Tobolowsky headed the publicity for the project. One temple member was so drawn to the inquiring minds of the Rhoads Terrace students that, despite her husband's nearly incapacitating illness, she resolved never to miss her day at the pre-school.[24] For its work at Rhoads Terrace the *Dallas Times Herald* awarded Temple Emanu-El Sisterhood its Club of the Year Award in 1970 for distinguished service in the area of youth education.

In March 1967, Rabbi Olan appeared before the Dallas school board to urge the administration to establish public kindergartens with local funds "in those areas of the community where the need for them is most acute, and where parents cannot afford tuition in such private institutions as already exist and thrive in the more prosperous areas of the city."[25] The school board listened to the rabbi, but it stood firmly by its position that Dallas would not start a public kindergarten program until the state legislature required it and supplied the funds. Public opinion mandated a change of legislative policy, and in 1971 the State of Texas began to provide money for some state-supported kindergartens. But by that time, because of the temple's farsighted desire to tackle a community problem, 300 children had already attended half-day sessions at the Rhoads Terrace Pre-School, effectively increasing their adjustment and achievement in the first grade. Moreover, Gerry Beer, the vice-chairman of the community project for the first two years and its second chairman in 1967, concluded that parental involvement with the pre-school made parents more adept at decision-making and helped them realize that they could take action to improve their lot. (Applying these same principles to the predicament of battered women and their children, Beer would later found The Family Place.) At Rhoads Terrace parents successfully petitioned the Dallas Housing Authority to grant the pre-school more space in order to admit thirty additional children. They also appeared before the school board to ask for a railroad warning system for a track close to neighboring H. S. Thompson Elementary School, that their children had to cross every day, a request which, after three years of prodding, the school board finally granted.[26]

With the establishment of public kindergartens in Dallas, the Rhoads Terrace Pre-School concentrated on pre-kindergarten education and later evolved into the Institute for Early Childhood Education and Developmental Day Care, a full-time day-care center partially funded by the Texas Department of Public Welfare. Local matching funds still comprised thirty percent of the center's budget. So donations from individual temple members, a temple allocation of $1,000, and foundation gifts remained mandatory for support. The Dallas Section, National Council of Jewish Women, also contributed a one-time gift of $5,000. In 1972 the Dallas Housing Authority authorized $300,000 for the construction of a new building for the Child Care Institute in the Rhoads Terrace project. Sonya Bemporad, the wife of Jack Bemporad, rabbi at Temple Emanu-El from 1972–1983, became director of the Rhoads Terrace Institute in 1974. A child care specialist, she had been a member of the psychology faculty at Sarah Lawrence College and director of its laboratory nursery school. The Rhoads Terrace Institute merged in 1976 with the Dallas Day Care Association and was renamed the Child Care Association of Metropolitan Dallas. Despite the changes, Temple Emanu-El continued to support the concept of early childcare development, donating funds for the new facility.[27]

The success of the temple's initial pre-school project was gratifying because individual members proved that with effort and commitment it was possible to effect a desirable social change in the community. During the time Temple Emanu-El was defining its goals and programs, led by its candid, liberal rabbi, however, the city of Dallas began to be known as a center of conservative, even right-wing activity. Organizations such as the American Legion and the Public Affairs Luncheon Club objected to the inclusive policies of the Dallas Museum of Art and the Public Library. These ultra-conservative groups insisted that the cultural institutions ban works by world renowned artists Pablo Picasso and Diego Rivera on the grounds of their "known Communist affiliations."[28] When the trustees of both public facilities yielded to the demands of the arch-conservative groups, John Rosenfield, the entertainment critic of the *Dallas Morning News* and the son of former president of the temple Max Rosenfield, scoffed in his column, "The Passing Show," that the city's code to govern "the exhibition of paintings, the performance of music and drama, the circulation of books or any other expression of mankind's creative spirit or mental processes . . . should be 'If anybody objects, yank it down, or ban it from the halls, or burn it up.'"[29] Shortly thereafter, museum trustees reversed their position and endorsed a resolution stating that "the policy of the trustees of the Dallas Museum of Fine Arts is to exhibit and acquire works of art only on the basis of their merit as works of art."[30] Although the trustees at the public museum remained firm, the right-wing groups had reaped a great deal of publicity and support for their view.

After that nationally reported episode about Dallas' lack of artistic freedom, two unpleasant political incidents also marred Dallas' reputation. First, Democratic vice-presidential nominee Lyndon Johnson and his wife, Lady Bird, had the misfortune to collide with ultra-conservative Republican Congressman Bruce Alger leading a group of Republican women promoting the Nixon-Lodge ticket. In Dallas on November 4, 1960, to campaign, the Johnsons arrived to attend a noon luncheon at the Adolphus Hotel. They were roughly jostled as they attempted to enter the hotel, and Mrs. Johnson was visibly shaken by the "howling, chanting, jeering pro-Nixon" crowd.[31] A few years later, on October 24, 1963, when United Nations Ambassador Adlai Stevenson came to Dallas to speak at

Memorial Auditorium for United Nations Day, he had to pass through a gauntlet of anti-U. N. pickets to reach the auditorium door. Once inside the hall he could not make himself heard. Belligerent men heckled the ambassador by ruffling their programs and stomping their feet, while their wives, deliberately wearing bangle bracelets, noisily jiggled them. The final indignity occurred when an antagonistic placard bearer hit Stevenson on the head.[32] After this fiasco, the city fathers nervously began to worry about the next political arrival scheduled to ride into town, none other than the president of the United States.

When President Kennedy opted to come to Dallas in the fall of 1963, just one month after Stevenson was, in a symbolic sense, run out of town, the Dallas Citizens Council turned to Sam Bloom to smooth the way for the president's visit. Once again Bloom was given the job of "protecting the moderate image of Dallas" because, according to David Ritz in an article for *D* magazine about his experiences at the Bloom Agency in the 1960s, "if he could integrate our schools and keep the crazies away, he could get our liberal President in and out of town without an incident."[33] Sam Bloom worked out a non-partisan invitation list for the Market Hall luncheon on November 22, 1963, in the belief that "whatever feeling a person held for the President, he was still the President of the United States and must be treated with respect."[34] As the whole world knows, the expectant audience at that luncheon waited in vain for John F. Kennedy. The president was shot by an assassin as he, his wife, Jacqueline, and Texas Governor and Mrs. John Connally rode in an open convertible by the Texas School Depository on their way to the Trade Mart. Not able to find a viewing spot among the throng welcoming President and Mrs. Kennedy along Main Street, temple member Abraham Zapruder worked his way to Elm Street and the triple underpass in order to capture the president's visit with his movie camera. At that spot he filmed the only visual record of the assassination, footage that "was developed immediately and shown to the FBI, the Secret Service and police" and became the principal source for reconstituting the shocking and terrible event.[35]

Directly after the news of the president's death was confirmed, Vice-President Lyndon Johnson, who had ridden in a car behind the president, called his friend Irving Goldberg to ascertain whether as the *de facto* new president he should take the presidential oath in Dallas or Washington. The man whom Johnson later appointed as an appellate judge told him to locate Federal District Court Judge Sarah Hughes so she could rush to *Air Force I* at Love Field to administer the oath of office in Dallas to the next president of the United States.[36] After the assassination, David Ritz related, Dallas leaders again called on Sam Bloom to try to mend Dallas' fractured image. Bloom advised Judge Joe B. Brown on how to handle the media during the trial of Jack Ruby, the killer of Kennedy's presumed assassin, Lee Harvey Oswald.[37]

The realization that the assassination of a president could take place in Dallas was so shocking to the city that it jarred some segments of the population into reexamining the community in which they lived. Congregants of Temple Emanu-El and loyal listeners to Rabbi Olan's radio sermons, who wondered what the rabbi thought about the tragedy, finally had their answer during his January 19, 1964, radio broadcast. "What Should Dallas Do Now?" is worth quoting:

> The first question which must be resolved is psychological. Is Dallas guilty of anything because the President of our country was assassinated on her streets? In the beginning there was a strong current of guilt which the Mayor's prophetic call expressed in noble terms. Many people felt that there was something frightfully wrong with the city and some wanted to face the truth. This mood is passing, and now there is a growing resentment of all criticism from without and within the gates. The present tone is that of rejecting all responsibility and disclaiming all guilt. Dallas, it is said, is no different from other cities, and better than many. . . .

> There is a psychological axiom which holds that when a disturbed patient accepts responsibility and blame for his behavior, and attempts to do something about it, the prognosis is good. When, however, a patient tends to rationalize away his behavior and justify it, the prognosis appears to be poor. The present mood of Dallas

which is one of rejecting responsibility and blame is essentially the greatest psychological danger confronting the city. Time is an important factor here, and the longer the delay in assuming responsibility the worse the prognosis.

Rabbi Olan went on to discuss the frustration and anxiety felt by those citizens who wanted to stop the rapidly progressing revolution taking place in the country where the old values of religion, family, and society were "in radical transition," thereby creating an ethical dilemma for the community.

For years after the assassination of John F. Kennedy, Rabbi Olan was called the "conscience of the city," a role which he certainly fulfilled.[38] *Fortune* magazine published a widely read, detailed article, "How Business Failed Dallas," criticizing the business leadership of Dallas. *Fortune* also remarked, "Dallas churches, for all their affluence, have been criticized by some for being singularly unrealistic about the urgent problems of the city. Accordingly, the most powerful religious voice in the area is undoubtedly that of Levi Olan, rabbi of Temple Emanu-El."[39] Levi Olan assuredly represented one of the best minds and hearts in the Dallas community.

In the next few years the Dallas leadership tried to adjust and temper the political climate of the city. Mayor Earle Cabell ran for Bruce Alger's congressional seat in order to oust the Republican congressman who had been part of the nasty campaign incident involving Lyndon Johnson. Erik Jonsson, who was appointed by the city council to fill Cabell's unexpired term, inaugurated a "Goals for Dallas" committee, modeled after former President Eisenhower's "Goals for America" national committee. Eighty-seven participants from different backgrounds and with divergent professional abilities convened at the Stagecoach Inn at Salado, Texas, to discuss Dallas' flaws as well as its strengths. From the exchange of ideas the Goals for Dallas Committee sought to build for the future.

Participants had at least two traits in common: they had a genuine interest in the city, and they had been entwined in its workings in one way or another for many years. Before the meeting, they studied as "required

197

reading" essays relating to broad areas of civic interest such as "The Citizen and His City," "Culture," "Transportation," and "Elementary and Secondary Education."[40] Carl Flaxman, president of Temple Emanu-El from 1967 to 1969, wrote an essay on welfare, and Flaxman, Edmund Kahn, Rabbi Levi Olan and Hortense Sanger participated in the retreat. A former director of the Civil Rights Regional Office for the Health, Education, and Welfare Department, Flaxman believed that the "Goals" were an influential catalyst for change in the political and civil rights climate of the city, although he conceded that change might not have been as profound nor as fast as some segments of the community would have wished.[41] Hortense Sanger recalled that because the committees were heterogeneous by design, representing Dallas men and women of all races and all faiths, the participants felt that they were involved in a ground-breaking effort to examine the problems of all residents in the city and to bring their findings to the attention of all Dallasites from every walk of life.[42]

At the time Rabbi Olan was also an integral part of other local and state organizations devoted to the improvement of the community, particularly in education. In 1963, Governor John Connally appointed him a regent of the University of Texas, making him only the second Jewish regent from Dallas (Alexander Sanger was the first) and the second rabbi after Rabbi Maurice Faber from Tyler, who had served in 1915 and 1916. Before Olan's appointment, he had been part of the Committee of 75 of the University of Texas that conducted an intensive study of the university's needs. One of the first decisions of the new board of regents in 1963 was the desegregation of the undergraduate division of the university. At the same time Olan was also a member of the Advisory Committee of 50 at SMU, where he was a visiting lecturer and an almost daily visitor at his "hideaway" for study, a secluded carrel in Bridwell Library.[43] SMU feted him on his sixtieth birthday in 1963 when his friends presented a valuable collection of rare books on the Judeo-Christian tradition to Perkins School of Theology in his name. Friends of Dr. and Mrs. Lefkowitz had previously established the Sadie and David Lefkowitz Collection in 1952 in honor of their fiftieth wedding anniversary. The two collections commemorated the love of scholarly learning upheld by the traditions of the university and of Temple Emanu-El.

Throughout the turbulent decade of the 1960s the rabbis and the congregation invited the Dallas community to events at the temple and purposefully occupied themselves in trying to solve urgent community problems, especially in the area of education. Moreover, individual temple members participated in civic life, hoping to better the lot of everyone in Dallas. For instance, in 1948 when he was a twenty-five-year-old Navy veteran, Milton Tobian ran as a reform candidate for the Dallas school board, whose members' average age was seventy. He did not win, but nearly twenty years later he was among the initiators of a new organization formed to improve the quality of education in Dallas: the League for Educational Advancement (LEAD).[44] Although its effectiveness lasted for only a few years, LEAD demonstrated in 1967 its vote-getting abilities when its supporters elected reform candidates, including Dr. Emmett Conrad, an African American, to the school board. Establishment of kindergartens was one of LEAD's goals, and Milton Tobian, as president of the temple from 1965 to 1967, steadfastly supported the Rhoads Terrace Pre-School. In that decade, this pre-school, which enlisted so many congregants to assist it, remained the temple's most notable contribution to the welfare of the community.

In an era of change and confusion the values of the prophetic tradition held true for another generation. Stoked by the faith, fervor, and fears of the 1960s, Temple Emanu-El boldly initiated a large-spirited approach toward the divisions and dislocations of the community at a time rife with difficult, nagging contradictions. To the congregation of the sixties, a serious social welfare stance was a most legitimate part of their religious belief. ☫

CHAPTER 10

Change: The Only Constant

Through the years, because of the changing population in the city, because of the movement here of people from the East and the North and California, there have come into the temple many people whose backgrounds were different from those of the original people in the Temple, and the demand for some of the things they were at home with became obvious.

Levi A. Olan

During the twenty years Levi Olan served as rabbi at Temple Emanu-El, Reform Judaism "saw new theological ferment within its ranks, unprecedented social activism, a yet fuller appreciation of tradition, and the first appearance of women in positions of spiritual leadership. But there were also some years of nagging self-doubt and the emergence of new rifts every bit as severe as the earlier conflict over Zionism."[1] Sol Goodell, a lawyer whose active participation in the temple spanned forty years, felt that the horrors of World War II and the Holocaust fueled the desire of Jews in the armed services and at home to seek more from religion and, in some cases, to join a synagogue for the first time.[2]

As a consequence, many Reform Jews wanted to be more involved in their temples, and some wished to restore "some of the old customs that the Reform people had abandoned." As well, they wanted "just more going on at the temple, making it more of a community center."[3] In general, during the population surge to the Southwest after the war, new

201

members of the temple who hailed from different parts of the country, especially those reared in a more traditional synagogue, were receptive to liturgical and program changes. For example, many young parents were attracted to Emanu-El because they were stirred by Rabbi Olan's outspoken liberalism and, on a more practical note, also appreciated the inclusion of religious school expenses in their membership dues—an amenity offered at no other Dallas synagogue. Once accepted as members, they wanted a deepening of religious content, such as Bar and Bat Mitzvah preparation, in their children's education.

As much as Levi Olan was intellectually in tune with the Reform movement, his Orthodox upbringing provided the background and capacity to restore at Temple Emanu-El some of the beauty and color of the rituals being reintroduced at other American Reform congregations. In the course of the vast pendular swing from Orthodox to Reform Judaism, some Reform rabbis—and Levi Olan patently was one—felt that American Jews had lost touch with the evocative meaning inherent in traditional prayers, songs, and practices. Besides his feeling of affection and admiration for the new music director, Sam Adler, Rabbi Olan also brought Adler to Dallas so that he could introduce classic Jewish music in song and prayer into the service.[4] In the same vein, Rabbi Olan revived the *kiddush* blessing over the wine at Friday night services and included more prayer in ancient Hebrew. Soon he found that not everyone was receptive to the rabbi's prerogative to change the service as he wished. At Olan's first High Holy Day services, held at Fair Park Auditorium, he recited the *Avinu Malkeinu* (Our Father, Our King) prayer in Hebrew, prompting one woman to reproach him afterward, saying, "We never read so much Hebrew. Dr. Lefkowitz never read that in Hebrew." All the rabbi could do was look at her and retort, "And now we did."[5]

In the religious school, some parents, ordinarily not bothered about basic Hebrew as part of the curriculum, became perturbed by what they viewed as an emphasis upon Israel permeating their children's religious instruction. These parents, whose views were not sympathetic toward the establishment of a Jewish state, found objectionable such practices as wrapping Hanukkah presents in the blue and white colors of the Israeli flag.[6] When challenged at a meeting called by the unhappy parent group at the South Boulevard temple, Olan, who never embraced an ethnic outlook, nevertheless brooked no discussion of the issue and left the parents with no recourse for the expression of their opinion.[7] In due time, as identification with and strong support for the new state became an absorbing factor in national and local American Jewish life, the cultural influence of Israel, which still seemed foreign to some temple members, disappeared as a point in question in the religious school.

Initially, although Bar Mitzvahs were becoming more prevalent, Rabbi Olan did not propose an active program. In response to an inquiry in 1953 concerning procedures and requirements in connection with Bar Mitzvah, Rabbi Olan replied that "in our Temple we do not encourage Bar Mitzvahs, although we meet the demand when some family asks for it. We still feel that the Confirmation service is our chief introduction of the young person in Judaism."[8] Olan's predecessor, David Lefkowitz, did not prepare many boys for Bar Mitzvah because that tradition did not exist at the Dallas temple, but he had conducted frequent Bar Mitzvahs when he was the rabbi at Bene Jeshurun in Dayton and told his Dallas congregation that it was a practice which "we heartily recommend."[9]

During the thirties first Richard Albert and then Joseph Funk were Bar Mitzvah at Emanu-El when their families requested the coming-of-age ceremony designating a thirteen-year-old as "a man of responsibility" entitled to recognition as part of a *minyan*. The Albert family moved to Dallas just before Richard's thirteenth birthday, and since he had partially prepared for this rite of passage in San Antonio, he continued studying Hebrew with Rabbi Lefkowitz and Rabbi Brav and celebrated his Bar Mitzvah in December 1934. Joe Funk's background was Orthodox, but his parents enrolled him at Emanu-El's religious school since he could conveniently ride there with Sara and Bertha Hart, who lived across the street and taught on Sundays. Joe knew that he would follow his family's Orthodox tradition, and he studied with Rabbi Lefkowitz and Rabbi Brav as preparation for his Torah reading at his Bar Mitzvah in December 1935.[10]

In anticipation of his Bar Mitzvah ceremony in November 1940, Max Tonkon studied Hebrew several days each week with Dr. Lefkowitz.

203

Prior to his sessions with the rabbi, Max's father, I. Edward Tonkon, had enrolled his son at the Hebrew School of Dallas, originally established in 1885 as a congregational school of Shearith Israel.[11] During the summer when the temple was open only for Friday night and Saturday morning services, Max went to the Lefkowitz house almost every day for private lessons. Being together so often, young Max and the rabbi forged a close bond. Years later when Max told Dr. Lefkowitz he was scheduled to go into the army on Yom Kippur Eve, the rabbi said, "Maxie, you know I could get you postponed, but it's better that you go. And Maxie, you don't have to fast the next day."[12] During the decade of the 1950s, a few Bar Mitzvah ceremonies took place each year. But ten years later, twenty-seven boys, one almost every Saturday morning from fall until spring, became Bar Mitzvah in the sanctuary, a mark of the growing popularity of the initiation rite at Temple Emanu-El.

For individualized Bar and Bat Mitzvah preparation, young people enjoyed working with Edwin Tankus, the grandfatherly Bar Mitzvah coordinator who was an unusual and delightful combination of scholar and showman. Tankus infused in his students a love and respect for learning and delivering ancient Hebraic chants and prayers and imparted to them the subtle joy of performance when delivering their addresses from the pulpit. After Edwin and Molly Tankus moved to Golden Acres, Martin Yaffe, professor of philosophy at the University of North Texas at Denton, assumed the position of Bar/Bat Mitzvah Coordinator. During his time at Temple Emanu-El the Bar/Bat Mitzvah ceremonies attained importance in Reform congregations nationwide, and the number of Dr. Yaffe's pupils increased dramatically as more young people at Emanu-El chose to strengthen their connection to Judaism.

The first Bat Mitzvah of a young woman in America took place in 1922 when Judith Kaplan read from the Torah in her father's New York synagogue. She was the daughter of Rabbi Mordecai Kaplan, the founder of Reconstructionist Judaism, which sees Judaism as an "evolving religious civilization of the Jewish people." Forty years later Janice Brin, daughter of Carol and Royal Brin, celebrated the first Bat Mitzvah held at Temple Emanu-El, although neighboring Conservative synagogue Shearith Israel had initiated the Bat Mitzvah Service in 1953. Janice elected to take a Hebrew class taught by Shirley Fisher as part of her religious school program and expressed to her parents her desire to be Bat Mitzvah. Sam Adler taught her to chant the Hebrew blessings, and Rabbi Klein arranged for her to become a Daughter of the Commandment at the Sisterhood Mother and Daughter Sabbath on March 27, 1965. Later that afternoon both Rabbi Klein and Rabbi Olan celebrated the occasion with Janice at a Havdalah Service concluding the Sabbath.[13] Initially, all Bat Mitzvahs were assigned to the afternoon service.

During the era when Rabbi Olan, like many Reform rabbis, reintroduced some of the traditional ritual practices that the Reform movement had abandoned, he made clear his concern with the larger picture, the relationship of Emanu-El to Reform Judaism as a whole. Because he believed that Reform Judaism met the needs of "modern thinking people," Rabbi Olan wanted the congregation to strengthen the liberal movement in the Jewish community. He was particularly disturbed about the unaffiliated Jews in the city. Out of 18,000 Jews estimated to live in Dallas, 10,000 were associated with a temple or synagogue, but 8,000 were unallied. In Rabbi Olan's view, the Jewish community ought to address the needs of this group, particularly those single people and young married couples with children who were not being exposed to Jewish life. He was convinced that the temple should offer attractive opportunities for involvement to those born Jewish but with no affiliation, to those who had left the fold, and to practicing but dissatisfied Conservative or Orthodox Jews.[14] Accordingly, president Philip Silverberg appointed a committee to determine Emanu-El's responsibility to the unaffiliated.

Concurrent with the question of Temple Emanu-El's obligation to Dallas Jewry was the consideration of the optimal size of the congregation, now numbering over 2,000 families. In 1962 a investigative committee concluded that no constraints should be placed on the size of the temple family. Although the temple refused to restrict membership, it could not ignore the strain that the increasing numbers of new members produced upon the physical facilities and the staff.

Meanwhile, the committee examining primary issues facing the temple determined that the institution's obligation to serve the religious life of the community, primarily the unaffiliated, needed immediate attention. Therefore, the temple offered to help with the formation of a new congregation, whose existence would not just attract the unaffiliated but also relieve the pressure on the facilities of Temple Emanu-El. Newly elected president Milton Tobian sent a letter to Temple Emanu-El members and to about 150 unattached Jews in the suburbs of Richardson, Garland, Farmers Branch, and North Dallas extending an invitation to meet in Tobian Auditorium. The board decided that the participation of Temple Emanu-El would be confined to counsel, and the new organization would be completely independent. Tobian's letter clearly expressed the temple's position:

> In the event that such a congregation comes into existence, by far its major and predominant support must come from the unaffiliated in our area. We are justly proud of our Temple with its history, tradition, and accomplishment, and its varied and many-faceted programs, but we are not so arrogant as to suggest that no member of our congregation might want to participate in a different type of congregational life than that afforded by our beloved Temple. Anyone so motivated will be encouraged to join the new congregation.
>
> Whether or not it is determined that the need for such a Reform Congregation exists, we will have, in any case, discharged our duty to be vigilant at all times to the end that the Reform Jewish religious life of our community is served.[15]

Later, Milton Tobian said that enough people were dissatisfied with various aspects of the large and long-established congregation to make him realize that a new congregation would be formed, and he wanted it created with Emanu-El's blessing.[16]

One of the men most interested in assembling a new congregation was Henry Jacobus, Jr., a temple board member then in his middle thirties. Continually frustrated by his experience as a trustee, Jacobus, son of a former president of the temple, began to sense that the board did not welcome young, innovative leadership. He realized that "the board was not where the action was" because he knew that all decisions were made prior to board meetings. At one meeting during which board members were heatedly discussing some issue, Jacobus recalled that Louis Tobian rose to his feet and said, "Now boys, you can discuss it all you want, but here's what we're going to do."[17] Stymied for a reply because of his reverence for a man who had contributed so much to the temple, Jacobus knew he never could bring himself to contradict the older man. Shortly afterward, Jacobus remembered that Judge Irving Goldberg asked him and his wife, Gloria, and several other young couples who had expressed an interest in forming another congregation to create a steering committee for the new congregation. Gloria Jacobus later recalled that for each founding family the decision to leave Temple Emanu-El was a "real wrench for everyone involved."[18] When thirty-eight prospects signified their interest at the community meeting sponsored by Emanu-El, they convened with the steering committee and established the second Reform temple in Dallas, Temple Shalom.[19]

The new congregation, with Henry Jacobus, Jr., as president and Dr. Marvin Gerard as president-elect, assembled for its first services at Perkins Chapel on the SMU campus. After three weeks Temple Shalom changed its location to the chapel at St. Mark's School of Texas, where it remained for six months. Lay members Alex Zelenka and Louis Ralph Cohen conducted the services at the chapel and later at Northaven Methodist Church, the next home of the congregation, until Rabbi Hershel Jaffe arrived in the summer of 1966 as the congregation's first rabbi. In a spirit of interfaith cooperation, the leaders of Northhaven Methodist Church provided an office for Rabbi Jaffe and also allowed Temple Shalom to store a portable ark at the church. Meanwhile, two Emanu-El staff members assisted the new congregation. Sam Adler helped with music for services, and Ray Israel taught prospective religious school teachers how to write a curriculum.[20] The religious school first met at Hockaday School and then was housed in classrooms at Ursuline Academy. Out of the initial enrollment of ninety applicants for the religious

207

school, eighty children were concentrated in pre-school and kindergarten, a clear indication of the congregation's appeal to young families.

When Rabbi Jaffe left the congregation after three years, former Temple Emanu-El members, who recalled Saul Besser "with such affection," were determined to secure him as rabbi for Temple Shalom.[21] In 1965 Rabbi Besser had left Emanu-El to become director of the Mid-Atlantic Region for the Union of American Hebrew Congregations. With his wife Annette and two young sons, Jeremy and Ethan, Besser returned to Dallas in 1969 as rabbi of Temple Shalom. Soon thereafter, the Shalom congregation, numbering about 250 families, initiated a building drive for a permanent home to be located on fourteen acres of land on the corner of Alpha and Hillcrest roads in North Dallas. After the congregation moved to its new building, Shalom's membership spurted to over 600 families during the next decade. Ironically, although the overburdened older temple had been instrumental in creating a new congregation, some of its members began to fret over the fact that Shalom was attracting young families while Emanu-El's membership was noticeably aging.[22] Even allowing for a decreasing birth rate, the drop in Emanu-El's religious school enrollment from 1,500 in 1965 to 900 in 1972 seemed precipitously sharp. Plainly, young couples who were newcomers to Dallas more often than not chose youth-oriented Temple Shalom as their place of worship.

To make the older temple more attractive to young families, the board began to underscore the importance of youth activities. Stanley I. Robin, who became the assistant rabbi in 1966, had actively participated with temple youth in the Ohio area while at Hebrew Union College. After he served as a chaplain in the United States Army for three years during the Vietnam War, Rabbi Robin and his wife Etta with their two young children moved to Dallas. At the temple he directed the Bar Mitzvah program, and, with temple choir member Dottie Mandell, also advised the youth group, then called the Temple Teens. Over one hundred teenagers belonged to the Temple Teens, which was recognized by *Parents Magazine* in 1963 for its public service projects. This youth group, led by its president Richard Marks, traveled to Denton each month to give parties for blind children and also participated in UNICEF drives to raise money for needy children in foreign countries. When Mrs. Milton P. Levy in 1973 donated $250,000 for the new Ruth and Milton P. Levy Youth Building designed for cultural and educational activities for youth, a sum which was further augmented by the philanthropic Levy family, the board authorized the appointment of a youth director. Since 1986, Judi Ratner, a singer and guitarist who tongue-in-cheek considers herself a perpetual camper, has administered the lively youth program—the day camp, the Israel Teen tour, and retreats to Greene family camp—all activities outside of the religious school.

After Stanley Robin departed in June 1969 to become assistant rabbi at Temple Emanu-El in Tucson, Dallas' Emanu-El continued its practice of hiring young Hebrew Union College graduates for an "internship" and welcomed a new assistant rabbi, Irwin Goldenberg, and his wife, Joyce, to the congregation. Rabbi Goldenberg grew up in Newark, New Jersey, and received his B.A. degree from Rutgers University. Even before the decision of Hebrew Union College to require each rabbi to matriculate at its Jerusalem campus for a year, he had spent a year of study and work in Israel.

At this time, after a two-year term in the prestigious post of president of the Conference of American Rabbis, Rabbi Olan reached the conventional retirement age of sixty-five, prompting the recommendation to the board that he be given the opportunity to retire with emeritus status when he thought it advisable. He would be salaried for life.

On January 9, 1970, congregational president Robert Strauss read a letter from Rabbi Olan:

Dear Friends:

I prayerfully ask that you permit me to retire as Rabbi of the Congregation on August 31, 1970, and to avail myself of the title "Rabbi Emeritus" as described in a resolution of the Board of Trustees.

Please allow me to postpone to a later date an adequate expression of my affection and appreciation for our years together.

209

Faithfully,
Levi A. Olan

With profound regret, the board accepted Rabbi Olan's decision to retire, and on May 17, 1970, people of all faiths gathered at the temple to pay him tribute.

Upon retirement, Rabbi Olan used his leisure time for writing and preaching as well as for traveling. He also continued teaching at Perkins School of Theology and the Institute of Religion at the University of Houston. When he came to worship services, he and Sarita participated simply as ordinary members of the congregation, taking whatever seats were available. In 1971 he accepted a prestigious and challenging teaching post for a year at the Leo Baeck College in London, returning for the weekend of the 100th Anniversary Celebration in December of 1972. Olan's departure marked the end of his working association with Gerald Klein, a relationship tempered over two decades. A balance had been created between the scholar with the rapier-like wit who "was the best preacher in Dallas" (but had little patience with small talk) and his younger associate who was willing to make sick calls and form the pastoral connections wanted and needed by Emanu-El's members. Well-liked and highly respected in the community, the first rabbi elected president of the Dallas Pastors Group, Klein assumed the responsibilities of the senior rabbi of the temple.

At first, no real effort was made to look for another experienced rabbi to join Rabbi Klein and Assistant Rabbi Goldenberg. After a year, Bernard Hirsh, who had become president in 1971, appointed a small rabbinical search committee consisting of several past presidents, plus Rabbi Klein. This committee contacted the Rabbinical Placement Commission in New York, a practice outlined by the Central Conference of American Rabbis to prevent individual congregations from directly recruiting prospective rabbis. Rabbi Klein wrote to Rabbi Malcolm Stern, head of the Rabbinical Placement Commission, with the congregation's stipulations for the position. In reply, Rabbi Stern sent biographies of several potential candidates.

Among the numerous resumes, Hirsh remarked in retrospect, "one biography stood out." Rabbi Jack Bemporad seemed to be the perfect candidate. His age, thirty-eight, "was good and his credentials looked good."[23] A Phi Beta Kappa graduate of Tulane University with a major in mathematics, the Italian-born Bemporad was ordained at the Hebrew Union College in 1959 and then accepted a Fulbright scholarship at the University of Rome. His scholarly interests were manifested by the fact that he had taught at the University of Rome as well as the Hebrew Union College-Jewish Institute of Religion, the New School for Social Research, and the University of Pennsylvania. In 1972 he was the director of the Commission on Worship of the Union of Hebrew American Congregations and also acted as rabbi to a small experimental congregation in suburban New York. Not having had much experience as a congregational rabbi, at this stage in his career Bemporad wanted to become less academically oriented and involve himself in congregational life.[24]

Former president Carl Flaxman flew to New York to interview Bemporad, the only rabbi contacted for the post at Temple Emanu-El, and Bemporad flew to Dallas in the summer of 1972 to meet Rabbi Klein and the rabbinical committee. On that visit he planned to absorb the city's atmosphere and to envision the tenor of life in Dallas for his wife Sonya, a child education specialist, and his two young sons, Henry and Raphael. Rabbi Klein met him at the plane and took him home for dinner and a meeting with the committee. The next day Bernard Hirsh drove Bemporad around the city with an eye toward finding appropriate neighborhoods and good schools. Favorably impressed on his first visit, he returned with Sonya to meet the executive committee, former past presidents, and the rabbinical committee. On this occasion Bernard Hirsh felt that the rabbi "utterly charmed everybody." After a discussion about salary and title—for Bemporad "wanted to be called 'rabbi,' not assistant or associate rabbi"—the president and the rabbi reached an oral agreement. Then the entire board and Rabbi Klein agreed to ask Rabbi Bemporad to leave New York for Dallas in August 1972.[25]

When Bemporad joined the congregation, members were busy with preparations for the celebration of the temple's 100th anniversary. The president and the board knew that a gala jubilee was appropriate for such an important milestone, one involving the community at large, as well as for special events for Dallas Jewry. For the opening event on April 7, 1972, the trustees had agreed to engage jazz virtuoso Dave Brubeck after Shirley Tobolowsky and Rabbi Klein heard him play in concert at a union biennial convention in Miami and shared their excitement about the performance with the board.

The production called for bass baritone McHenry Boatwright and Cantor Harold Orbach from Detroit, as well as the temple choir, the East Texas State University Chorale, and the Dallas Symphony Orchestra musicians. Combining jazz, the twelve-tone scale, the oratorio form, and the African American spiritual, Dave Brubeck and his wife Iola adapted the libretto for Gates of Justice from the Torah, from the *Union Prayer Book*, and from words by Dr. Martin Luther King, Jr. After the concert, members of the congregation expressed their delight at being present at such a "spine-tingling, majestic, genuine celebration."[26]

The major celebration occurred on the first weekend of December 1972. At the Friday night service, all the past presidents or their family surrogates walked down the sanctuary aisles in a Torah processional led by President Bernard Hirsh, Sisterhood President Blanche Steinberg, Brotherhood President William Schwartz, and Dallas Area Federation of Temple Youth (DAFTY) President Gary Udashen. On the pulpit with Temple Emanu-El's rabbis was Dr. Alfred Gottschalk, the newly installed president of Hebrew Union College-Jewish Institute of Religion, who preached on "Judaism in the World of Tomorrow."

On Saturday evening Joan and Milton Loeb, Jr., and Nita Mae and Sam Tannebaum chaired a program featuring an inspiring video presentation, "Temple Emanu-El—The First Hundred Years." Not only were the vintage pictures a handclasp from the past, but present-day congregants narrated the documentary while Edward Stern related the story of the congregation. After the show the congregation enjoyed cotton candy, popcorn, and a towering anniversary cake in Tobian Auditorium, transformed through the embellishment of lattice work and flowers into an 1872 garden party.

On Sunday afternoon Jeanne and Sanford P. Fagadau, Emme Sue and Jerome Frank, Carl Flaxman, and Billie Stern (Frauman) invited the

Dallas community to an open house featuring a symposium which addressed "The Future of Religion in Western Civilization." Noted religious scholars presented Protestant, Catholic, and Jewish perspectives. That day visitors to the temple also viewed a display in Linz Hall commemorating 100 historic years of vigorous Jewish life in Dallas. Its curators, Emily Hexter, granddaughter of Rabbi David Lefkowitz, and Shirley Pollock, granddaughter of former temple president Ludwig Philipson, had gathered photographs from members and from the temple's archives for the exhibit, "The First Hundred Years—God Has Been With Us."

As an additional contribution to the anniversary celebration, on December 6, 1972, Sisterhood and Brotherhood invited the public to hear Dr. Margaret Mead. The renowned professor of anthropology at Columbia University and curator of ethnology at the American Museum of Natural History spoke eloquently and trenchantly about "The American Family—Present and Future" to a "standing room only" crowd, who savored her scholarly opinions punctuated with examples highly pertinent to everyday life. In committee chair Joan Loeb's opinion, 100th anniversary events attracted the participation of so many people—congregants helping in the planning stages and attending the events— because there was "a feeling of excitement" and "a feeling of accomplishment" in attaining the 100-year milepost.[27] Unequivocally, the celebration imparted to the participants a sense of being at home with and integrated into their heritage.

After the gala anniversary year, Bernard Hirsh knew that it was time to contend with the multiplicity of problems—programmatic and financial—facing the congregation. He appointed a small committee to investigate every facet of temple life: the religious school, the music and adult education programs, and the financial deficit. In Hirsh's mind this committee would "do those things that needed to be done, not just file a report away."[28]

The trustees summoned Sam Bloom, president in 1949, to assume the office in 1973. Bloom was already in charge of a committee to energize the lay leadership and give direction to every department of the temple, particularly problem areas like the religious school, whose attendance kept dropping, and the music program, led only by a part-time music director.

The board's attention was drawn to the floundering music department, which had flourished so brilliantly under the energetic direction of Sam Adler. Adler, Emanu-El's first music director in 1953, had resigned in 1966 to accept the post of professor of composition at the Eastman School of Music of the University of Rochester. The choir was delighted with the choice of Simon Sargon, a charming and gifted composer, conductor, and pianist, who brought a rich and varied background to the temple. Born in Bombay, India, to an Indian father and an American mother who had met each other in Jerusalem, Sargon's family left for safer shores when he was a baby, sailing for America on the last boat allowed to travel through the Suez Canal before the outbreak of World War II. A Phi Beta Kappa graduate of Brandeis University, where he was also class valedictorian in 1959, Sargon held a master's degree in composition from the Juilliard School and had studied at Tanglewood, Aspen School of Music, and Columbia University. After two years as head of the vocal department of the Rubin Academy of Music in Jerusalem, Sargon and his wife, vocalist Bonnie Glasgow, with daughter Olivia, decided in 1973 to return to the United States. While he was seeking a position, Sargon paid a chance courtesy call on Herbert Fromm, the synagogue composer and music director of Temple Israel in Boston. That contact led him to music committee Chairman Rhea Wolfram, who called Simon in Michigan, where he was staying, met him at the Chicago airport, and then invited him to interview in Dallas.[29] Because the Yom Kippur War erupted, making his return journey to Jerusalem impossible, Simon was able to spend a week at the Wolfram home. Assured by Rhea Wolfram that the temple was a place that respected and nurtured creativity (Sargon wanted to compose), he accepted the invitation to assume his new post in August 1974.

Sargon heightened "the emotional component of the service" by introducing more songs by Jewish composers, injecting traditional folk songs, and adapting music from the Conservative and Orthodox traditions.[30] He immediately changed the Ashkenazic (German and East European) Hebrew sung by the choir to the Sephardic (Spanish and Portuguese) Hebrew spoken as a living language in Israel, and he began to create an anthem repertoire with more Jewish content. Besides directing the adult and the junior choirs, Sargon expanded the temple's role as a leading proponent of Jewish music in North Texas. *At Grandmother's Knee*, in which he captured the moods and feeling of the Yiddish heritage; *Elul: Midnight* and *Flame of the Lord*, which he wrote and conducted; and *Shabbat S'Farad*, a collection of magnificent Sabbath liturgy which he researched and arranged, were presented in performances starring guest soloists and ensembles. Under his direction, the choir also traveled to other parts of the United States, Mexico, Israel, and London to participate in special concerts. In 1983 Sargon took a sabbatical and accepted an appointment as associate professor of composition and theory at SMU. While at the university he composed his *Symphony No.1. Holocaust*, which Dallas symphony conductor Eduardo Mata premiered at the Morton H. Meyerson Symphony Center on March 28, 1991. Rejoining Emanu-El as music director in 1985, Sargon also continued his association with SMU.[31]

With the task force committees' fervor for improvement, adult education was the next department revised and rejuvenated. The committee inaugurated the two-part Olan Lecture in 1975 scheduled as closely as possible to Rabbi Olan's March birthday, featuring on different dates an address by Rabbi Olan and then a talk by a scholar of his choice. The first Olan lecturer, Dr. Hans Jonas of the New School for Social Research in New York, discussed the ethical courage essential to confront and survive the rigors of the modern technological world. The 1984 Olan lecturer was Elie Wiesel, the articulate survivor of Auschwitz and Buchenwald and the voice of the Jewish conscience, who chose the evocative topic, "When the Unthinkable Happens: Implications of the Holocaust for the Nuclear Arms Race."

In 1976 the Sam R. Bloom Scholar in Residence program was established in recognition of his service to the congregation and to the community at large. To honor Bloom, the adult education committee invited a qualified scholar and lecturer to address the temple staff and congregants as well as the general public on topics of interest. Dr. Charles Hartshorne, professor of philosophy at the University of Texas, was the first Sam Bloom Scholar.

Improving the quality of programs at the temple was essential to keep the congregation's interest and participation, but finding the financial strength to support the enlarged professional staff and enhanced agenda was crucial. The financial problem had badgered the trustees through the decade of the 1960s, and by 1969 Temple Emanu-El, like other Reform congregations across the United States, had capped its growth spurt and entered a static membership period. Because dues did not cover programming and maintenance, out of sheer necessity the temple continued to practice deficit spending.

It would take another generation of leadership before the trustees drew up a long-range financial plan instead of relying upon a few generous members to contribute sums necessary to balance the budget. Moreover, some Jews considered money for Israel, which had paid dearly for the 1967 War, as well as Jewish Welfare Federation projects such as a Jewish home for the aged, their first concern. In truth, to the temple membership, funds for a religious house of worship were not deemed an immediate priority, perhaps because of the reluctance of the board and Rabbi Olan to face up to the need for aggressive steps to resolve financial problems. Under a budget that was only minimally maintaining the temple, contributing what had been designated as its fair share to the Union of American Hebrew Congregations and Hebrew Union College was out of the question. In fact, the readiness to consider full payment of the temple's union dues a negotiable part of its budget contributed to a crisis with the national Reform organization.

Emanu-El's rocky association with the Union of American Hebrew Congregations was a commitment that directly affected the budget's bottom line and a conflict that had been brewing for years. Even though the trustees always found a way to fund many worthwhile and popular programs for its membership, the leadership, with only a few exceptions, balked at the dues calculated by the union as Emanu-El's share of the organization's overhead. For reasons unknown, Temple Emanu-El had not rushed to join the national alliance of Reform congregations when it was founded by Isaac Mayer Wise in 1873. The congregation waited until 1906 to affiliate. Even though the southwestern regional office of the

216

union was established in Dallas in 1936, the temple never developed the bond with the union that it enjoyed with Hebrew Union College. That congenial relationship was based on the compatibility of the temple's rabbis, who were alumni of the college, with college presidents—Dr. Lefkowitz with Dr. Julian Morgenstern, and Rabbi Olan with Dr. Nelson Glueck and Professor Jacob Marcus—as well as Rabbi Klein's rapport with Dr. Marcus.

After World War II, when union President Maurice Eisendrath moved the offices from Cincinnati to New York in the expectation of aggressively expanding the Reform movement into the mainstream of Jewish life, its policies irritated temple board members. Of uppermost consideration was the union's supposed role as spokesman for all of Reform Judaism when it was clearly moving away from what Emanu-El practiced as Reform Judaism. True, the Dallas congregation had accepted some changes such as the emphasis on the Bar Mitzvah rite and the inclusion of more Hebrew in the service. But the union went beyond reviving "old ceremonies and rituals" in the synagogue and in the home; it also sanctioned the introduction of a cantor to chant the synagogue service and in 1975 would set aside the classic *Union Prayer Book* in favor of the contemporary *Gates of Prayer*.[32]

The long-lived domination of union President Maurice Eisendrath, elected for life, was galling to many temple trustees.[33] Eisendrath was an emblematic Jew to the Christian community, one who zealously supported liberal causes such as integration and social action projects, issues not readily accepted in the conservative South, and his views also trod heavily upon the deeply patriotic feelings of American Jews when he spoke scathingly against the United States' role early in the Vietnam War. In 1965 Congregation Emanu-El of New York, whose conservative leadership first objected to the union's Religious Action Center for Reform Judaism in Washington, D. C., dropped its membership for a year because of Eisendrath's anti-Vietnam statements.[34] By 1968 the Central Conference of American Rabbis led by its president, Levi Olan of Dallas, also called for an immediate halt to the U. S. bombing of North Vietnam, decrying the conflict by stating that "our military intervention has never

217

been justified."[35] But that dovish view was not espoused by a majority of Jews in the United States. Statistics revealed by a 1968 Gallup poll showed that American Jews were evenly divided on their opinion of the Johnson administration's hawkish role in Vietnam. Indeed, the Union of Orthodox Congregations and the Jewish War Veterans strongly supported President Johnson's aggressive policy in Vietnam.[36]

Ironically, the causes championed by the Union of American Hebrew Congregations were the same ones Levi Olan preached on his radio broadcast and from Emanu-El's pulpit. Olan's views were not always endorsed by his congregation, but his right to say them was accepted because of his moral and intellectual stature. The union, on the other hand, was perceived to be in the mold of eastern liberalism as well as in the forefront of the return to traditionalism. More to the point, its financial demands were considered onerous. In 1965 the union expected the temple to pay $32,000—a hefty ten percent of its operating budget—but the temple trustees, working within a tight budget, voted to pay only $14,000. Irving Goldberg brought home the salient point believed by Emanu-El: many other congregations did not pay the specified ten percent dues, and for the temple to do so "would impose a burden upon our current and future budgets which we are not prepared to meet and for which we can not at this time plan with any degree of fiscal responsibility."[37] Comments often voiced in support of this decision were along the lines that "The union doesn't do anything for us. It doesn't give us anything we need. We're large enough to go it alone."[38]

One of the most telling arguments for backing the UAHC was the undeniable need of small congregations for the organized assistance provided by its dissemination of educational materials and programming information. Milton Tobian, a member of the UAHC regional board, felt that as an integral and essential part of the Reform movement, Temple Emanu-El should not plead financial hardship as an excuse for failure to pay the dues stipulated by the central United States agency for Reform Judaism.[39] Even Sam Bloom conceded that the temple "has an obligation to send delegates to union meetings."[40] Nevertheless, the temple leadership cared to be associated with the union only on Emanu-El's own terms.

Possibly provoked by Temple Emanu-El's intransigence, the Maintenance of Union Membership Committee (MUM) ruled that Temple Emanu-El must meet with the union's regional representatives to formulate a plan for the discharge of past debts or face possible suspension. Furthermore, the union pronounced the congregation immediately ineligible for biennial representation because of the dereliction of its payments.[41] After this ultimatum, the board unanimously adopted a financial plan to "accommodate" the union and negotiated an agreement which forgave all back dues and gave the temple three years, until 1972, to pay its full $39,000 assessment.[42]

In 1969, after this compromise, Robert Strauss assumed the office of temple president. Politically astute, Strauss had co-chaired the Humphrey-Muskie presidential campaign in Texas in 1968 and functioned as treasurer of the Democratic Party while serving as temple president. Later Strauss served as chairman of the Democratic National Committee in 1976 under President Jimmy Carter and accepted the post of ambassador to Russia in the Republican administration of fellow Texan George Bush. While temple president, Strauss adjusted dues to reflect the union fee and appealed to the members to honor Temple Emanu-El's assessment, to which it had agreed.[43] A few temple members refused to pay the surcharge, but most acquiesced to the augmented dues with good grace. The trustees then increased its payment to the union, but demurred at paying the temple's full share, remonstrating that since the union adopted special plans and arrangements for other congregations which, like Emanu-El were having financial problems, the congregation should also enjoy similar leeway.[44]

That state of affairs lasted for five years until union Treasurer Harold W. Dubinsky informed Sam Bloom that unless the temple honored the agreement established while Bob Strauss was president, Dubinsky would advise suspension of all services to Temple Emanu-El by the date of the union's fall meeting in 1974. Rabbi Charles D. Mintz, director of membership for the union, also recommended curtailment of services to Emanu-El, but at the request of Leo Davis, a trustee of both organizations, he wrote to Bloom inquiring once more whether the temple

219

board would accede to the union's demands.[45] Bloom replied, "As a matter of good faith, I must relate to you that my recommendation to the board will be the acceptance of your ultimatum," preferring suspension than submission to the dues agreement previously made by the UAHC and Emanu-El.[46]

The board assembled November 19, 1974, to consider its options. Before the meeting, board member Leo Davis, who had been closely associated with temple's negotiations for the past two years and who currently served on the union's southwestern region board of trustees, had sent a letter to all temple trustees, asking them to take a reasoned approach to the stalemate. He felt that if the temple's premise for negotiation were based on its desire to be part of the Reform movement and assist smaller congregations, then it should pay the required dues and join for only one year—contingent on union acceptance of a representative of Emanu-El on the national board and a complete revision of the entire dues structure for presentation at the 1975 union convention scheduled in Dallas.[47] Noting the receptive attitude to negotiation and compromise held by Rabbi Alexander Schindler, president after Maurice Eisendrath's death in 1973, Davis added that if Temple Emanu-El were still not satisfied after a year then, it should prepare to withdraw. Board member I. A. Victor agreed with Leo Davis and, since he could not attend the crucial meeting, wrote Davis asking him to indicate their mutual moderate point of view.[48]

At the November meeting president Sam Bloom read letters from a few unavoidably absent board members and Rabbi Klein, who all counseled remaining a part of the national Reform body. In her letter, Sisterhood President Janie Rosenthal reminded the board of the strong connection Sisterhood and DAFTY enjoyed with the Reform Jewish movement through the union.[49] Rabbi Klein recorded his conviction that the temple's association with the national bodies of Reform Judaism represented by the Union of American Hebrew Congregations, Hebrew Union College-Jewish Institute of Religion, National Federation of Brotherhoods, National Federation of Sisterhoods, and National Federation of Temple Youth "go far beyond fiscal obligations and implications." He avowed that "these relationships determine, to a significant degree, the kind of congregation we are and to what we aspire." He hoped that the temple would resolve "a hard money matter" with "reconciliation and dialogue," fully agreeing with the opinions expressed by Rosenthal, Davis, and Victor.[50] In opposition to these conciliatory views, Rabbi Bemporad, a former union staff member now severely critical of that organization, advised withdrawing for one year and predicted that the union would then "come back to us."[51] Willing to detach itself from the national association, Temple Emanu-El's trustees voted 26–12 in favor of accepting the suspension forced by the union board.

After two more meetings with union representatives and "a lengthy discussion" at the temple board meeting on March 23, 1975, the trustees voted 29–3 with one abstention to withdraw from the union.[52] One member stepped down from the board because of its decision to leave the union. Leo Davis, who had been a temple leader for twenty years, was "unable to support what may be the most important decision our Board has made in a decade."[53] Affronted at not being included in the second meeting with UAHC representatives, Davis wrote to Sam Bloom: "As it says in our Book, there comes a time for everything, including when a person should get off the train." He then reiterated his disinclination to believe "that the best interests of Temple will be served in isolation from our national movement" or "that every effort has been made to accommodate the differences without benefit of the results of the Biennium to be held in Dallas in November 1975."[54] Since his congregation was no longer a part of the union, Davis also felt obliged to resign from the national board and as chairman of the local arrangements committee for the convention in Dallas.

Delegates from 127 congregations converged on Dallas for the Biennial, which had been scheduled since Emanu-El accepted the assignment in 1972.[55] Sisterhood and Brotherhood, who had close ties to their national bodies, proceeded as if Emanu-El's resignation had never materialized and participated fully in the union's meetings. Bernard Hirsh had recently ascended to the presidency of the National Federation of Temple Brotherhoods, and he had presided over its fall board meeting in Dallas one week prior to the union assembly. Board member Shirley Tobolowsky was the Biennial chairwoman of arrangements for the National Federation of Temple Sisterhoods, who convened its membership in conjunction with the UAHC convention. Once the delegates had arrived, Emanu-El's board, in a show of good will, allowed them to visit and tour the temple at appointed times and in turn relayed to the membership the union's invitation to attend UAHC programs.

Most important from Temple Emanu-El's standpoint, the Biennial committees seriously addressed the problems brought to the fore by the Dallas congregation's resignation. In October (just before the Biennial) the board fired off a six-page letter to the union enumerating its reasons for withdrawal. Much to the surprise of the union, the temple aired the controversy by distributing the letter to other Reform congregations as well as to Emanu-El's membership.[56] In fact, Sol Goodell was told by members who attended the convention "that [Emanu-El's] letter outlining the reasons for [its] resignation gave clear, honest, and forceful expression to the problems, disappointments and frustrations that had been troubling many congregations, large and small, for many years."[57] As its staff personnel had changed, a new committee was appointed to study the structure of the union and to recommend modifications. Moreover, Alexander Schindler recommended to the General Assembly that it mandate fully publicized membership committee guidelines and permit full disclosure of all dues.

Shortly after its resignation, Emanu-El learned firsthand about one glaring disadvantage of a Reform congregation's religious life conducted outside the national Reform body. Irwin Goldenberg, who had served as assistant rabbi from 1969–1973, had left Emanu-El to join Temple Beth Israel in York, Pennsylvania. In 1976, the board tried to obtain a third rabbi to lead the religious school, supervise adult education, and create a young adult group. Since Temple Emanu-El was no longer a union member and ineligible for aid offered by the UAHC to its affiliates, the Rabbinic Placement Commission headed by Rabbi Malcolm Stern refused to help find a rabbi for the congregation. As a matter of fact, Rabbi Stern told Carl Flaxman that employing a rabbi would not be easy, for anyone who accepted a position with Emanu-El would "be in trouble" and face possible suspension by the Central Conference of American Rabbis. Undaunted, the rabbinic search committee, chaired by Sam Bloom, found a promising young man, Rabbi Jay Holstein, a Ph.D. from Hebrew Union College who was an associate professor at the University of Iowa. After Holstein and his wife came to visit and he met with the board and spoke to the congregation and the religious school, the board offered him the position. Subsequently, Rabbi Malcolm Stern did, in fact, report Rabbi Holstein to Rabbi Jack Stern, the chairman of the committee on ethics, because, by circumventing the placement bureau, Holstein had not "played the game honorably."[58] After several phone calls to Rabbi Holstein from Rabbi Malcolm Stern warning him of a dismal rabbinic fate, the young rabbi declined Emanu-El's proposal.

After that unpleasant incident, attempts at rapprochement with the Union of American Hebrew Congregations resumed in 1977 under new president Ronald Mankoff, a young lawyer who had taken part in the negotiations. The consensus among Emanu-El's lay leadership was that it was time for the temple to rejoin the major Reform body in the United States.[59] The board, with the abstention of four members, unanimously voted on April 10, 1978, to rejoin the UAHC and Temple Emanu-El reentered the union on July 1, 1978. When temple reaffilated, it, like many other congregations, received certain dispensations applicable to its needs and never was held to the full twelve percent dues. The union also appointed temple President Ronald Mankoff to its board of directors for two years and its executive committee for one year and further assured the congregation of representation in union deliberations when it later designated Herbert (Buddy) Rosenthal a member of its board.

The clash with the Union of American Hebrew Congregations in 1975 was pigeonholed by most of the temple leadership as a financial, as opposed to philosophical, problem. Incontrovertibly, union membership was a budget breaker, as evidenced by the fact that during the three years the temple did not pay dues it was able to balance its budget. But other undercurrents related to a fear of change also came into play as the national group forged ahead in its social action stance and its support of integration. Shirley Tobolowsky remembered attending the 1963 Biennial with

Rabbi Olan at which Martin Luther King, Jr., was a featured speaker. King's sponsorship by a Jewish organization worried many southern delegates, who feared for the status and safety of merchants in small southern towns if they were perceived as integrationists, a point which did not mesh with Levi Olan's moral standards.[60]

Even when the union's stand on contemporary issues reflected the feelings of some Temple Emanu-El members, its position fell on unsympathetic ears because Emanu-El's leadership resented its dictatorial stance and its imperious claim to be agent for all Reform Jews. Eventually the issue was resolved because, as subsequent temple President Harold Kleinman recalled, "when wounds healed and finances got better . . . we negotiated our way back into the union."[61]

Emanu-El's amicable reentry was an acknowledgment by its leadership in 1978 that the Dallas congregation could not continue as a separate but equal part of the Reform movement. The congregation's ability to access the union's programs and services, especially with regard to rabbinical selection, was necessary for its future growth and development. After a few years, the quarrel, in retrospect, waned in importance as challenges within Emanu-El's ranks and the direction of the national Reform Jewish movement propelled Emanu-El toward further change.

Rabbi Levi A. Olan

Rabbi Jack Bemporad, Philip Glassman, and Edwin Tankus
celebrated Philip's Bar Mitzvah in 1974.

Brotherhood President Ben Rosenthal, Jr., Rabbi Levi A. Olan, and
Rabbi Gerald J. Klein met Supreme Court Justice William O. Douglas,
second from left, before his Brotherhood lecture in 1974.

Dallas Area Federation of Temple Youth (DAFTY), about 1974. First row: Alex Goldstein,
Cindy Schenkler, Gary Udashen, John Rosenberg, Alan Hoffman, Steve Greene,
Marilyn Shosid, Gary Leva. Second row: Alice Bergman, Barbara Edenbaum, Carole Wiener,
Mike Stokie, Carol Shosid, Amy Fine, Wayne Lindauer, Cliff Friedman, Janet Karpeles,
Aunt Dottie Mandell. Third row: Lisa Brachman, Margarite Winer, Janie Harrison,
Richard Naftalis, Danny Ball, Mrs Kitzie Ball, Mrs. Lorelei Marks. Fourth row:
Mrs. Carolyn Edenbaum, Carolyn Schenkler, Kerry Silver, Joey Morris, Howard Menaker,
Jodie Siegel, Barry Bubis, Tina Lazato, Mark Lazato, Marc Byers

Ambassador Abba Eban spoke at the Israel Bond dinner
honoring Rabbi Gerald J. Klein in 1976.

Rabbi Ellen Lewis in 1980 was the first woman to
serve a Jewish congregation in Dallas.

Noted musician and composer Simon Sargon has led the Temple Emanu-El choir since 1974.

CHAPTER 11

TRANSITION AND RENEWAL

How do we get the members active? A lot of us felt that we were sitting on a sleeping giant.

Herbert (Buddy) Rosenthal

From 1972 until 1983, the decade when Gerald Klein and Jack Bemporad shared a co-rabbinate and divided responsibilities, the congregation, as well as the rabbis, suffered through an unsettling and difficult period. The hoped-for connection and counterbalance between rabbis was nonexistent. In fact, soon after Rabbi Bemporad's arrival, the tension between him and Rabbi Klein was obvious; it eventually deepened into a complete lack of communication.[1] Faced with an uncomfortable situation and unwilling to grant ultimate rabbinical authority to either rabbi, the special committee to address the deteriorating relationship created the co-rabbinate, officially dividing rabbinical responsibilities. Under this arrangement, both rabbis held joint responsibility for preaching and pastoral duties, but each maintained his own earmarked spheres of interest. Rabbi Bemporad took charge of the religious school, adult education, youth activities, and the music program; Rabbi Klein oversaw Sisterhood and Brotherhood activities, rabbinical relations with the temple office, and general administrative concerns. Ideally, even though one rabbi or another had primary responsibility in an area, the other would be consulted, attend meetings, and "express his views on matters of interest." Instead of helping the impasse, the divided arrangement solidified the gulf between the two rabbis; each turned for support to his constituency within the temple.

At first, these constituencies continued to function in their usual way, particularly Sisterhood and Brotherhood, who yearly involved their membership in projects and felt a strong affinity with Rabbi Klein. The Sisterhood started an annual interfaith service in conjunction with Dallas churches and welcomed newly arrived Russian Jewish families fortunate enough to escape the Soviet Union, which had slowly begun to permit Jewish emigration. The Brotherhood instituted a Christmas Mitzvah Program so that Jewish volunteers could fill in for Christian members of hospital staffs on Christmas Day, enabling them to celebrate the holiday with their families.

Temple committees under Rabbi Bemporad's jurisdiction also found an audience. For example, the adult education committee initiated a well-attended, provocative film series highlighted by speakers who offered preliminary comments and then led a lively discussion after the movie. The music committee welcomed the gifted Russell Hellekson as organist after Rabbi Bemporad had recommended him upon hearing him play at SMU. And the choir, directed by Simon Sargon, created a moving and memorable recording, *Our Father, Our King*, which featured selections of High Holy Day liturgy.

Naturally, many events revolved around the celebratory participation of the membership and both rabbis, most often at Friday night services. President Ronald Mankoff created a special events committee which broke into various subcommittees to orchestrate each celebration. For instance, Dovie and Irvin Jaffe hosted a special tribute in 1978 to Morris I. Freedman to express the congregation's appreciation for his continued leadership of the cemetery committee for twenty-eight years. On the occasion of Rabbi Klein's twenty-fifth anniversary at Temple Emanu-El, the congregation honored him at a special Sabbath Service and reception in 1977. On that night Rabbi Klein was pleased to welcome his friend, American Jewish Archives Director Jacob Marcus, Klein's professor at Hebrew Union College, as guest speaker.

Though the rabbis were astir in activities within and without the temple, it was becoming apparent to many members, and especially to the leadership, that they were working at cross purposes. The congregation was suffering under the divided and diluted rabbinical leadership created by the dissension between them, and their lack of strong leadership was responsible for dwindling interest and diminished activity among the members. Clearly, the two rabbis' inability to achieve a working relationship was taking its toll on congregants' participation. To ease the strain two presidents of the congregation attempted to create a more companionable atmosphere. Attorney Ronald Mankoff emphasized communication and conciliation. Mankoff found Rabbi Bemporad a "very engaging, warm person" and felt that the rabbinic conflict might be a breakdown in communication. So he invited Rabbi Klein and Rabbi Bemporad to breakfast with him every Tuesday morning in an effort to create "an opportunity, [he] hoped, to share information and open topics (because they weren't necessarily talking to each other during the week), and hopefully to get them to know each other and to like each other a little better." In Mankoff's opinion, his effort to reconcile them was hardly "a magic solution," but the meetings were "predictable and would happen on a regular basis."[2] Four years later when Herbert (Buddy) Rosenthal was president, he also had breakfast with the rabbis one day a week, sometimes inviting another congregant to join them.[3] But the distressing relationship between the rabbis never improved.

Beside the difficult problem of the co-rabbinate, Ronald Mankoff faced another delicate rabbinical issue during his term as president. In August 1978 the board had hired Rabbi Bernard Schachtel, son of revered Rabbi Hyman Schachtel of Beth Israel Congregation in Houston, to run the religious school. The younger Schachtel had been in charge of the school for only a month when he became embroiled in a controversy concerning the direction of the Hebrew program. After less than a year the board realized that Rabbi Schachtel was in the wrong place. In order to allow him time to seek other opportunities, it agreed to pay his salary for the remainder of his two-year contract through June 1980.[4]

Schachtel's departure underscored the need for a third rabbi at Temple Emanu-El, one who would be "interested in and enjoy working

231

with youth and young adults" and who would have primary responsibility for the religious school.[5] When one member, Harry Goodman, expressed his dissatisfaction with the religious school and the Hebrew program, he was advised that "changes [were] to be made in this area for the coming year to relieve current problems."[6] Attorney Harold Kleinman and his wife Ruth, an experienced religious school teacher, were so firmly convinced that Emanu-El's school was educationally lax that they enrolled their youngest son Max in Shearith Israel's more stimulating and accelerated Hebrew school. Even though his four older brothers had celebrated their Bar Mitzvah at Temple Emanu-El, Max celebrated his at Shearith Israel.[7]

To bolster Temple Emanu-El's religious education program, Lawrence S. Pollock, Jr., president in 1980, appointed Buddy Rosenthal to chair the search committee for a rabbi to strengthen the religious school. When Rosenthal and Pollock, along with Rabbi Klein and Rabbi Bemporad, flew to Cincinnati to meet with five applicants graduating from Hebrew Union College, Rosenthal remembers how out of place he and Pollock felt when they walked into services which "were more Orthodox than [he] had ever seen." Yet that service was "an awakening to [him] that Reform Judaism was moving back [to being] more traditional."[8] The Dallas group invited two candidates to meet the entire search committee, the executive committee, and the religious school committee in Dallas. Ellen Lewis, also an alumna of Brown University who was married to Rabbi William Kraus, stayed with Buddy and Rita Rosenthal when she and her husband visited Dallas. One morning while the Rosenthals and their guests were sitting around the breakfast table, Uri Rosenthal telephoned to talk to his son in order to scotch a "nasty rumor" circulating about "Buddy's chairing a committee that is considering a female rabbi," a fact immediately confirmed when Rita Rosenthal said, "Would you like to talk to her?" Ruffled, the senior Rosenthal hung up, but he met the likable Ellen Lewis on that visit, and they eventually became friends.[9]

Because at that time hiring a women rabbi was a controversial departure from both the American and Jewish societal norm, Rosenthal credits "a great search committee" for unanimously recommending that

Lewis be offered a two-year contract.[10] While in Dallas, Lewis served as co-chair of the Women's Rabbinic Network, the national women's group of the Central Conference of American Rabbis, and her term at Emanu-El was sprinkled with "firsts." The Lewis-Kraus' seven-month-old son Gideon was the first child born to two ordained rabbis from Hebrew Union College, and Rabbi Lewis was the first rabbinic mother to work full time as a rabbi. By engaging Rabbi Lewis, the temple could be perceived as being in the vanguard of women's coming presence in the rabbinate. Only a decade before Lewis joined Temple Emanu-El as the first woman rabbi in Dallas, females, although not prohibited completely from study, were barred from ordination.

The advent of a female rabbi was a signal of the acceptance of women's changing role in society. This recognition had been underlined by the invitation to speak at the 1963 Sisterhood Donor Luncheon that two forward-looking chairwomen, Miriam Feinberg and Ruth Golman, extended to feminist leader Betty Friedan. Friedan, the controversial author of *The Feminine Mystique*, later founded the National Organization of Women (NOW). Shirley Tobolowsky recalled the consternation rippling through the audience, who "really dressed up in those days," when the guest of honor arrived at the sellout event in a somewhat dowdy outfit she obviously had not taken the time to "put together." Immediately, Betty Friedan challenged the volunteers, "What are you doing here?" Then she nettled them with her next words: "You ought to be out in the work place. Why are you giving up your energy, your time, and your talent to do this kind of work that doesn't pay you anything?" Friedan's fiery speech, which also included her admonition to "send your kids to school in cabs" if you have to and to "find someone in the yellow pages to clean your house" if necessary, ended in dead silence.[11] Even the usually unflappable Rabbi Olan was nonplussed and quickly closed the program without asking for questions. Nonetheless, there was no doubt in the minds of some educated attendees, who had been conditioned to feel guilty because they wanted to work, that troubadour Bob Dylan's song of the 1960s, "the times they are a changing," revealed the truth.

At the time of Betty Friedan's visit, the mostly male temple board had just opened its ranks by nominating more females than the two or three token women trustees who had served in addition to the two designated Sisterhood representatives. Dorothy Lewis, whose husband Ben often acted as trustee, was the first woman board member, serving from 1948 until 1952. Hortense Sanger, Marie Weisberg (the widow of former president Alex Weisberg) and Minnie Marcus (a former Sisterhood president and widow of former president Herbert Marcus) were the next women invited on the board. As an officer of the congregation from 1956 to 1961, Hortense Sanger was the only woman who participated in both the decisions of the executive committee and the new building committee as the two bodies outlined the future direction of the temple.

By 1964 six women had seats on the forty-two-member board. By the end of the 1970s, former Sisterhood President Shirley Tobolowsky and school counselor Rhea Wolfram were vice-presidents, and ten other women had served as board members. By the 1980s the board selection criterion was not gender but competence. When in 1987 clinical psychologist Carmen Michael was elected as the first woman president of the congregation, fifty years after her father Henry S. Miller, Sr., presided in that office, the nominating committee picked her because of her qualifications, regardless of her sex.

Shortly after Rabbi Ellen Lewis arrived at Temple Emanu-El, the board decided to "offer a quality child development program for its members." Besides acknowledging a need faced by women of all economic strata, the trustees also wanted to induce younger members of the community to join the temple.[12] Unlike the first attempt to establish a pre-school a decade earlier, when working mothers were scarce in the congregation, the trustees gave full support to the project. To underline Sisterhood's support, its president Ruth Pines pledged $3,000 for initial funding. For the vital position of director, the pre-school steering committee selected former Sisterhood president and temple board member Nita Mae Tannebaum. Coordinator of the Mother's Day Out Program at the temple with Barbara Silberberg, Tannebaum possessed a master's degree in early childhood education from North Texas State University and taught a course in child development at Brookhaven Community College.

Starting with eight children, the pre-school "exceeded all expectations in performance and growth" by filling its limit of thirty-five children its second year and more than doubling its enrollment to eighty-five children in four years. Since Emanu-El had always stalwartly supported public kindergarten education, the board thoroughly discussed the propriety of adding a private kindergarten to the facility.[13] Both a kindergarten and afternoon day care were eventually provided by the pre-school because, as women's role in the work place changed and amplified, young working mothers depended heavily upon the professional quality of pre-school education offered at the temple. Buddy Rosenthal and Nita Mae Tannebaum credited Rabbi Lewis' wholehearted support as a major reason for the successful launch of the pre-school. As staff liaison to the board, "she went to bat in terms of the budget and [also] helped the pre-school staff visualize" the program.[14] Eventually, in the way the trustees had anticipated, some young families, who were pleased with the nurturing care their children received in the pre-school, became members of the congregation.

In 1987 Temple Emanu-El Pre-School was a part of a pilot demonstration project directed by the National Association for the Education of Young Children to establish criteria for pre-school and day-care accreditation. Pre-school Chairman Bob Weiss was a member of the national committee that selected only thirty-two pre-school and day-care centers across the country to participate. To honor the pre-school's accomplishments, Mayor Annette Strauss, the first woman elected as Dallas mayor (and sister-in-law of former president of the temple Robert Strauss), presided over the accreditation ceremony at the temple. In 1991 Nita Mae Tannebaum decided to step down after ten years of administering the pre-school. During those years it had expanded to an enrollment of 170 children from across the community.

In an effort to heed the concerns of other diverse groups within the congregation, Buddy Rosenthal brought the concept of "The Caring Congregation" before the board and the rabbis. While attending a UAHC Biennial, Rosenthal was first exposed to the outreach program developed on a national level by the Union of American Hebrew Congregations.

235

Anticipating that the Caring Congregation would promote a "comprehensive approach to serving the human needs of the 8,000 people who are the Temple family," the temple introduced the concept in 1983 during Rosenthal's term as president.[15] Hospice volunteer Gay Mallon-Frank guided the Caring Congregation with the intention of utilizing trained volunteers. The total UAHC Caring Congregation program incorporated a newcomers' welcome committee, bereavement support group, a peer support group for children of aging parents, and discussion groups for Jews by choice as well as a hospital, home, and nursing home visitation committee. Former religious school director Ray Israel had already inaugurated a pastoral services program to accommodate senior adults; it sponsored luncheons one day a month for older people. Beverly Tobian and Joan Kramer enlarged that project and formed the Leisure Club.

As effectively as the lay leadership might try to function, the co-rabbinate still remained a profound and pressing problem. From the outset it was a concept whose success hinged on near-perfect harmony between the two rabbis and an impossible amount of selfless altruism. The ongoing impasse culminated in the polarization of the trustees and many members of the congregation into pro-Klein and pro-Bemporad camps.[16] In an attempt to ensure his continuity as rabbi at Emanu-El, Rabbi Bemporad appeared before the executive committee to request tenure. However, the trustees were unwilling to grant him permanent status.[17] When the executive committee did not recommend Bemporad's request, the younger rabbi announced his decision to resign at the 1983 annual meeting and accepted the offer of Kehillath Israel, a congregation of 300 families in Pacific Palisades, California.

With Rabbi Bemporad's departure and the resultant heavier responsibilities thrust upon Rabbi Klein and Rabbi Lewis, the lay leadership felt constrained to increase its role in the temple, becoming even more involved in administration and programming. The most urgent task for the lay leadership was the selection of a rabbi to assume the mantle of congregational leadership.

Following Central Conference of American Rabbis procedure compulsory for all congregations looking for a rabbi, the search committee, led by Henry Schlinger and Shirley Pollock, carefully studied the resumes sent by the Rabbinic Placement Commission. Several candidates were interviewed at great length by telephone, and their qualifications inspected and debated. Then a few rabbis were invited to visit Dallas for "in-depth interviews" and the opportunity to meet for several days with the committee and temple staff. As the final phase in the selection process, a group from the committee traveled to different cities to attend services at the select few candidates' temples and visit with their families, always informing them of their arrival but trying to appear inconspicuous. After several months of scrutiny and investigation, a period that Shirley Pollock felt "took much longer than originally anticipated," the committee still "didn't feel that they had met the right person."[18] Finally, temple President Irwin Grossman suggested that if the prescribed process did not produce a viable candidate, then members of the search committee were "going to put on [their] coonskin caps and go hunting."[19] By sounding out contacts at the Union of American Hebrew Congregations and Hebrew Union College to "find out who were the outstanding people" in the rabbinate, "not just those who sent resumes," the committee received favorable word about Rabbi Sheldon Zimmerman at Central Synagogue in New York.[20]

After ordination from Hebrew Union College in New York, Rabbi Zimmerman had come to Central Synagogue in 1970 as assistant to Rabbi David Seligson. Zimmerman was born in Toronto on February 21, 1942, to a large family of Russian and Polish Jews. He could trace ten generations of Russian rabbis on his father's side, and he hailed from an equally traditional, though not rabbinic, matriarchal family who emigrated from Poland before World War I. As a very young boy, Shelly, as he was called, alternated between the Orthodox *shul*, where his paternal grandfather was the rabbi and spoke Yiddish, and his maternal grandfather's more modern Orthodox congregation. As he grew older, he began to frequent a new Conservative congregation that, although still very traditional, had "decorum and dignity" as well as mixed seating, sermons in English, and a teenage boys' group, The Tephillin Club, that Shelly joined. When he was proposed for president, an honor possible only if his parents were members of the congregation, Morris Zimmerman realized the importance of the office to his son, and the elder Zimmerman affiliated with the Conservative synagogue. Later Shelly joined the B'nai B'rith Youth Organization (BBYO) Chapter that met at his Canadian synagogue and rose to the presidency of the international B'nai B'rith youth organization.[21]

Upon graduation from the University of Toronto, Zimmerman married Judy Baumgarten, a fellow youth group member from Buffalo, New York, whom he had met at an international B'nai B'rith Youth Convention. The couple remained in Toronto, where Shelly studied for his master's degree in philosophy and he and Judy became parents of a son, Brian. Declining the offer of a doctoral fellowship from the University of Rochester, he decided to enter rabbinical school, but he ruled out attending the traditional Jewish Theological Seminary because all applicants had to pledge to observe Jewish rituals according to the school's interpretation. Instead, he chose Hebrew Union College-Jewish Institute of Religion (HUC-JIR) in New York, entering the Reform movement intent on his "right to make choices."[22] While attending HUC-JIR, Shelly taught religious school, organized youth groups, acted as an assistant rabbi on weekends, and joined the philosophy faculty of Hunter College as an instructor. In Zimmerman's first post in 1970 at Central Synagogue, the buoyant young assistant rabbi invigorated the aging congregation by instituting a program of adult education. He also enlivened the religious school, introduced festival celebrations, and encouraged the reactivation of the Sisterhood. When Rabbi Seligson expressed his desire to retire in the fall of 1972, Central's board elevated Sheldon Zimmerman to the position of senior rabbi even though he had only two years' experience and was just thirty. The years in New York were animating, but the strain of being in an exacting position at so young an age and "the toughness" of living in a very costly city (especially so for the Zimmermans, who by the early 1980s were looking at the prospect of costly private school tuition for their four children) "took its toll." Rabbi Zimmerman began to consider a change.[23]

When the search committee, seasoned by now, contacted Sheldon Zimmerman, the rabbi had also been through the placement process but had decided to stay at Central Synagogue for the time being. Still, he agreed to a "preliminary talk" with the Dallas group. During the rabbi's first conference call, he related certain facts about himself that he wanted to be certain they knew. In his words, "One, I keep kosher; two, I use the new prayer book; three, my kids go to a Jewish day school." He added candidly that "if any of these are a problem, let's not get involved." In retrospect, Rabbi Zimmerman recollects that he and the long-distance phone conferees agreed to a Dallas visit with the sensible stipulation that it was "just a trip for them to take a look at me and me to take a look at them."[24]

On that first trip in July 1984, on the way from the airport into Dallas, Rabbi Zimmerman asked Shirley Pollock to stop at a grocery store so he could check the kosher product selection and satisfy himself that resources for obeying Jewish dietary laws were readily available. That visit also afforded him a chance to take stock of the temple and meet some of the staff. When he saw the sanctuary, he said to Shirley, "This is beautiful, but the pulpit is too high." His second observation was the absence of activity in the building. Puzzled, he inquired, "Why is it so quiet? Why is there nothing going on?"[25] She explained that it was summer, the time for the usual vacation lull. That day he also had a chance to chat with Levi Olan, who years ago had dropped in at Central Synagogue one summer morning and stayed to listen to the suddenly nervous—with the noted rabbi in attendance—Assistant Rabbi Zimmerman read and teach the Torah. Zimmerman's visit with Rabbi Olan was necessarily brief because the elderly rabbi was very frail.

For Rabbi Zimmerman's first evening in Dallas, Ruth and Harold Kleinman hosted a kosher dinner. When Shelly came in the door, the Kleinman's son Mark added to the informality and spontaneity of the evening by greeting him by his first name. Mark, who had deferred his freshman year in college to lead the international B'nai B'rith Youth Organization, had met Sheldon Zimmerman when Zimmerman was honored as BBYO Alumnus of the Year at the B'nai B'rith camp in Starlight, Pennsylvania. Relishing the evening, Shelly recounted later that what he remembered most vividly was that he "loved the people from the minute [he] came down—that was really the fit."[26] Like many another northerner, he was enchanted by the southern hospitality showered on a

239

welcome visitor. Even the rabbi's desire to jog was considerately taken into account. Eugene Sanger, Jr., made sure Zimmerman was at the Aerobics Center at Preston Road and Willow Lane early in the morning to beat the July heat, already 83 degrees at 6:00 A.M.

Undaunted by the searing weather, Judy and Shelly Zimmerman looked at schools for Kira, David, and Micol (Brian was in college) and began to relax in the less tense and wearing atmosphere of the southwestern city. The Zimmermans also liked the appealing "can do" attitude permeating the city in 1984, an atmosphere that evaporated only a year later when the bottom fell out of the Dallas real estate market and the three most prominent and seemingly unassailable banks—Republic National, First National, and Mercantile National—collapsed.[27] The "big three banks" had been the linchpins of the economic boom in Dallas and the Southwest, and their failure presaged the precipitate decline of the spiraling 1980s real estate pyramid and the exposure of the savings-and-loan debacle.

Upon returning to New York, Rabbi Zimmerman telephoned Rabbi Charles Kroloff of Temple Emanu-El in New Jersey, whom Zimmerman deemed a prime candidate for the position in Dallas, to sound out his reasons for withdrawing his name. Kroloff replied that by the time he introduced the new prayer book, brought in a cantor, and initiated more traditional practices, he would have made too many enemies in the congregation, a situation that he was loath to engender. Zimmerman replied that, in his opinion, Kroloff "underestimated the capacity of the congregation to change—slowly, but to change."[28]

During the year-long search for a rabbi, the committee began to understand how far Temple Emanu-El lagged behind the mainstream Reform movement as expressed by the new generation of Reform rabbis. For example, one question always asked of a candidate was his feeling about performing a "mixed" marriage, one between a Jew and a member of another faith. Although marriage between Jew and non-Jew had become common practice, none of the rabbis seriously considered indicated that they would perform the marriage unless the non-Jewish partner converted. Other aspects of Reform religious life had taken on a much more traditional tone as well. In their visits to Reform congregations, the committee witnessed both congregants and rabbis wearing head coverings and prayer shawls (in one instance the *yarmulkes* to cover the men's head were a lilac color to coordinate with the decorative scheme), listened to cantors, and of course read from *Gates of Prayer* instead of the *Union Prayer Book*. When several members flew to New York to observe Rabbi Zimmerman conduct a Friday night service, they were impressed by his great warmth and the congregation's wholehearted participation in the service. After that trip the representatives concluded that they had found a dedicated, vigorous leader with a proven success record at his congregation, a rabbi who could revitalize the somewhat rudderless congregation in Dallas. Unanimously, the committee agreed that Sheldon Zimmerman's vision of "increased levels of learning and religious practice was appropriate" for Temple Emanu-El.[29]

Rabbi Sheldon Zimmerman arrived at Temple Emanu-El in July 1985 and was formally installed in September. Members of the search committee supervised the weekend-long events. Rabbi Jack Stern, of Westchester Reform Temple in Scarsdale, New York, Rabbi Zimmerman's close friend who was current president of the Central Conference of American Rabbis, addressed the congregation at the Friday night Sabbath Service. At this ceremony the choir presented an especially composed liturgy featuring the gifted daughter of former music director Sam Adler, Debbie Adler, as guest flutist. Following the service, the congregation gathered at a reception arranged by former Sisterhood President Rosalee Cohen.

The next day a Saturday evening Selichot service, a recitation of centuries-old penitential prayers based primarily on poetry in the Book of Psalms, marked the beginning of the High Holy Days. A commentary by the new rabbi, "Reflections on Being Human," also preceded the 10:30 P.M. reception. On Sunday, Rose Marion Berg and Denna Ely directed a celebratory reception hosted by the congregation to introduce Rabbi Zimmerman to the religious and lay leaders of Dallas.

Immediately after his installation, Rabbi Zimmerman began to introduce his agenda to make the temple "the nucleus of Judaism." He advised the trustees that "traditionalism alone will not keep the children Jewish . . . membership in Temple Emanu-El must make a difference in the lives of its members . . . we must be an educated, caring, believing community."[30] True to his deep-rooted belief in the wisdom of a membership well versed in Judaism, Zimmerman immediately scheduled classes on Saturday morning to discuss the weekly Torah reading. Even though Rabbi Zimmerman was told, "No one will come on Saturday morning to study," his class filled quickly.[31] Without delay, he offered another opportunity for Bible study on Sunday morning. Since the rabbis at Emanu-El had always taught adult education classes, what was unique about these sessions and the later Talmud and theology seminars taught by Rabbi Zimmerman? Former Sisterhood President Shirley Tobolowsky felt that the difference between Sheldon Zimmerman and Levi Olan was that "Levi didn't make the demands that Shelly makes. . . . Levi said, 'it's there for you, go get it.' Shelly says, 'it's there for you, and I want to see you there next Monday night.'"[32] Because of the "high priority" the Reform movement placed on "individual autonomy," Rabbi Zimmerman believed that an "equivalent priority" or counterbalance must be laid on Jewish education.[33] The freedom, and even the stability of Reform Judaism, must be based upon a Jew's knowledge of Judaic tradition enabling the individual to make informed choices about life's significant decisions. In Zimmerman's mind, one such resolution might entail the serious choice of marrying within a person's religion or even the consideration of keeping a kosher home.

Rallied by Rabbi Zimmerman's dynamic leadership, many more congregants participated in religious services and temple programs. Part of their ardent interest evolved because the rabbi "wanted to reduce the distance between the pulpit and the audience" in order to inspire rapport. One of his first acts was to replace the "big, foreboding lectern" on the pulpit which, in his opinion, not only separated the congregation from the rabbi but blocked a view of the ark, the holy emblem of their faith.[34] As shocking as the idea of any alteration to the sanctuary seemed at first, after temple architect Howard Meyer approved the new, unembellished table-like lectern, it looked visually harmonious, a fact not too surprising as it was similar to Meyer's original design in 1955. Instead of striding in majestically and aloofly from the robing room behind the pulpit, Rabbi Zimmerman walked into the sanctuary and down the aisles greeting people as he made his way to the pulpit. Services became more informal and more celebratory as people with a knowledge of Hebrew chimed in with the service, as babies were named, and as festival days were emphasized. Not only was the business office closed for festivals such as Sukkot, but the congregation also enjoyed the option to share personally in a multi-sided celebration of the holiday. As an example, members could attend a Sisterhood family supper and a service on the eve of Sukkot as well as a Sukkot breakfast, a service, and an adult study program on the following day. The festival represents the Israelites' journey through the desert after the exodus from Egypt, when they lived in impermanent booths, plus the final reaping of the harvest. As the enlargement of programmatic activities proceeded, Harold Kleinman, temple president from 1991 to 1993, recalled that "every activity involved twice as many people as expected." Family dinners and Sabbath celebrations were sell-outs, and adult education lectures were packed.[35] With the growing emphasis upon holiday festivals and family celebrations to enhance congregational life, social secretary Teresa Parker became life-cycle celebrations coordinator so that she could work directly with the rabbis, the celebrations committee, and individual families to envision and present imaginative activities for special occasions. In 1994 only one other American Reform temple, Wilshire Boulevard in Los Angeles, boasted the same kind of comprehensive staff positioning.

In order to induce lay participation and discussion about possible changes in religious services, Rabbi Zimmerman asked Henry Schlinger to assemble a worship committee. Schlinger appointed as chair of the new committee Josephine Goldman, a former Sisterhood president whose grandfather August Israelsky in 1875 had signed the original charter of Congregation Emanu-El. Willing to modify the accustomed procedure of religious services and aware that Rabbi Zimmerman, while in Manhattan, had conducted a well-attended early evening service for worshipers who stopped at Central Synagogue on their way home from work, the worship committee decided to experiment with a 6:00 P.M. Friday service held twice monthly in Lefkowitz Chapel and an intimate 10:30 A.M. service in the chapel on some Saturdays. These "extra" services appealed to congregants who appreciated the option of worshiping in a small group apart from a larger special Sabbath or Bar/Bat Mitzvah ceremony in the sanctuary.[36] The worship committee also recommended utilizing *Gates of Prayer* once a month at the regular 8:15 evening service in the sanctuary to acclimate the congregation to its eventual adoption. At that time the new—to Temple Emanu-El—prayer book published in 1975 was in use in almost every Reform congregation in the United States. At Emanu-El it soon supplanted the *Union Prayer Book*, although the rabbis read the old prayer book at evening and morning services once a month because some congregants were uncomfortable with the alteration of worship services, whose changelessness had brought them spiritual ease, and preferred the familiar words of the old prayer book.[37]

In this era of examining, extending, and enriching ceremonial observances, the possibility of building a mausoleum at Emanu-El's cemetery struck a responsive chord among interested members. For years two private mausoleums for the families of Hyman Pearlstone and Asher Silberstein had resided on the sacred premises. In the 1960s temple architect Max Sandfield had drawn up a plan for a mausoleum, but the project languished. Congregants opting for burial above ground chose mausoleums open to all faiths at Hillcrest or Restland cemeteries. Max Edward Tonkon, chairman of the cemetery committee, felt that Temple Emanu-El's cemetery should have a place for those Jews who wished to be interred in crypts on consecrated land. Tonkon enlisted Lyra Daniels to head the committee for a mausoleum and Leo Fields to secure funds for its construction. Irwin Grossman, who was acquainted with architects Duane and Jane Landry, asked them to plan a mausoleum that would include a chapel to shield mourners from the weather as well as serving as a spiritual haven. The Landrys, for a time associated in San Antonio with renowned architect O'Neil Ford, had designed buildings at St. Mark's School, the University of Dallas, and Skidmore College. Searching for direction, Jane Landry found inspiration while reading a meditation in

Gates of Repentance written by concentration camp survivor Rabbi Leo Baeck:

> "World and eternity are here one word, both signify the same unendingness."

Three separate wedge-shaped segments of the triangular mausoleum represent the architects' concept of infinity. Connected and yet open, the crypts, columbarium, and chapel, all surrounding a courtyard, are entered by beautiful bronze open-work gates.

When he was at Central Synagogue, Rabbi Zimmerman's congregation had tried to alleviate the problem of the homeless by operating a food kitchen in New York City, volunteering to cook and serve a hot breakfast and also distributing a brown bag lunch to the hungry. Many days congregants served 200 street people.[38] Sadly enough, by the time of Rabbi Zimmerman's arrival in Dallas, the plight of the homeless had accelerated in urban areas across America. To address the issue of child care for the homeless, Doris Budner, a member of Temple Emanu-El's social action committee, helped Thelma Vogel, a Shearith Israel congregant, found the Dallas Jewish Coalition for the Homeless, an association of twenty-six synagogues and organizations which amalgamated in 1986 to relieve the plight of homeless families living in family shelters.[39] The program, first known as The Alcove, was later named in memory of Thelma and Phil Vogel after their untimely and tragic death in a plane crash. In the present home of the Vogel Alcove on Griffin at Akard Street as many as 102 children daily are attended by a professional staff and by volunteers while their parents seek employment or attend night classes which may make them employable. All expenses for child-care staff are funded by the coalition, which also ensures homeless families access to food, clothing, and other necessities. In 1996, the Alcove was one of five recipients of a two-year grant for social services from Crystal Charity.

In addition to supporting the Jewish Coalition for the Homeless, Temple Emanu-El's social action committee led by Sylvia Benenson had addressed the needs of medically underserved and uneducated refugees

245

from Southeast Asia living in East Dallas, the third largest center for Southeast Asian refugees in the United States. Initiating the project with a contribution of $5,000 from the Rabbis' Good Works Fund, in 1984 Benenson convened approximately forty disparate church groups, organizations, and health providers, and the congregation responded generously to a letter from Rabbi Klein asking for its assistance to mitigate a critical community problem. To assure the basic health requirements of thousands of families from varied cultural backgrounds, the East Dallas Health Coalition employed a mobile medical clinic owned by the city of Dallas, staffed it with doctors, nurses, translators, and community volunteers, and opened a part-time clinic at the Magnet High School for Health Professions located at Ross and Carroll. After five years of funding by Temple Emanu-El and by individual contributors and foundations, the East Dallas Health Coalition (EDHCO) moved to permanent facilities at the East Dallas Health Center on Haskell and became part of the Community Oriented Primary Care Program (COPC). Temple Emanu-El continued to raise needed funds for the Health Coalition, and a number of members serve on its advisory board. For its work with EDHCO, Temple Emanu-El in 1985 won the Outstanding Volunteer Award sponsored by the Volunteer Center of Dallas, Atlantic Richfield Company, and Sun Exploration and Productions Company.

Recognizing the need to forge bridges to other religious institutions in the city, Temple Emanu-El also pledged to support the North Dallas Shared Ministries, which provides emergency assistance to people in a temporary crisis who live within the northwest sector of Dallas County. When Emanu-El accepted the invitation to join as the first non-Christian member, the temple committed itself to supplying food supplies for the pantry and sending volunteers to staff the center. With the aim of demonstrating that compassionate and empathetic individuals can and do make a difference in the greater Dallas community, in 1994 Temple Emanu-El held a Mitzvah Day, engaging its families in the work of non-profit agencies in both the Jewish and the secular community. Over 1,000 people participated in Mitzvah Day. Volunteers, directed by members of the Social Action Committee and staff program coordinator Renee Karp, scattered to their assignments at the AIDS Resource Center, the Family Place, Golden Acres, the North Texas Food Bank, or the Vogel Alcove. Choosing from forty-nine volunteer opportunities arranged by the Mitzvah search committee, the workers of Emanu-El prepared meals, cleaned, repaired, and decorated rooms and houses, planted vegetable and flower gardens, and took children to the Holocaust Memorial at the Jewish Community Center and to the African American Museum at Fair Park. As the rabbis wished, in the Jewish belief that our purpose as human beings is to work with God to repair the world, Temple Emanu-El members attempted to be an exemplar of the Caring Congregation in the community.

During this era of intense activity, the rabbinical staff at the temple underwent several changes. Rabbi Klein had graciously paved the way for a new rabbi by writing a letter to the congregation in 1984 outlining his "complete, enthusiastic, sustained cooperation and support" for the new administration.[40] Klein became emeritus in 1988, but the veteran rabbi expected "to continue all of [his] pastoral, life-cycle and counseling duties when called upon by a congregant or a family" and would remain in his "accustomed place" at services.[41] That year he also celebrated thirty-five years as rabbi with Temple Emanu-El, and his many friends established the Dorothy and Rabbi Gerald J. Klein Garden in the temple atrium to honor the rabbi's decades of dedicated attentions on the congregation's behalf.

A few months before Rabbi Zimmerman arrived, Associate Rabbi Ellen Lewis left to assume the pulpit of Temple Sinai in Summit, New Jersey. The assistant rabbi, Richard K. Harkavy, a San Franciscan who had graduated from Claremont Men's College and Hastings College of Law at the University of California, had joined the congregation in 1984 after ordination from Hebrew Union College. While at the temple, he initiated the adult B'nai Mitzvah classes for those adults who wanted to study Hebrew, learn more about Judaism, and also experience the preparation of a Bar/Bat Mitzvah well after the customary age of thirteen. The success of the program was evident at a Sabbath service in December 1987 when, after fifteen months of study, twenty-three adults celebrated their B'nai Mitzvah, making their transition, as Carol Brin expressed it, "not from

247

childhood to adulthood, but from one level of Jewish commitment to another."[42] Rabbi Harkavy remained at Emanu-El for two years until he accepted a position at Congregation Knesseth Israel in Philadelphia.

Elisabeth Weiss Stern, a graduate of Vassar who had been ordained in 1984, then accepted the post of assistant rabbi, relocating from Oklahoma with her husband, Rabbi Keith Stern, and their two young children. While in Tulsa, Rabbi Elisabeth Stern had split her time between the pulpits of United Hebrew Congregation in Joplin, Missouri, and Beth Ahaba Congregation in Muskogee, Oklahoma. At Emanu-El she became involved in *chavurot*, groups of individuals and families who together shared Jewish learning and holiday experiences, almost like a family, in a heightened feeling of fellowship. Rabbi Keith Stern first taught at Solomon Schechter Academy and then became rabbi of the growing Beth Shalom congregation in Arlington. After completing the standard five-year period for associate rabbis at Emanu-El (assistant rabbis customarily advanced to associate rabbis after two years with the congregation), Rabbi Stern left the congregation in 1991. By then approximately 150 members were active in eleven *chavurot*, and three additional groups were being formed under the auspices of the Caring Congregation. Liza Stern (as she was called) remained in Dallas for several years, first associating with Shearith Israel and later with Temple Shalom.

Before Rabbi Stern left the congregation, David Eli Stern (no relation to Liza Stern) joined the rabbinic staff in 1989 as assistant rabbi. David Stern's credentials were impressive: *magna cum laude* and Phi Beta Kappa from Dartmouth College and master's degrees in Hebrew letters in 1986 and in Jewish education in 1988 from the New York and Los Angeles campuses of Hebrew Union College-Jewish Institute of Religion, plus an internship at Central Synagogue in New York and service as a student rabbi at Congregation Shomrei Torah in Santa Rosa, California. Undoubtedly, David Stern was an appealing candidate for many pulpits. His reasons for choosing Temple Emanu-El were twofold. First, like most of his fellow graduates, he wanted to work with an activist like Sheldon Zimmerman. Second, even though he never thought of accepting a post in the Southwest or at a large congregation, once he met the search committee, he felt challenged by the "interesting and stimulating" mix of people.[43]

At the temple, Stern's ability to communicate his love of learning and of teaching, together with his involvement with the members, endeared him to the congregation. His pursuits included teaching congregants of all ages at his Monday afternoon Alice Liebman Bible Class, overseeing the youth program, guiding programming for singles, young couples and young leadership, and directing the many activities of the Caring Congregation committee. David Stern's father, Rabbi Jack Stern, who had installed his friend Sheldon Zimmerman at Temple Emanu-El in 1985, spoke at his son's "official" welcoming service. After David Stern and Nancy Kasten married in 1990, Rabbi Kasten, who also received her master's degree in Hebrew letters and Jewish education from Hebrew Union College-Jewish Institute of Religion in New York, affiliated with SMU as associate chaplain and director of the Campus Jewish Network.

In 1991 Rabbi Debra J. Robbins also joined the rabbinical staff at Temple Emanu-El. The Boston native had attended Colby College in Maine before graduating from the University of California at Berkeley. Then she enrolled at the Los Angeles campus of HUC-JIR and upon graduation received the Jack and Audrey Skirball Award in Homiletics and the Louis and Minnie Raphael Award for Outstanding Service to a Small Congregation. After Debra Robbins and her husband Larry Robins (spelled with one b), who grew up attending Temple Emanu-El, came to Dallas so that Rabbi Zimmerman could bless their marriage, Debra decided to interview for a position at Emanu-El. She was selected as assistant rabbi after eighteen candidates were interviewed at the New York and Cincinnati Hebrew Union College campuses and three invited to visit in Dallas.[44]

In an attempt to bring "a new sort of energy" to the upper grades of the religious school and cut the dropout rate of students after Bar Mitzvah, Robbins enlivened Kadima! (Forward), an alternative study program for ninth and tenth grade students. Instead of attending religious school classes on Sunday, young people choose innovative ways to earn credit such as joining Rabbi Zimmerman's Torah class, taking a Joys of

Jewish Learning course at the Jewish Community Center, or attending a learning session in the archives. Rabbi Robbins, as well as Rabbi Stern and Rabbi Zimmerman, also taught classes for the adult B'nai Mitzvah program. At Emanu-El the emphasis on injecting more Hebrew into the religious service, and the affirmation of studying and reading Torah, in the opinion of religious school and education director Rabbi Barry Diamond, intensified the appreciation of Jewish education among the members. Therefore, Diamond, a Californian who graduated in 1991 from Hebrew Union College's Los Angeles campus with concentrated work in Jewish education and joined Emanu-El in 1993, believed that the task of teaching both Hebrew and Torah, the bedrock of the Jewish faith, was an interlocking process of education starting in the religious school.[45]

With highly competent rabbinical support and a surge of programming by an expanded staff, by 1993 the temple leadership had to address the urgent request for more classrooms and meeting rooms. The most glaring examples of the desperately cramped conditions were the utilization of Rabbi Zimmerman's private office as an additional meeting room and the use of the stuffy choir robing room for religious school classes. The primary reason for the crowded school quarters was the school committee's mandate for classes to meet only on Sunday morning. Prior attempts to solve the space limitations by staggering classes on different days proved inconvenient and unpopular as parents complained that scheduling religious classes on Wednesday or Saturday interfered with their children's school and extra-curricular activities.

The executive committee appointed Adlene Harrison, chair of the house and grounds committee, to oversee the reorganization of the physical plant and agreed to commission the firm of Phillips and Ryburn to conduct a space plan study. When the architects devised a plan to add more classrooms as well as to improve the existing physical arrangement within the present structure, the planning committee engaged architect James L. Hendricks, partner in the firm Hendricks and Brantner, to draw up detailed specifications for additional construction.[46] James Hendricks had worked on the renovation of the SEDCO building in Dallas, previously the original Cumberland School, and the restoration of the

Governor's Mansion in Austin, both projects of Governor William Clements.

On a cold but sunny winter day, February 12, 1995, well-wishers gathered in the atrium for the second groundbreaking ceremony at the Hillcrest site. Forty years after the original groundbreaking ceremony, Rose Marion Berg, temple's indefatigable president and persevering fund raiser, Adlene Harrison, the strong-willed and resolute leader of the building and restoration project, and Carolyn Clark, aesthetics committee head and tireless keeper of architect Howard Meyer's legacy, would act as a team to supervise the new wing and the remodeling of the existing structure. A capital campaign headed by Stanley Rabin and Ronald Steinhart raised $7,000,000 for the project, more than three times as much as the cost of the original building.[47]

As Temple Emanu-El forged ahead with plans to build another wing as well as to remodel its 1957 structure, the lay people, by their efforts to enrich congregational life, reinforced the concept of the synagogue as the primary focus in American Jewish life. In the view of Rabbi Zimmerman, the importance assumed by the American synagogue is strictly an American phenomenon because it has no historical precedent. In Europe the synagogue was almost exclusively a place to pray. Abroad, the needs of the Jewish community from birth to death were met by the organized lay community, by its own school system, and by the home and family. In America, participation in the Jewish community was voluntary, Jewish schools were only an adjunct to the synagogue, and the extended family became undermined by the end of cohesive neighborhoods and dispersal to suburbia. Only one major institution endured to which Jews gave their allegiance—the synagogue. In this unprecedented environment the challenge of the synagogue is to replace the unified Jewish community of the past.[48] Rabbi Zimmerman's avowed goal was to create a model or exemplar for the temple of the future.

When Rabbi Sheldon Zimmerman arrived at Temple Emanu-El in 1985, the temple was known as a "classical Reform" congregation. To Zimmerman that definition connoted special redeeming qualities, a clearly delineated, unique consciousness, including

A sense of standards, a sense of the spiritual, a sense of the aesthetic, and a sense of the rational . . .and we've lost some of that. The question for us is can we bring some of those wonderful parts of classical Reform into an encounter with a desire for more tradition, if you will, more participation, more involvement. Young people don't want to be an audience.[49]

In Sheldon Zimmerman's mind the problem was how to bring it all together, to retain a fidelity to the sense of what Temple Emanu-El "is all about." Because Emanu-El is an institution which is "sui generis," it must build on its own history and its sense of self. But Rabbi Zimmerman has also tried to respond "in terms of some of the color, in terms of the ritual, in terms of some of the observance" in answer "to people's legitimate spiritual needs." Most important to the rabbi and for the future of Temple Emanu-El was the reality that in Dallas the finest Jewish leadership was still involved at the temple. Zimmerman felt that whereas leadership in other communities had been stripped from the synagogue and lodged in other Jewish organizations like the Jewish Welfare Federation, Dallas Jewry did not suffer that conflict.[50] Historically, presidents and officers of Temple Emanu-El have alternated in service to the temple and to the federation, the other dominant Jewish organization in Dallas. Since the founding of the federation in 1911, fourteen presidents of temple have also served as federation presidents. In that time-honored practice, recent temple presidents Harold Kleinman, president from 1991 to 1993, Sanford P. Fagadau, president from 1995 to 1997, and Stanley Rabin, president in 1997, had all presided as federation presidents.

In 1993 Rabbi Zimmerman was named president of the Central Conference of American Rabbis, at fifty-one the youngest rabbi to be elected to the post. Not surprisingly, the rabbinical organization had changed radically from the era when Dr. Lefkowitz and Rabbi Olan were its heads and the membership was composed of mostly congregational rabbis. During Zimmerman's stint as president, one-third of its 1,700 rabbis were military or hospital chaplains, academicians, or people in communal service work, and a large number were retired. The advent of more women in the rabbinate—in 1994 approximately fifty percent of Reform rabbinic students were women—raised questions concerning maternity leave, child care, dual professions (especially when both spouses were rabbis), along with the basic rights of equal pay and equal opportunity.[51] In short, the altered rabbinate in microcosm reflected the changing American society.

As president of the conference, Zimmerman became one of the most recognized and influential Jewish leaders in the United States, his presence at public affairs an affirmation of his fellow Jews' role in American and global history. He recited the opening prayer at Texas Governor Ann Richards' inauguration in 1991, traveled to Poland with Vice-President Al Gore for the fiftieth anniversary commemoration of the Warsaw Ghetto uprising in 1993, and witnessed the Israeli-Palestinian accord with President Bill Clinton on the White House lawn in 1994.

Sustained and stimulated by the continued succession of outstanding lay and rabbinic leadership, members of the congregation were understandably distressed to learn suddenly in August 1995 that Rabbi Zimmerman had accepted the presidency of Hebrew Union College-Jewish Institute of Religion. Initially, Zimmerman had served on the college's search committee formed to replace Dr. Alfred Gottschalk, who was slated to become the university's chancellor. When one of the two top candidates for the presidency withdrew his name, the board of governors reopened the search, and Stanley P. Gold, chairman, convinced Zimmerman to allow his name to be put up for the presidency. In short order Emanu-El's rabbi was chosen. In Zimmerman's letter to the congregation, the rabbi expressed his "bittersweet" regrets at leaving "home" but looked forward to the prospect of leading "the ideological, spiritual, and educational center of world Reform Judaism."[52]

When president Sanford P. Fagadau appointed past presidents Carmen Michael and Harold Kleinman to lead the quest for a rabbi to guide the congregation into the next millennium and beyond, the diverse committee's common bond proved to be its deep commitment to the temple and the determination to build upon the momentum created during Rabbi Zimmerman's eleven-year tenure.[53] The one question temple members optimistically (albeit doubtfully) asked each other was, "Would David Stern take the job?" Granted, he was young, only thirty-four, to be senior rabbi of the third largest Reform congregation in the United States. But everyone, in a rare show of unanimity, agreed that virtually the entire congregation responded to his intellectual gifts, his sincere dedication, and his personal warmth and wished he would express a desire to remain permanently in Dallas.

Meanwhile, in order to assist Rabbi Stern, Rabbi Robbins, and Rabbi Klein in their duties, Charles D. Mintz joined the congregation on June 1, 1996, as interim rabbi, with a possible extension of his six-month term. Emanu-El considered itself fortunate, as Rabbi Mintz was exceptionally well-qualified. In 1991, at sixty-five, he had retired after serving fourteen years at Temple Ohev Sholom in Harrisburg, Pennsylvania, and had been "retired for a whole week, bothering no one" when a call came from Minneapolis. The congregation had lost its rabbi under difficult circumstances and invited Mintz to serve during a transition period. Natalie and Charles Mintz stayed for fifteen months. The rabbi found that he "was able to give people time to catch their breath . . . so that they could make rational decisions without feeling rushed."[54] Then he was asked to act in a similar position for congregations in Miami and Milwaukee and now looked forward to helping cover the large congregation in Dallas. For two months before Rabbi Mintz's arrival Rabbi Lawrence "Jake" Jacofsky, regional director, Southwest Council, Union of American Hebrew Congregations, lent his assistance to the rabbinical staff, visiting hospitalized congregants, teaching classes, and officiating at life cycle events as needed.

At the same time, the search committee began to "scour the country" in a conscientious quest for excellence while congregants grumbled, "why are you even considering somebody else" other than David Stern.[55] During the ensuing year, the committee reviewed a list of nearly fifty qualified and interested rabbis, talked to more than fifteen applicants, and then invited three strong candidates to come to Dallas. When two candidates emerged as excellent possibilities, the committee felt that finally the time had come to ask Rabbi Stern if he were interested in the position.

Unbenownst to the committee, "Every day throughout that year after Rabbi Zimmerman announced" his departure, David Stern and Nancy Kasten had asked themselves the question, "Did we want to stay?" and "kept coming up with the answer, 'no'. We would then ask the question the next day because it was a tremendous possibility to consider, and it was not a door that was easily closed." Later Stern readily admitted, "I had never really seen myself being senior rabbi of a congregation this size. We had never seen ourselves staying in Dallas forever; we had always imagined ourselves going back up to the northeast or to a smaller congregation in a suburban setting."[56] Underlying any discussion was David's awareness that it might be "foolhardy to have one's first experience as senior rabbi at a congregation of this size and complexity." On the other hand, Nancy was very happy with both her professional situation as associate chaplain at SMU and her active role as a Jew in the Dallas community.

As David Stern assumed more responsibility in the wake of Sheldon Zimmerman's departure, he began to see the professional challenges in Dallas as less daunting and infinitely more exciting. By the time the couple, vacationing in July with their families in Massachusetts, received the formal offer for consideration, they had made their decision. If there were one definitive factor, it may have been the congregation's averred awareness of and sensitivity to the uncommon situation of a thirty-five-year-old first-time senior rabbi with children only three-and-one-half and two years old. By advancing to senior rabbi at Temple Emanu-El, Rabbi Stern knew that he represented continuity to the congregation. He felt challenged to reap all of the benefits of knowing and being familiar to his congregants while looking at his new position with a fresh eye.

On Thanksgiving weekend, November 29, 1996, Rabbi Sheldon Zimmerman installed David Stern as senior rabbi of Temple Emanu-El. In the tradition of the rabbis who "transformed" the temple for their time, Rabbi Stern accepted the challenge to lead the congregation into the next chapter of the congregation's life posing "new possibilities and new promise" in the Jewish people's continuing covenant with God.[57] At the start of his tenure the congregation included over 2,700 families, ranking it third among Reform congregations in the United States. When one reflects on Temple Emanu-El's record of civic accomplishment spanning a century and a quarter, it is evident that the history of the congregation has been synonymous with the progress of the Jewish community in Dallas. Simultaneously, temple's religious development has mirrored the currents of Reform Judaism in America. Bound to their ancestral faith and to their own communal organizations, Emanu-El's members also devoted themselves to the promotion of Dallas' civic and cultural growth. From the first Jews' entry into Dallas with the coming of the railroad, Dallas Jewry has represented only a fraction of the city's population, in 1990 numbering a mere 38,000 out of a greater Dallas population of over two and a half million. Even so, Jews in Dallas, benefiting from the opportunities inherent in an open society, continuously reaffirmed their stake in the welfare and vitality of their city. From Temple Emanu-El's beginning as the first Jewish organization in Dallas, its history has been intertwined with the history of Dallas, and its members role in this southwestern city has illustrated the experience of the Jews in America, a history at once unique, yet one that has much in common with the collective experience of all Americans. ᛘ

The search committee that brought Sheldon Zimmerman to Temple Emanu-El. Left to right: Morton Prager, Carl Lee, Harold Kleinman, Kathi Baum, Paul Salzberger, Carmen Michael, Adlene Harrison, Robert Fine, Co-Chairmen Shirley Pollock and Henry Schlinger, Rabbi Zimmerman, Joan Loeb, Irwin Grossman, Shirley Tobolowsky, Herbert (Buddy) Rosenthal, Samson Weiner, and Joseph Rosenstein. Not pictured are Henri L. Bromberg, Jr., and Nancy Szor.

Adlene Harrison and President Rose Marion Berg, building project leaders with Carolyn Clark (not pictured), celebrate the groundbreaking for the new wing with former President Henri L. Bromberg, Jr., 1995.

Some of the well-wishers at the appreciation service held in May 1996 for Rabbi Sheldon Zimmerman. Dr. Don R. Benton, president of the Kindness Foundation and former senior pastor of Lovers Lane United Methodist Church, Jay D. Hirsch, national chancellor of the Jewish Chatauqua Society of the National Federation of Temple Brotherhoods, Sanford P. Fagadau, president of Temple Emanu-El, Rabbi Zimmerman, Annette Strauss, former mayor of Dallas, David Zimmerman, and Rabbi Lawrence "Jake" Jacofsky.

Courtesy Marci Benson.

Judy and Rabbi Sheldon Zimmerman received the plaudits of the congregation at the appreciation service before they left for Hebrew Union College in Cincinnati.

Courtesy Marci Benson.

An all-rabbinic celebration at David Stern's installation in 1996 as senior rabbi of Temple Emanu-El: Nancy Kasten, David Stern, Sheldon Zimmerman, Jack Stern, Lawrence Jacofsky, David Cohen, Debra Robbins, and Charles D. Mintz.

Courtesy Marci Benson.

Members of Temple Emanu-El's Executive Committee, 1997. Left to right, Andrea Statman, vice-president; Harold Kleinman, past president; Beverly Bonnheim, vice-president; Stanley Rabin, president; Bernard Raden, secretary; Ladd Hirsch, vice-president; Suzi Greenman, first vice-president; Sanford P. Fagadau, past president.

Courtesy Marci Benson.

APPENDIX

RABBIS OF TEMPLE EMANU-EL

Aaron Suhler	1875–1879
Herman M. Bien	1879–1882
Henry Schuhl	1882–1883
Joseph Silverman	1884–1885
Edward M. Chapman	1885–1887
George Alexander Kohut	1887–1889
Oscar Joseph Cohen	1900–1901
William H. Greenburg	1901–1919
David Lefkowitz	1920–1950
Emeritus	1950–1955
Stanley Brav	1934–1937
David Lefkowitz, Jr.	1937–1940
Joseph L. Ginsberg	1940–1943
	1946–1948
Lou H. Silberman	1943–1945
J. Aaron Levy	1948–1949
Herbert M. Yarrish	1949–1950
Levi A. Olan	1949–1970
Emeritus	1970–1984
Gerald J. Klein	1952–1988
Emeritus	1988–
Saul Besser	1962–1965
Stanley Robin	1966–1969
Irwin Goldenberg	1969–1972
Jack Bemporad	1972–1983
Ellen Lewis	1980–1985

Richard Harkavy	1984–1986
Sheldon Zimmerman	1985–1996
Elizabeth Weiss Stern	1986–1991
David E. Stern	1989–
Debra J. Robbins	1991–
Charles D. Mintz	1996–
Mark Kaiserman	1997–

PRESIDENTS OF TEMPLE EMANU-EL

Presidents of the Hebrew Benevolent Association

Moses Ullman	1872–1873
Alexander Sanger	1873–1874
George Myers	1874
Emanuel Tillman	1874–1875

Presidents of Temple Emanu-El

David Goslin	1875–1879
Samuel Klein	1879–1881
Unknown	1881–1883
Sigmund Loeb	1883–1884
Adolph Metzler	1884–1886
Emanuel Tillman	1887–1889
Philip Sanger	1889–1894
Emanuel Kahn	1894–1896
Ludwig Philipson	1896–1897
Alex Ortlieb	1897–1899
Alexander Sanger	1899–1901
Rudolph Liebman	1901–1903
Victor Hexter	1903–1904
Rudolph Liebman	1904–1912

Jules K. Hexter	1912–1918
Max J. Rosenfield	1918–1919
Herbert Marcus	1919–1922
Arthur L. Kramer, Sr.	1922–1926
Lawrence Miller, Sr.	1926–1928
Charles L. Sanger	1928–1929
Henri L. Bromberg, Sr.	1929–1931
Julius H. Pearlstone	1931–1933
Nathan E. Mittenthal	1933–1935
Henry S. Miller, Sr.	1935–1937
Herbert Mallinson	1937–1939
Louis Tobian	1939–1941
Eli Wiener	1939–1943
Julius Purvin	1943–1945
Winfield S. Myers	1945–1947
Eugene M. Solow	1947–1949
Sam R. Bloom	1949–1950
Alex F. Weisberg, Sr.	1950–1951
Louis Tobian	1951–1953
Lewis B. Lefkowitz	1953–1955
Irving L. Goldberg	1955–1957
Henry S. Jacobus, Sr.	1957–1959
Henri L. Bromberg, Jr.	1959–1961
Richard Liebman	1961–1963
Philip Silverberg	1963–1965
Milton Tobian	1965–1967
Carl Flaxman	1967–1969
Robert S. Strauss	1969–1971
Bernard Hirsh	1971–1973
Sam R. Bloom	1973–1975
Sol Goodell	1975–1977
Ronald M. Mankoff	1977–1979
Lawrence S. Pollock, Jr.	1979–1981
Herbert S.(Buddy) Rosenthal	1981–1983

Irwin Grossman	1983–1985
Henry D. Schlinger	1985–1987
Carmen M. Michael	1987–1989
Joseph Rosenstein	1989–1991
Harold Kleinman	1991–1993
Rose Marion Berg	1993–1995
Sanford P. Fagadau	1995–1997
Stanley Rabin	1997–

NOTES

Unless otherwise indicated, Temple Emanu-El correspondence, minutes, records, and taped interviews may be found in the Dorothy M. and Henry S. Jacobus Temple Emanu-El Archives.

FOREWORD

1. Levi A. Olan, *Maturity in an Immature World* (New York: KTAV Publishing House, 1984), pp. 49–54.

2. E. Brooks Holifield, "Toward a History of American Congregations," in *American Congregations*, eds. James P. Wind and James. W. Lewis (Chicago: University of Chicago Press, 1994), vol. II, p. 47.

CHAPTER 1

1. William L. McDonald, *Dallas Rediscovered* (Dallas: The Dallas Historical Society, 1978), p. 19; an eyewitness, John Milton McCoy, in a letter to his parents, July 22, 1872, estimated the crowd at no more than 2,000 people, John Milton McCoy, *When Dallas Became a City: Letters of John Milton McCoy, 1870–1881*, ed. Elizabeth York Enstam (Dallas: The Dallas Historical Society, 1982); *Dallas Daily Herald*, July 20, 1872, p. 1, described the crowd as numbering 7,000.

2. Robert Seay quoted by John William Rogers, *The Lusty Texans of Dallas* (New York: E. P. Dutton and Company, Inc., 1951), p. 117.

3. McDonald, *Dallas Rediscovered*, p. 19.

4. *Dallas Herald*, May 8, 1858.

5. Rogers, *Lusty Texans*, p. 45.

6. McDonald, *Dallas Rediscovered*, pp. 7–9.

7. Frank Marion Cockrell, "History of Early Dallas," *Dallas Sunday News*, May 15, 1932, p. 29.

8. Rogers, *Lusty Texans*, p. 83.

9. Cockrell, "History of Early Dallas," p. 29.

10. Conversation with Jesse Fosse, great-granddaughter of Dr. Albert M. Levy, March 25, 1995.

11. Dallas County Census for 1850 and 1860; John Henry Brown, *History of Dallas County, Texas from 1837-1887* (Dallas: Milligan, Cornett & Farnham, 1887); Julia Simon obituary, *The Banner* (Brenham, Texas) February 25, 1931, and other newspaper clippings from the Texas Jewish Historical Society Archives, Center for American History, University of Texas.

12. *Dallas Herald*, June 13, 1860.

13. Barrot Steven Sanders, *The Caruths: Dallas Landed Gentry* (Dallas: Sanders Press, 1988). NorthPark Center was developed in 1965 by noted art collector, Raymond D. Nasher.

14. A. C. Greene, *Dallas: The Deciding Years-A Historical Portrait* (Austin, Texas: The Encino Press, 1973), p. 17.

15. Julia Simon obituary, *The Banner*.

16. *Archives Israelites*, vol. 26, no. 7 (April 1, 1865), p. 277, American Jewish Archives, Hebrew Union College, Cincinnati, Ohio.

17. E. M. Kahn, "Looking Backward Fifty Years and More, 1873–1923," memoir in Dorothy M. and Henry S. Jacobus Temple Emanu-El Archives, Dallas (hereafter cited as TEA).

18. *Ibid.*

19. Lehman Sanger quoted by Leon Joseph Rosenberg, *Sangers': Pioneer Texas Merchants* (Austin: Texas State Historical Association, 1978), p. 16.

20. *Ibid.*, pp. 13–26. Lehman Sanger quoted on p. 18.

21. "Alex Sanger: Widely Known Merchant Answers Last Call," *Dallas Morning News*, September 14, 1925, p. 1.

22. Robert Seay as quoted by Rogers, *Lusty Texans*, p. 118.

23. McDonald, *Dallas Rediscovered*, p. 21.

24. Alex Sanger as quoted by Rogers, *Lusty Texans*, p. 121.

25. Rosenberg, *Sangers': Pioneer Texas Merchants*, pp. 61, 76.

26. *Ibid.*, p. 33; "Flowers that Never Wither," obituary of Alexander Sanger reprinted from *Dallas Times Herald*, September 13, 1925.

27. Hebrew Benevolent Association Minute Book 1872–1878, Prologue (TEA).

28. *Ibid.*

29. *Ibid.*

30. Hebrew Benevolent Association Minute Book Bylaws (TEA).

31. *Dallas Herald*, December 28, 1871; Congregation Emanu-El Cemetery Records, 1884–1889 (TEA).

32. "Emanuel Tillman," *Memorial and Biographical History of Dallas County, Texas* (Chicago: The Lewis Publishing Company, 1892), pp. 709–710.

33. Rosenberg, *Sangers': Pioneer Texas Merchants*, p. 30.

34. Hebrew Benevolent Association Minute Book Prologue (TEA).

35. Hebrew Benevolent Association Minute Book, August 7, 1872, February 2, 1873, May 4, 1873.

36. *Ibid.*, February 2, 1873, May 4, 1873.

37. *Ibid.*, April 6, 1873, April 5, 1874, April 4, 1875.

38. *Ibid.*, September 14, 1872, April 6, 1873.

39. Hasia R. Diner, *A Time for Gathering: The Second Migration, 1820–1880*, vol. 2 of *The Jewish People in America* (Baltimore: The John Hopkins University Press, 1992), p. 109.

40. *Ibid.*

41. Letter from Nat Strauss to D. A. Eldridge, March 30, 1904 (TEA).

42. William H. Greenburg, "History of the Jews of Dallas," *Reform Advocate* (January 24, 1914), p. 4. David Lefkowitz, "History of Temple Emanu-El, Dallas, Texas 1873–1933," (4-page pamphlet in TEA).

43. Hebrew Benevolent Association Minute Book, September 14, 1872, December 1, 1872.

44. *Ibid.*, March 2, 1873, May 7, 1873.

45. *Directory of the City of Dallas*, F. E. Butterfield and C. M. Rundlett, 1875, pp. 81–137.

46. Jacob Rader Marcus, *United States Jewry 1776–1985*, vol. 2 (Detroit: Wayne State University Press, 1991), p. 201.

CHAPTER 2

1. Michael A. Meyer, *Response to Modernity: A History of the Reform Movement in Judaism* (New York: Oxford University Press, 1988), p. 54.

2. *Ibid.*

3. Leon A. Jick, *The Americanization of the Synagogue, 1820–1870* (Hanover, New Hampshire: Published for the Brandeis University Press by the University Press of New England, 1976), p. 7.

4. Charles Reznikoff and Uriah Z. Engelman, *The Jews of Charleston* (Philadelphia: The Jewish Publication Society of America, 1950), p. 124.

5. *Ibid.*, p. 125.

6. *Ibid.*, p. 126.

7. *Ibid.*; Meyer, *Response to Modernity*, pp. 229–234; Jick, *Americanization of the Synagogue*, pp. 12–14.

8. Arthur Hertzberg, *The Jews in America* (New York: Simon & Schuster, 1989), p. 122.

9. Meyer, *Response to Modernity*, p. 238.

10. Isaac M. Wise quoted by Kenneth Libo, *We Lived There Too* (New York: St. Martin's, 1984), p. 208.

11. Hertzberg, *The Jews in America*, p. 122.

12. Isaac M. Wise, "The World of My Books," Translated with an Introduction and Explanatory Notes by Albert H. Friedlander, *Critical Studies in American Jewish History*, Selected Articles from American Jewish Archives (New York: KTAV Publishing House, 1971), pp. 166–167.

13. *Ibid.*, Explanatory note by Albert H. Friedlander, p. 166.

14. Hertzberg, *The Jews in America*, pp. 119–123; Meyer, *Response to Modernity*, pp. 239–244; Libo, *We Lived There Too*, p. 209.

15. David Philipson, *My Life as an American Jew* (Cincinnati: John G. Kidd & Son, Inc., 1941), p. 23.

16. "The Jewish Synagogue," *Dallas Herald*, May 30, 1876, p. 3.

17. Reznikoff and Engelman, *Jews of Charleston*, p. 140.

18. "The Jewish Synagogue," *Dallas Herald*, May 30, 1876, p. 3.

19. Virginia Rosenthal Metzler's memoirs (TEA).

20. *American Israelite*, November 12, 1875.

21. *Ibid.*; "Jewish Synagogue," *Dallas Herald*, May 30, 1876.

22. *American Israelite*, November 12, 1875.

23. *Ibid.*

24. Robert Strauss to Felicia Zeidenfeld, September 27, 1991; Heinrich Schwarz's obituary, clipping with handwritten *Galveston Post*, 1900 (TEA).

25. "The Jewish Synagogue," *Dallas Herald*, May 30, 1876.

26. *Ibid.*; Greenburg, "History of the Jews of Dallas," *Reform Advocate*, p. 9.

27. *American Israelite*, February 14, 1879.

28. John Henry Brown, "Rabbi Herman M. Bien," *The Encyclopedia of the New West*

(Marshall, Texas: The United States Biographical Publishing Company, 1881), p. 181.

29. *American Israelite*, August 18, 1878.

30. *Ibid.*, Secondary sources such as *American Israelite* are used as references for Temple Emanu-El's early years. From the formation of the congregation in September 1875. Until 1883 no records kept by Temple Emanu-El exist. Leo Wolfson, the secretary of Emanu-El in 1898, reported in "Fair Leaflets: A Literary Souvenir of the Jahrmarkt, 1898" that "the congregation was unfortunate in losing their records twice since their first formation" (TEA).

31. Edward Chapman to Officers and Board of Directors of Temple Emanu-El, May 3, 1896 (TEA).

32. W. Gunther Plaut, *The Growth of Reform Judaism* (New York: World Union for Progressive Judaism, LTD, 1965), p. 14.

33. *American Israelite*, August 26, 1881.

34. William H. Greenburg, "History of the Jews of Dallas," *Reform Advocate*, p. 11.

35. *Ibid.*

36. David Philipson, *My Life as an American Jew*, p. 25.

37. Greenburg. "History of the Jews of Dallas," *Reform Advocate*, p. 11.

38. Joseph Stolz, *Central Conference of American Rabbis Yearbook* (no place: CCAR, 1931), p. 93.

39. McDonald, *Dallas Rediscovered*, p. 23.

CHAPTER 3

1. "The Generosity of the Jews," *The Dallas Herald*, September 27, 1873.

2. C. D. Morrison & Company's General Directory of the City of Dallas for 1878–1879 (Marshall, Texas: 1878), pp. 21–22.

3. *Dallas Morning News*, November 19, 1885; *Red Book of Dallas 1895–1896* (Dallas: Holland Brothers Publishing Company), pp. 30–31.

4. *Dallas Morning News*, November 19, 1885.

5. David Goslin's obituary, *Dallas Morning News*, August 13, 1889.

6. "Samuel Klein," *Memorial and Biographical History of Dallas County, Texas* (Chicago: The Lewis Publishing Company, 1892), p. 407.

7. John Henry Brown, *History of Dallas County from 1837–1887*, pp. 58–59.

8. John H. Cochran, *Dallas County: A Record of its Pioneers and Progress* (Dallas: Service Publishing Company, 1928), pp. 226–234.

9. Interview with Joseph Sanger Linz, May 10, 1989.

10. Rosenberg, *Sangers'*, p. 71; Morris Lasker to Alex Sanger, January 1, 1909 (TEA); McDonald, *Dallas Rediscovered*, p. 108.

11. "Philip Sanger," *Baptist Standard* (Baptist Standard Publishing Company: Published Weekly at Dallas, Texas, J. B. Cranfill, president, March 9, 1889), pp. 5–6 (TEA).

12. *The WPA Dallas Guide and History*, p. 281; Elizabeth York Enstam, "The Forgotten Frontier: Dallas Women and Social Caring, 1895–1920," *Legacies: A History Journal for Dallas and North Central Texas* (Spring 1989), p. 21.

13. Rosenberg, *Sangers'*, p. 74.

14. 1897 Annual Report to the Congregation by Ludwig Philipson (TEA).

15. 1895 Annual Report to the Congregation by Emanuel Kahn (TEA).

16. *Ibid.*

17. *Ibid.*

18. Rev. E. M. Chapman to the President and Board of Directors of Temple Emanu-El, November 11, 1894 (TEA).

19. *Ibid.*, June 22, 1895.

20. Resolutions Adopted by the Board of Directors of Congregation Emanu-El, January 10, 1897 (TEA).

21. 1897 Annual Report by Ludwig Philipson (TEA).

22. Rebekah Kohut, *His Father's House: The Story of George Alexander Kohut* (New Haven: Yale University Press, 1938), p. 78.

23. David de Sola Pool, "George A. Kohut,: *Dictionary of American Biography*, ed. Harris E. Starr, vol. 21 (New York: Charles Scribner's Sons, 1946), pp. 473–474.

24. George Alexander Kohut to Board of Directors, April 19, 1899 (TEA).

25. 1897 Annual Report (TEA).

26. Alex Sanger to A. Harris, May 23, 1891 (TEA).

27. Rosenberg, *Sangers'*, p. 69.

28. Interview with Minnie Marcus by Polly Crossman and Gerry Cristol, November 29, 1973.

29. *Beau Monde, A Journal Devoted to Art, Drama, Literature, Music, Society, Current Gossip*, April 16, 1898, (TEA).

30. Virginia Rosenthal Metzler memoirs (TEA).

31. *Beau Monde*, April 16, 1898.

32. George Alexander Kohut to Board and Directors of Temple Emanu-El, April 19, 1899 (TEA).

33. "Dedicated New Temple," *Dallas Morning News*, December 2, 1899.

34. Alexander Marx, "George Alexander Kohut," *The American Jewish Year Book*, ed. Cyrus Adler (Philadelphia: The Jewish Publication Society of America, 1903), p. 56.

35. "Dedicated New Temple," *Dallas Morning News*, December 2, 1899.

36. Lawson and Edmonson's Dallas City Directory and Reference Book (Springfield, Missouri: The Missouri Patriot Book and Job Printing House, 1873), p. 9.

37. McDonald, *Dallas Rediscovered*, p. 115.

38. *Ibid.*, p. 108.

CHAPTER 4

1. McDonald, *Dallas Rediscovered*, p. 85.

2. Interview with Blanche Mittenthal Lefkowitz, March 29, 1974.

3. "Jews in the United States," *American Jewish Year Book*, September 17, 1917–September 6, 1918, ed. Samson D. Oppenheim for the American Jewish Committee (Philadelphia: The Jewish Publication Society of America, 1917), p. 412.

4. Greenburg, "History of the Jews of Dallas," p. 20.

5. *American Israelite*, May 24, 1900.

6. Alex Sanger to William H. Greenburg, July 25, 1901 (TEA).

7. William H. Greenburg unpublished autobiography, William H. Greenburg Papers (TEA).

8. *Ibid.*

9. Levi Olan, Introduction to *Medicine for a Sick World* (Dallas: Southern Methodist University Press, 1952); Greenburg autobiography (TEA).

10. Greenburg autobiography (TEA).

11. *Ibid.*

12. 1901 Annual Report by Alex Sanger (TEA).

13. 1906 Annual Report by Rudolph Liebman (TEA).

14. Nat Strauss to D. A. Eldridge, March 30, 1904 (TEA).

15. 1906 Annual Report by Rudolph Liebman (TEA).

16. Isaac M. Wise, editorial in *American Israelite* quoted by W. Gunther Plaut, *The Growth of Reform Judaism*, p. 277.

17. Meyer, *Response to Modernity*, pp. 290–292.

18. Greenburg, "History of the Jews of Dallas," p. 17.

19. Meyer, *Response to Modernity*, p. 290.

20. Isaac Meyer Wise quoted in Plaut, *Growth of Reform Judaism*, p. 269.

21. Temple Emanu-El Minutes, November 10, 1903 (TEA).

22. *Ibid.*

23. Faith Rogow, *Gone to Another Meeting: The National Council of Jewish Women, 1893–1993* (Tuscaloosa: The University of Alabama Press, 1933), p. 15.

24. *Ibid.*, p. 21.

25. *Ibid.*

26. Greenburg, "History of the Jews of Dallas," p. 17.

27. Temple Emanu-El Minutes, October 26, 1909 (TEA).

28. Temple Emanu-El Minutes, January 25, 1910 (TEA); Temple Literary and Musical Society Programs, 1910-1912 (TEA).

29. William H. Greenburg to Herbert Marcus, December 14, 1915 (TEA).

30. Herbert Marcus to Jules K. Hexter, December 15, 1915 (TEA).

31. Meyer, *Response to Modernity*, p. 264.

32. Kaufmann Kohler quoted in Plaut, *Growth of Reform Judaism*, pp. 311–312.

33. Meyer, *Response to Modernity*, p. 286.

34. *Ibid.*, pp. 287–288.

35. William Greenburg to Godcheaux Levi, May 20, 1911 (TEA).

36. Interview with Godcheaux L. Levi by Gerry Cristol, April 26, 1993.

37. Greenburg, "History of the Jews of Dallas," pp. 19–20.

38. Federated Hebrew Charities Minutes, 1911–1920, Dallas Jewish Historical Society, Jewish Community Center.

39. Enstam, "The Forgotten Frontier: Dallas Women of Social Caring, 1885–1920," p. 23.

40. Blanche Greenburg's scrapbook of the Dallas Infants Welfare and Milk Fund, 1911–1919 (TEA).

41. Greenburg autobiography.

42. "Many Return Thanks," *Dallas Morning News*, November 29, 1907, p. 5.

43. People's Thanksgiving Service programs, 1907–1918 (TEA); Mayor Henry D. Lindsley to Dr. William H. Greenburg, November 9, 1916 (TEA).

44. Greenburg autobiography.

45. Herbert Gambrell, "The Critic Club, 1908–1965," Dallas Historical Society, Hall of State, Fair Park.

46. Greenburg autobiography.

47. Rogers, *Lusty Texans*, p. 233.

48. Greenburg autobiography; *Dallas Morning News*, October 27, 1912.

49. Mrs. Morris Liebman to Board of Directors, January 19, 1913 (TEA).

50. Jeffrey S. Gurock, "The Emergence of the American Synagogue," *The American Jewish Experience*, ed. Jonathan D. Sarna (New York: Holmes and Meier Publishers, Inc., 1986), p. 199.

51. William H. Greenburg, "The Growth and Purpose of the Institutional Synagogue," April 27, 1913, William H. Greenburg papers (TEA).

52. Rabbi's Report, 1913 (TEA).

53. Greenburg, "Growth and Purpose of the Institutional Synagogue."

54. 1913 Annual Report by Jules K. Hexter (TEA).

55. *Ibid.*

56. Darwin Payne, *Dallas: An Illustrated History* (Woodland Hills, California: Windsor Publications, 1982), p. 171.

57. Temple Emanu-El Minutes, December 5, 1913.

58. *Ibid.*, February 23, 1914, March 3, 1916; Rabbi's Report at the 1915 Annual Meeting (TEA).

59. Solicitation letter from J. K. Hexter, Chairman, and William H. Greenburg, Secretary-Treasurer, October 26, 1917 (TEA).

60. *Dallas Morning News*, January 31, 1916.

61. Telephone conversation with Herman Philipson, Jr., by Gerry Cristol, 1994.

62. Clifton Linz to Mr. and Mrs. Simon Linz, July 28, 1918 (TEA).

63. Rabbi's Annual Message, June 10, 1917 (TEA).

64. Meyer, *Response to Modernity*, p. 296.

65. Rabbi's Annual Message, 1917; Special Committee Report, December 5, 1917; Temple Emanu-El Minutes, December 5, 1917 (TEA).

66. *Ibid.*

67. *Ibid.*

68. 1917 Annual Meeting Report by Jules K. Hexter; Temple Emanu-El Minutes, September 22, 1917.

69. Rabbi's Annual Message, 1917.

70. Special Committee Report, December 15, 1917 (TEA).

71. Temple Emanu-El Minutes, June 6, 1915, March 26, 1918, April 7, 1918, April 12, 1918, April 14, 1918, April 28, 1918, May 7, 1918; Annual Meeting Report June 10, 1917 (TEA).

72. 1919 Annual Report by Max Rosenfield; Temple Emanu-El Minutes, March 25, 1919.

73. *Dallas Morning News*, August 15, 1919.

74. Temple Emanu-El Minutes, March 19, 1918.

CHAPTER 5

1. Stanley Marcus to Gerald J. Klein, June 16, 1989 (TEA).

2. *Dallas Morning News*, April 12, 1940, p. 12.

3. *Dallas Times Herald* obituary, June 6, 1955; David Lefkowitz to Dr. Harry Lefkowitz, April 4, 1935 (TEA).

4. David Lefkowitz to Rabbi Abraham Cronbach, October 19, 1920 (TEA).

5. Levi A. Olan, Introduction to *Medicine for a Sick World*.

6. *Ibid.*

7. Interview with Rabbi David Lefkowitz, Jr., by James R. Alexander and Gerry Cristol, June 3, 1990.

8. David Lefkowitz to Henry A. Howard, December 19, 1929 (TEA).

9. Olan, Introduction to *Medicine for a Sick World*.

10. Leon Harris, "Dallas and the Marci," *Merchant Princes* (New York: Harper & Row, 1979), pp. 167–172; Stanley Marcus, *Minding the Store* (Boston: Little, Brown & Company, 1974), pp. 4–14; Interview with Minnie Marcus, May 16, 1974.

11. Harris, "Dallas and the Marci," *Merchant Princes*, pp. 188–189.

12. Frank X. Tolbert, "The *News* Brought Goettinger Here," *Dallas Morning News*, March 16, 1955.

13. Speech given by Edna Kahn Flaxman at the Dallas Jewish Historical Society,

Jewish Community Center, May 10, 1989 (TEA).

14. Minnie Hexter, unpublished History of Sisterhood (TEA).

15. *Ibid.*

16. Interview with Hortense Sanger by Gerry Cristol, June 8, 1990.

17. *Emanu-El Bulletin*, September 14, 1922 (TEA).

18. David Lefkowitz to Mr. Gutman, September 23, 1920 (TEA).

19. David Lefkowitz to Robert Stern, November 21, 1932 (TEA).

20. *Emanu-El Bulletin*, November 17, 1920.

21. *Ibid.*, March 23, 1921.

22. David Lefkowitz to Jeanette Goldberg, November 23, 1920 (TEA).

23. *Emanu-El Bulletin*, December 15, 1920.

24. Nathan Mittenthal's Report at the Annual Meeting, April 1, 1921; *Emanu-El Bulletin*, December 15, 1920.

25. *Emanu-El Bulletin*, April 1, 1923.

26. Shawn Lay, ed. *The Invisible Empire in the West: Toward a New Historical Appraisal of the Ku Klux Klan of the Twenties* (Chicago: University of Illinois Press, 1952), pp. 5–7.

27. "Klan Marches in Awesome Parade," *Dallas Morning News*, May 22, 1921.

28. Conversation with M. J. Mittenthal by Gerry Cristol, 1993.

29. David Lefkowitz to George B. Dealey, June 16, 1921 (TEA).

30. Charles Alexander, *Ku Klux Klan in the Southwest* (Lexington: University of Kentucky Press, 1965), p. 201.

31. Hortense Sanger interview, 1990.

32. Marilyn Wood Hill interview with Mrs. Helman Rosenthal, February 23, 1967; "A History of the Jewish Involvement in the Dallas Community" (M.A. thesis, Southern Methodist University, 1970).

33. *Dallas Morning News*, March 8, 1922, p. 1, March 9, 1922, p. 1.

34. Tommy Stringer, "The Zale Corporation: A Texas Success Story" (Ph.D. dissertation, University of North Texas, 1985), pp. 9–12.

35. *Dallas Morning News*, April 2, 1922, p. 1.

36. *Ibid.*, April 5, 1922, p. 1.

37. *Ibid.*, October 25, 1923, p. 8.

38. *Ibid.*, October 28, 1923, p. 4; David Lefkowitz to George Dealey, April 11, 1922; David Lefkowitz to Mrs. Thomas S. Hart, November 1, 1923 (TEA).

39. David Lefkowitz, Jr., interview, 1990.

40. *Ibid.*

41. Jacob Marcus, *United States Jewry 1776–1985*, vol. 4, p. 697.

42. Arthur Kramer was president from 1922 until 1926.

43. David Lefkowitz to Dr. Norman Crozier, September 6, 1933 (TEA).

44. The *Emanu-El Bulletin* featured a monthly section entitled "The Rabbi in the Community."

45. David Lefkowitz to Robert Stern, November 21, 1932 (TEA).

46. Random letters from 1929–1940 in "Radio Broadcasts" file (TEA).

47. *Dallas Morning News*, October 23, 1927, Alex Weisberg file (TEA).

48. *Dallas Morning News*, September 28, 1927, Martin Weiss scrapbook (TEA).

49. Rogers, *Lusty Texans*, pp. 242–243.

50. John Rosenfield, "Program Notes," *Dallas Morning News*, 1951, Eli Sanger file (TEA).

51. David Lefkowitz to Henry Englander, April 6, 1930 (TEA).

52. David Lefkowitz to Dr. Joseph Stolz, May 26, 1930; Abraham I. Schechter, "Message of the President," "The Kallah: An Annual Convention of Texas Rabbis," Beaumont, Texas, March 1928–March 1929, p. 8 (TEA).

53. David Lefkowitz to Rabbi Ferdinand Isserman, April 1939 (TEA).

54. Interview with Rabbi Gerald J. Klein by Jerry Whitus, September 1972.

CHAPTER 6

1. Harold Wineburgh, *The Texas Banker: The Life and Times of Fred Florence* (Dallas: Harold Wineburgh, 1981), pp. 30–32; *Dallas Morning News* quoting Adolph Ochs, March 12, 1933.

2. *The WPA Dallas Guide and History*, Written and Compiled from 1936–1942 by the Workers of the Writers Program of the Works Projects Administration in the City of Dallas (Denton: University of North Texas Press, 1992), p. 96.

3. *Ibid.*

4. Charles Silberman, *A Certain People: American Jews and Their Lives Today* (New York: Summit Books, 1985), pp. 23, 48–49.

5. "Immigration to the United States and Canada," *The American Jewish Year Book*, October 2, 1913–September 20, 1914, ed. Herbert Friedenwald and H. G. Friedman for the American Jewish Committee (Philadelphia: The Jewish Publication Society of America, 1913), pp. 427–431.

6. Bernard Marinbach, *Galveston: Ellis Island of the West* (Albany: State University of New York Press, 1983), pp. 10–11.

7. Federated Hebrew Charities Board Minutes, June 17, 1914, Dallas Jewish Historical Society, Jewish Community Center.

8. 1939 Annual Report by Herbert Mallinson (TEA).

9. David Lefkowitz to Earle Johnson, March 13, 1933 (TEA).

10. David Lefkowitz to Julius Pearlstone, April 25, 1934 (TEA); "NRA Victory Jubilee," *Dallas Morning News*, March 3, 1933; Ted Morgan, *FDR* (New York: Simon & Schuster, 1985), p. 401.

11. David Lefkowitz to R. Sternberger, December 29, 1938 (TEA).

12. David Lefkowitz to L. H. Cohn, July 29, 1932 (TEA); interview with Louis Tobian by Jerry Whitus, September, 1972.

13. Temple Emanu-El Board Minutes, June 12, 1933.

14. *WPA Dallas Guide*, p. 97.

15. *Ibid.*, p. 98.

16. "Fred Florence Says," reprinted from *American Business Magazine*, April 1953 (TEA).

17. David Lefkowitz to Dallas Rabbis, October 9, 1936 (TEA).

18. Plaut, *Growth of Reform Judaism*, p. 86.

19. David Lefkowitz to Rabbi Henry Cohen, September 3, 1936; Lefkowitz to Dr. Stephen S. Wise, October 13, 1936 (TEA).

20. David Lefkowitz to Rabbi Samuel Rosinger, November 19, 1928 (TEA).

21. David Lefkowitz to Dallas Rabbis, October 9, 1926.

22. David Lefkowitz to Dr. Julian Morgenstern, May 22, 1934 (TEA).

23. Stanley Brav to James R. Alexander, April 1, 1990 (TEA).

24. Interview with Henri L. Bromberg, Jr., by Gerry Cristol, 1993.

25. David Lefkowitz, Jr., interview, 1990.

26. David Lefkowitz to Herman Lefkowitz, September 18, 1949 (TEA).

27. Program of Temple Lyceum Course, 1935–1936; Report of R. C. Knickerbocker, Executive Director, Community Course, to SMU Committee of the

Board of Trustees Investigating Charges made by John O. Beaty. This report was read to Temple Emanu-El's Board of Trustees, May 25, 1954 (TEA). Beaty was a professor of English at SMU who asserted that "a certain powerful non-Christian element in our population" was trying to dominate SMU. Dr. Umphrey Lee, president of SMU, took full responsibility for the cooperation of the university with Jewish organizations and SMU professors backed him by a vote of 50 to 1. *Dallas Morning News*, February 11, 1954, February 16, 1954, February 18, 1954.

28. "Threats Made of Boycotting Jewish Stores" *Dallas Morning News*, March 28, 1933, p. 1; Howard M. Sachar, *A History of the Jews in America* (New York: Alfred A. Knopf, 1992), p. 468.

29. David Lefkowitz to Richard E. Gutstadt, September 11, 1933 (TEA).

30. Sachar, *A History of the Jews in America*, p. 468.

31. "Nazis Boycott Against Jews Observed in Holiday Style," *Dallas Morning News*, April 2, 1933, p. 1; David Wyman, *Paper Walls: America and the Refugee Crisis 1938–1941* (New York: Pantheon Books, 1985), p. 28.

32. Interview with Gerda Yaffe by Gerry Cristol, 1994.

33. "Threatened Flight of Jews Prevented by German Decree," *Dallas Morning News*, April 4, 1933, pp. 1–2.

34. David Lefkowitz to May Baar Solomon, April 3, 1933; Lefkowitz to Umphrey Lee, May 3, 1933; Lefkowitz to Charles Selecman, May 3, 1933, Lefkowitz to George Truett, October 25, 1936 (TEA); "Protests Made by All Creeds at Nazi Policy," *Dallas Morning News*, April 3, 1933, p. 1.

35. David Lefkowitz to Rabbi Abram V. Goodman, November 22, 1938; *Temple Bulletin*, December 1, 1938 (TEA).

36. Interview with Trude Shakno by Gerry Cristol, May 9, 1990.

37. *Ibid.*

38. Interview with Irmgard Brooksaler by Gerry Cristol, April 30, 1990.

39. *Ibid.*

40. Martin Fruhman, Henry Jacobus, and Nathan Mittenthal to George A. Levy, January 13, 1938, Jewish Federation for Social Services Minutes, Dallas Jewish Historical Society, Jewish Community Center.

41. Report to the Board of Directors of Jewish Federation for Social Services, February 22, 1940, Dallas Jewish Historical Society, Jewish Community Center.

42. February 19, 1939, Annual Meeting, Jewish Federation for Social Services; Jewish Federation for Social Services Board Minutes, September 26, 1939, Dallas Jewish Historical Society, Jewish Community Center.

43. George A. Levy Report to Board of Directors, Jewish Federation for Social

Services, October 25, 1939, Dallas Jewish Historical Society, Jewish Community Center.

44. Irmgard Brooksaler interview, 1990.

45. Interview with Fannie and Stephen Kahn by Gerry Cristol, September 20, 1993.

46. Irmgard Brooksaler interview, 1990.

47. Wyman, *Paper Walls*, p. 209.

48. *Ibid.*, p. 211.

49. *Ibid.*, p. 212.

50. David Lefkowitz to Senator Tom Connally, May 2, 1939 (TEA).

51. *Dallas Morning News*, April 12, 1940.

52. David Lefkowitz to Rabbi Wolf Macht, May 1, 1940 (TEA).

53. David Lefkowitz to Allan Merriman, September 12, 1939 (TEA).

CHAPTER 7

1. David Lefkowitz to Rabbi Samuel R. Bacon, October 23, 1939 (TEA).

2. Joseph Sanger Linz to David Lefkowitz, September 22, 1942 (TEA).

3. Interview with Henry Jacobus, Sr., by Joan Loeb and Frances Tocker, March 19, 1974; written remarks from a talk given by Henry Jacobus, March 26, 1942 (TEA).

4. *Dallas Morning News*, June 30, 1971, 1C.

5. Interview with Blossom Myers by Hortense Sanger, 1974.

6. Edward Titche newspaper article, no date or newspaper name on clipping (TEA).

7. Conversation with Valerie Aronoff, 1993; interview with Helen Loeb by Joan Loeb and Gerry Cristol, May 15, 1974.

8. Vivian Anderson Castleberry, "Adlene Nathanson Harrison," *Daughters of Dallas: A History of Greater Dallas Through the Voices and Deeds of its Women* (Dallas: Odenwald Press, 1994), p. 435.

9. Interview with Frances Bernstein by Gerry Cristol, May 2, 1994.

10. Private First Class Abe Levin to David Lefkowitz, April 10, 1944 (TEA).

11. Conversation with Rosalee Cohen, 1993.

12. David Lefkowitz to Lieutenant Charles A. Levi, Jr., November 4, 1943 (TEA).

13. David Lefkowitz, Sr., to David Lefkowitz, Jr., March 23, 1943 (TEA).

14. David Lefkowitz to Private First Class Carol Miller, June 1, 1943; Carol Miller to Rabbi Gerald J. Klein, May 21, 1990 (TEA).

15. David Lefkowitz, Sr., to David Lefkowitz, Jr., March 23, 1943 (TEA).

16. David Wyman, *The Abandonment of the Jews* (New York: Pantheon Books, 1984), p. 3.

17. Interview with Sam Milstein by Gerry Cristol, October 24, 1994.

18. William J. vanden Heuvel, "The Holocaust Was No Secret," *The New York Times Magazine*, December 22, 1996, p. 31.

19. Lieutenant Lee H. Berg to David Lefkowitz, May 23, 1945 (TEA).

20. Rudy Baum, speech before the Leisure Club of Temple Emanu-El, April 11, 1994; speech for the 50th anniversary of the liberation of the camps, February 12, 1995 (TEA).

21. *The Zionist Idea: A Historical Analysis and Reader*, ed. Arthur Hertzberg (New York: Atheneum, 1986), pp. 202–203.

22. Sacher, *History of the Jews in America*, p. 240.

23. Meyer, *Response to Modernity*, p. 293.

24. David Lefkowitz to Dr. W. H. Kittrell, Sr., February 10, 1931 (TEA).

25. Meyer, *Response to Modernity*, p. 331.

26. *Ibid.*

27. *Ibid.*, p. 332.

28. Thomas A. Kolsky, *Jews Against Zionism: The American Council for Judaism* (Philadelphia, Temple University Press, 1990), p. 78.

29. David Lefkowitz to Dr. Morris Lazaron, April 21, 1943; Lefkowitz to Jake Mossiker, November 30, 1943 (TEA).

30. Temple Emanu-El Board Minutes, February 18, 1964.

31. David Lefkowitz, Jr,. interview, 1990.

32. Carmen Miller Michael conversation with Gerry Cristol, December 30, 1995.

33. Kolsky, *Jews Against Zionism*, p. 83.

34. Robert I. Kahn to Officers and Board of Congregation Beth Israel, "late 1943 or early 1944" handwritten across copy (TEA); Anne Nathan Cohen, *The Centenary History of Congregation Beth Israel of Houston, Texas, 1854–1954* (Houston: Beth Israel, 1954) pp. 53–58.

35. Cohen, *The Centenary History of Congregation Beth Israel of Houston, Texas, 1854–1954*, p. 58.

36. David Lefkowitz to Fred Florence, April 11, 1945 (TEA).

37. David Lefkowitz to Alex Geisenberger, May 1, 1946 (TEA); interview with Levi A. Olan by Hortense Sanger, August 5, 1972.

38. Interview with Fannie Schaenen by Gerry Cristol, August 17, 1994.

39. Jewish Welfare Federation Board Minutes, June 10, 1948, Dallas Jewish Historical Society, Jewish Community Center.

40. Interview with Jack Kravitz by David Zeff, Council of Jewish Federations, September 23, 1986 (TEA).

41. Jewish Welfare Federation Board Minutes, October 9, 1941, Dallas Jewish Historical Society, Jewish Community Center.

42. Conversation with Hortense Sanger by Gerry Cristol, 1994.

43. Interview with Fannie Schaenen by Gerry Cristol, August 17, 1994.

44. Jan Ginsberg Flapan to James R. Alexander, May 29, 1990 (TEA).

45. David Lefkowitz to Chaplain Joseph Ginsberg, January 9, 1945 (TEA).

46. David Lefkowitz to Chaplain Henry Tavel, January 26, 1946 (TEA).

47. Rabbi Harvey Wessel to Temple Emanu-El, March 20, 1947 (TEA).

48. Meyer, *Response to Modernity*, p. 357.

49. *Ibid.* p. 358; David Lefkowitz to Harvey Wessel, February 6, 1948 (TEA).

50. Rabbi Sylvan D. Schartzman to Rabbi Gerald J. Klein, April 30, 1991 (TEA).

51. David Lefkowitz to Rabbi Louis Witt, April 23, 1948 (TEA).

52. *Dallas Morning News* clipping, no date (TEA).

CHAPTER 8

1. Joshua Loth Liebman to Eugene Solow, March 3, 1948 (TEA).

2. Interview with Louis Tobian by Jerry Whitus, September 1972.

3. Interview with Rabbi Levi A. Olan by Gerry Cristol, July 22, 1974.

4. Levi Olan interview, 1974; "Outspoken Rabbi Levi Olan Dies," *Dallas Times Herald*, October 18, 1984, p. 22A.

5. Levi Olan interview, 1974.

6. Levi Olan to Thomas S. Roy, December 19, 1950 (TEA).

7. Levi Olan interviews, 1972, 1974.

8. *Ibid.*

9. *Ibid.*

10. Temple Emanu-El Board Minutes, June 6, 1949.

11. Interview with Rabbi Gerald J. Klein by Gerry Cristol, May 24, 1988.

12. Personal recollections of Rabbi Herbert M. Yarrish, August 1990 (TEA).

13. Gerald Klein interview, 1988.

14. *Ibid.*

15. *Ibid.*

16. McDonald, *Dallas Rediscovered*, p. 126.

17. Interview with Rabbi Gerald J. Klein by Jerry Whitus, September 1972.

18. Temple Emanu-El Board Minutes, April 5, 1950, May 3, 1950.

19. Board Minutes, January 8, 1950, June 6, 1950; Louis Tobian interview, 1972.

20. Building Committee Meeting with Eric Mendelsohn, July 21, 1951 (TEA).

21. Interview with Irving Goldberg by Joseph Rosenstein, August 22, 1972.

22. Temple Emanu-El Board Minutes, January 29, 1963.

23. Louis Tobian interview, 1972.

24. *Ibid.*

25. Irving Goldberg interview, 1972.

26. Warranty Deed for Hillcrest and Northwest Highway property, August 16, 1952.

27. Gerald Klein interview, 1988.

28. David Dillon, "Howard Meyer was the Epitome of the Gentleman Architect," *Dallas Morning News*, January 17, 1988, p. 13.

29. Gerald Klein interview, 1988.

30. Telephone conversation with Carol Sandfield, 1994.

31. Levi Olan to Rabbi Philip S. Bernstein, November 10, 1958; William Wurster to Sam Bloom, September 12, 1957 (TEA).

32. Levi Olan, "What the Temple Should Do for Its Members," April 13, 1951 (TEA).

33. Interview with Raymond Israel by Gerry Cristol, 1993.

34. Interview with Samuel Adler by Dottie Mandell, Norma Schlinger, and Helen Stuhl, June 19, 1978.

35. *Ibid.*

36. *Ibid.*; "40th Anniversary of the Volunteer Choir," 1993 (TEA).

37. Samuel Adler interview, 1978.

38. Interview with Elizabeth Olan Hirsch by Gerry Cristol, January 6, 1994.

39. Howard Meyer, "Art and Architecture of Temple Emanu-El," Panel with Rabbi Levi A. Olan, Max Sandfield, and John Lundsford taped at Temple Emanu-El, February 10, 1974.

40. *Ibid.*

41. Gerald Klein interview, 1988.

42. Howard Meyer, "Art and Architecture of Temple Emanu-El," 1974.

43. Gyorgy Kepes to Hannah C. Boorstin, June 9, 1960 (TEA).

44. Gerald Klein interview, 1988.

45. Howard Meyer, "Art and Architecture of Temple Emanu-El."

46. Gerald Klein interview, 1988.

47. Howard Meyer, "Art and Architecture of Temple Emanu-El."

48. Gerald Klein interview, 1988.

49. Louis Tobian interview, 1972; interview with Irving Goldberg by Hortense Sanger and Gerry Cristol, September 21, 1994.

50. Hertzberg, *The Jews in America*, p. 321; Edward S. Shapiro, *A Time for Healing: American Jewry Since World War II*, vol. 5 of *The Jewish People in America* (Baltimore: The John Hopkins University Press, 1992), p. 193.

51. Levi Olan speech, Temple Emanu-El groundbreaking ceremony, June 1955.

52. Lewis Lefkowitz speech, Temple Emanu-El groundbreaking ceremony, June 5, 1955.

53. Louis Tobian speech, Temple Emanu-El groundbreaking ceremony, June 5, 1955.

54. Conversation with Ira L. McColister by Gerry Cristol, 1968.

55. Collection of letters and newspaper articles by and about Julius Schepps (TEA).

56. Levi Olan to Irving Goldberg, December 16, 1954 (TEA).

57. David Lefkowitz to Eli Wiener, March 11, 1941 (TEA).

58. *Temple Bulletin*, February 9, 1955.

59. Conversation with Hortense Sanger, 1994.

60. Temple Emanu-El Board Minutes, September 28, 1955.

61. Building Committee Report, submitted by Louis Tobian at the May 23, 1956,

Annual Meeting.

62. William Parker McFadden to Howard Meyer, January 28, 1957 (TEA).

63. *Life*, "Lofty Shrine," February 25, 1957, p. 62.

64. O'Neil Ford to Irving Goldberg, February 15, 1957.

65. Elizabeth Olan Hirsch interview, 1994.

Chapter 9

1. Hertzberg, *Jews in America*, pp. 301–303; Silberman, *A Certain People*, p. 114.

2. 1957 Annual Report by Irving Goldberg.

3. Conversation with Hortense Sanger, 1994.

4. Interview with Rabbi Olan by Helen Stuhl, March 22, 1978.

5. Adolphus Cummings, Letter to the Editor, *Dallas Morning News*, November 8, 1984.

6. Conversation with Paul Salzberger by Gerry Cristol, May 28, 1997.

7. Levi A. Olan, WFAA radio broadcast reprinted in *The Texas Observer*, June 7, 1957.

8. Irving Goldberg interview, August 22, 1972.

9. Elizabeth Olan Hirsch interview, 1994.

10. Stanley Marcus to Lois Kravitz, December 14, 1993 (copy in TEA).

11. Interview with Sam Bloom by Joan Loeb and Gerry Cristol, March 26, 1974.

12. Glenn M. Linden, *Desegregating Schools In Dallas* (Dallas: Three Forks Press, 1995), p. 61.

13. Mayor Adlene Harrison, "Statement on United States District Court Order," March 10, 1976 (TEA).

14. *Dallas Morning News*, January 30, 1994, 24A; Louis Tobian to Mayor Starke Taylor, April 21, 1976 (TEA).

15. Resolution Adopted by the Inter-Racial Committee, June 28, 1951 (Louis Tobian file TEA).

16. "Ceremony Dedicates Home Area," *Dallas Morning News*, October 5, 1953, III-1; Louis Tobian to Starke Taylor, April 21, 1976 (Louis Tobian file TEA).

17. Report to the Temple Emanu-El Board by Bernard Hirsh, 1959.

18. Temple Emanu-El Board Minutes, February 25, 1959.

19. *Ibid.*

20. Temple Emanu-El Board Retreat (no date) held in 1960 or 1961.

21. Temple Emanu-El Board Minutes, January 29, 1963.

22. *Ibid.*, March 2, 1963.

23. Report of the Temple Emanu-El Pre-School Project, November 23, 1965.

24. *Ibid.*; Temple Emanu-El Board Minutes, July 7, 1965, May 28, 1969; conversation with Elissa Sommerfield, 1994.

25. Temple Emanu-El to Dallas Board of Education and Dr. White, 1967; Public Pre-School for Poor Urged," *Dallas Morning News*, March 9, 1967, 1D.

26. Telephone conversation with Gerry Beer by Gerry Cristol, 1994.

27. Report of the Temple Emanu-El Pre-School Project, November 23, 1965 (TEA).

28. "Women's Group Protests Policy of Art Presentation at Museum," *Dallas Morning News*, March 15, 1955, part 2-1.

29. John Rosenfield, *Dallas Morning News*, November 30, 1956, p. 18.

30. Dallas Museum of Fine Arts Board Minutes, December 7, 1955, Dallas Museum of Art.

31. "LBJ Calls Pro-Nixon Fans at His Rally 'Discourteous,'" *Dallas Morning News*, November 5, 1960, p. 1.

32. Darwin Payne, *Dallas: An Illustrated History* (Woodland Hills, California: Windsor Publications, 1982), p. 243; conversation with Hortense Sanger, 1994.

33. David Ritz, "Remembering Bloom," *D The Magazine of Dallas* (July 1985) p. 59.

34. *Ibid.*, p. 60.

35. Ruth S. Brodsky, "A Man and His Camera," *Dallas Jewish Life* (November 1994), p. 5.

36. Interview with Irving Goldberg by Hortense Sanger and Gerry Cristol, September 21, 1994. Goldberg told Johnson that he was already the president by virtue of the Constitution. The reason "people get sworn in is that they want witnesses."

37. Ritz, "Remembering Bloom," p. 60.

38. "Conscience of the City," *Dallas Times Herald* editorial, October 20, 1984.

39. Richard Austin Smith, "How Business Failed Dallas" *Fortune,* July 1964, p. 163.

40. Erik Jonsson to Carl Flaxman, June 3, 1966; Goals for Dallas Essays (14 essays describing current city problems), May 1966 (TEA).

41. Interview with Carl Flaxman by Gerry Cristol, April 3, 1974.

42. Conversation with Hortense Sanger, 1994.

43. Gerald J. Klein, "The Lefkowitz Years, 1920–1955," written for the Rabbi Levi A. Olan Lecture, March 9, 1990, Temple Emanu-El, p. 15.

44. Interview with Milton Tobian, November 1975.

CHAPTER 10

1. Meyer, *Response to Modernity*, p. 353.

2. Interview with Sol Goodell by Gerry Cristol, April 26, 1994.

3. *Ibid.*

4. Levi Olan interview, 1974.

5. *Ibid.*

6. Levi Olan interview, 1972.

7. Conversation with Eugene Sanger, December 22, 1994.

8. Levi Olan to Selig Salkowitz, December 17, 1956 (TEA).

9. *Temple Bulletin*, September 1940.

10. Conversation with Richard Albert, 1994; conversation with Joe Funk, 1994.

11. Ginger Chesnick Jacobs, *The Levin Years: A Golden Era, 1929–1951* (Dallas: Taylor Publishing Company, 1989).

12. Interview with Max Tonkon by Gerry Cristol, May 31, 1994.

13. Conversation with Carol Brin, 1994.

14. Temple Emanu-El Board of Trustees Minutes, May 12, 1963.

15. Board Minutes, July 27, 1965.

16. Conversation with Milton Tobian, 1994.

17. Interview with Henry Jacobus, Jr., March 30, 1994.

18. Conversation with Gloria Jacobus, April 25, 1997.

19. Henry Jacobus, Jr., interview, 1994.

20. *Ibid.*

21. *Ibid.*

22. *Ibid.*; interview with Bernard Hirsh by Gerry Cristol, October 17, 1974.

23. Bernard Hirsh interview, 1974.

24. Interview with Rabbi Jack Bemporad by Carl Flaxman, August 15, 1975.

25. Bernard Hirsh interview, 1974; Jack Bemporad interview by Gerry Cristol, May 19, 1994.

26. Rabbi Gerald J. Klein to Charles Nelson, Maurice Thompson, and every member of the East Texas State University Choral and the Temple Emanu-El Choir, November 11, 1972; 100th Anniversary Program.

27. Interview with Joan and Milton Loeb, May 11, 1994.

28. Temple Emanu-El Board Minutes, January 31, 1972; Bernard Hirsh interview, 1974.

29. Untaped interview with Rhea Wolfram, November 26, 1994.

30. Interview with Simon Sargon, October 23, 1994.

31. The Morton H. Meyerson Symphony Center was named through a generous gift by Ross Perot, founder of Electronic Data Systems, for symphony fund raiser Morton H. Meyerson, a temple member who was president of EDS from 1979 to 1986.

32. Jacob Marcus, *United States Jewry, 1776–1985*, vol. 4, p. 779.

33. Irving Goldberg interview, 1994.

34. Meyer, *Response to Modernity*, p. 366.

35. Levi A. Olan, The President's Message to the 70th Annual Convention, Boston, Massachusetts, June 17, 1968; Clipping from *Boston Herald Traveler*, June 18, 1968, Levi A. Olan file (TEA).

36. *Boston Herald Traveler*, June 18, 1968.

37. *Ibid.*

38. Report to the Temple Emanu-El Board by Bernard Hirsh, 1959; conversation with Hortense Sanger, 1994.

39. Temple Emanu-El Board Minutes, December 15, 1964.

40. *Ibid.*, January 29, 1963.

41. Robert S. Rosow to Carl Flaxman, May 26, 1969; Temple Emanu-El Board Minutes, May 28, 1969.

42. Board Minutes, May 28, 1969.

43. *Ibid.*, October 7, 1969.

44. *Ibid.*, January 21, 1974.

45. Charles D. Mintz to Sam Bloom, October 22, 1974 (TEA).

46. Sam Bloom to Charles D. Mintz, October 25, 1974 (TEA).

47. Leo M. Davis to Sam Bloom, November 15, 1974 (TEA).

48. I. A. Victor to Leo Davis, November 18, 1974 (TEA).

49. Janie Rosenthal to Temple Emanu-El Board, November 14, 1974 (TEA).

50. Gerald J. Klein to Sam Bloom, November 19, 1974 (TEA).

51. Notes taken by Leo Davis at the November 19, 1994, Temple Emanu-El Board meeting (TEA).

52. *Ibid.*, March 23, 1975.

53. Leo Davis to Sam Bloom, April 11, 1975 (TEA); interview with Leo Davis by Gerry Cristol, October 25, 1994.

54. Leo Davis to Sam Bloom, April 11, 1975.

55. Temple Emanu-El Board Minutes, May 28, 1969, October 7, 1969.

56. Sol Goodell to the Union of American Hebrew Congregations: Matthew H. Ross, Rabbi Alexander M. Schindler, Rabbi Arthur J. Lelyveld, Rabbi David Jacobson, Rabbi Malcolm Stern, Dr. Jules Backman, Rabbi Alfred Gottschalk, October 2, 1975; Rabbi Alexander Schindler and Matthew H. Ross to Sol Goodell, October 22, 1975 (TEA).

57. "A Message from Temple Emanu-El's President," *Window of Our Temple*, December 6, 1976.

58. Sol Goodell to Ross, Schindler, Lelyveld, Jacobson, Stern, Backman, Gottschalk, March 2, 1977; Rabbi Malcolm Stern to Rabbi Jack Stern, Jr., November 19, 1976 (TEA).

59. Sol Goodell interview, 1994; Ronald Mankoff interview, 1994; interview with Harold Kleinman by Gerry Cristol, April 28, 1994.

60. Shirley Tobolowsky interview, 1994.

61. Harold Kleinman interview, 1994.

CHAPTER 11

1. Jack Bemporad interview, 1994.

2. Ronald Mankoff interview, 1994.

3. Interview with Herbert (Buddy) Rosenthal, April 29, 1994.

4. Temple Emanu-El Board Minutes, July 16, 1979; Executive Committee Minutes, July 20, 1979; Bard Schachtel to Lawrence S. Pollock, Jr., July 27, 1979.

5. Report from the Committee on Personnel Needs Assessment, Temple Emanu-El Board Minutes, November 13, 1979.

6. Temple Emanu-El Board Minutes, July 14, 1980.

7. Harold Kleinman interview, 1994; interview with Ruth Kleinman by Gerry Cristol, May 17, 1994.

8. Buddy Rosenthal interview, 1994.

9. *Ibid.*

10. Search committee for Ellen Lewis: banker Jack Bell, community volunteers Sharlene Block and Sharan Goldstein, former Councilwoman and Mayor Adlene Harrison, attorney Carl Lee, hospice volunteer Gay Malon-Frank, Dr. Morton Prager, professor of surgery at Southwestern Medical School, Joseph Rosenstein, associate professor in the College of Business, University of Texas at Arlington, Dr. Jay Todes, teacher of economics and business at Dallas Community College, college counselor Rhea Wolfram.

11. Shirley Tobolowsky interview, April 5, 1994.

12. Temple Emanu-El Board Minutes, February 9, 1981.

13. *Ibid.*, November 10, 1981; interview with Nita Mae Tannebaum by Gerry Cristol, May 31, 1994.

14. Buddy Rosenthal interview, 1994; Nita Mae Tannebaum interview, 1994.

15. Caring Congregation Report to the Temple Emanu-El Board, October 14, 1986.

16. Temple Emanu-El Executive Committee Meeting, March 6, 1977.

17. Interview with Jack Bemporad by Gerry Cristol, May 19, 1994; Buddy Rosenthal interview, 1994.

18. Interview with Shirley Pollock by Gerry Cristol, May 5, 1994; interview with Adlene Harrison, April 30, 1994.

19. Interview with Irwin Grossman by Gerry Cristol, March 15, 1994.

20. *Ibid.*; Harold Kleinman interview, 1994, Adlene Harrison interview, 1994.

21. Interview with Rabbi Sheldon Zimmerman by Gerry Cristol, April 14, 1994.

22. *Ibid.*

23. *Ibid.*

24. *Ibid.*

25. Interview with Rabbi Sheldon Zimmerman by Gerry Cristol, May 10, 1994.

26. *Ibid.*

27. *Ibid.*

28. *Ibid.*

29. Interviews with Shirley Pollock, Harold Kleinman, Adlene Harrison, and Joan Loeb, 1994; interview with Joseph Rosenstein by Gerry Cristol, June 8, 1994.

30. Temple Emanu-El Board Minutes, September 10, 1985.

31. Harold Kleinman interview, 1994.

32. Shirley Tobolowksy interview, 1994.

33. Sheldon Zimmerman interview, May 10, 1994.

34. *Ibid.*

35. Harold Kleinman interview, 1994,

36. Interview with Josephine Goldman by Gerry Cristol, August 9, 1994.

37. Temple Emanu-El Executive Committee Minutes, February 25, 1991; *Window*, November 1986.

38. "Temple Appoints New Rabbi," *Dallas Morning News*, November 22, 1984, 39A.

39. Conversation with Doris Budner by Gerry Cristol, 1994.

40. Gerald J. Klein to the congregation, August 24, 1984.

41. Carmen Michael to the congregation, October 11, 1988.

42. Carol Brin article in *Window*, February 19, 1988.

43. Interview with Rabbi David Stern, December 2, 1994; Search committee: attorney Andrew Baker, social worker Beverly Bonnheim, Dr. Roy Elterman, businessman Robert Pollock, community volunteer Hortense Sanger, former Sisterhood President Shirley Tobolowsky, clinical psychologist Carmen Michael, Joseph Rosenstein, former associate professor in the College of Business, University of Texas at Arlington.

44. Interview with Rabbi Debra Robbins, December 7, 1994.

45. Interview with Rabbi Barry Diamond, November 23, 1994.

46. Temple Emanu-El Executive Committee Minutes, August 31, 1992; Adlene Harrison interview, 1994.

47. Capital Campaign Cabinet: Rose Marion Berg, Dolores Barzune, Sanford P. Fagadau, Suzi Greenman, Irvin Jaffe, Harold Kleinman, Lester Levy, Jeffrey Marcus, Morton H. Meyerson, Lawrence S. Pollock, Jr., Carole Shlipak, Liener Temerlin, Barbara Zale.

48. Sheldon Zimmerman interview, May 10, 1994.

49. *Ibid.*

50. *Ibid.*

51. *Ibid.*

52. Sheldon Zimmerman to members of Temple Emanu-El, August 7, 1995; notes taken by Gerry Cristol at August 1, 1995, staff meeting.

53. Search committee: Rose Marion Berg, Robin Elkin, Judy Foxman, Gilbert Friedlander, Alan Gold, Suzi Greenman, Adlene Harrison, Ladd Hirsch, Milton P. Levy, Jr., Stuart Morse, Cheryl Pollman, Stanley Rabin, Joseph Rosenstein, Herbert (Buddy) Rosenthal, Hortense Sanger, Michael Schwartz, Ellen Silverman, Ronald Steinhart, Shirley Tobolowsky.

54. "Temple Emanu-El Selects Interim Rabbi," *Dallas Morning News*, March 29, 1996, 34A; "Meet the Mintzes," *Moving Forward*, July 1996 (TEA).

55. Conversation with Harold Kleinman by Gerry Cristol, October 14, 1996; conversation with Carmen Michael by Gerry Cristol, August 27, 1996.

56. Interview with David Stern by Gerry Cristol, August 2, 1996.

57. Rabbi Jack Stern used "transform" in his speech and Rabbi David Stern spoke of "new possibilities and new promise" at the Installation Service, November 29, 1996.

BIBLIOGRAPHY

Primary Sources in the Dorothy M. and Henry S. Jacobus
Temple Emanu-El Archives

Baum, Rudy. Speech for the 50th Anniversary of the Liberation of the Camps, February 2, 1995. Speech at Temple Emanu-El, April 11, 1994.

Greenburg, Rabbi William Henry. William Henry Greenburg Papers.

Hebrew Benevolent Association Minute Book 1872–1878.

Hexter, Mrs. Victor. History of the Sisterhood of Temple Emanu-El.

Kahn, E. M. Reminiscences, Looking Backward Fifty Years or More, 1873–1923

Lefkowitz, David. Extensive correspondence and other material, 1920–1955.

Metzler, Virginia Rosenthal. Memoirs, 1848–1938.

Olan, Levi A. Letters, sermons, scrapbooks and other material, 1949–1970.

Temple Emanu-El Annual Reports, 1895–1996.

Temple Emanu-El Board of Trustees Minutes, 1901–1996.

Temple Emanu-El Bulletin and *Window*, 1920–1996.

Temple Emanu-El Cemetery Records, 1884–1889.

Temple Emanu-El Correspondence Book, 1898–1906.

Other Primary Sources

Cohen, Henry. Henry Cohen Papers. Rosenberg Library, Galveston, Texas.

Federated Hebrew Charities, later called Jewish Federation for Social Services and renamed Jewish Welfare Federation, Board Minutes from 1911–1950. Dallas Historical Society, Jewish Community Center.

Jacobus, Dorothy. "Growing up in Dallas." American Jewish Archives, Hebrew Union College, Cincinnati, Ohio.

Jewish Federation for Social Services Board Minutes, see Federated Hebrew Charities.

Jewish Welfare Federation Board Minutes, see Federated Hebrew Charities.

The Levi A. Olan Collection at the American Jewish Archives, Hebrew Union College, Cincinnati, Ohio.

CENSUS REPORTS AND DIRECTORIES

All census and directories are located at the Dallas Public Library.

C. D. Morrison & Company's General Directory of the City of Dallas for 1878–1879. Marshall, Texas: 1878.

Dallas County Census for 1850 and 1860. Copied from the original census records on file at Washington, D. C. Compiled and indexed under the auspices of the Dallas Genealogical Society by E. B. Comstock, 1932.

Directory of the City of Dallas. Carefully arranged and prepared by F. E. Butterfield and C. M. Rundlett for the year 1875.

Directory of the City of Dallas. Published by W. L. Hall & Company of Dallas, Texas. Dallas: Commercial Steam Printing House, 1877.

Lawson & Edmonson's Dallas City Directory & Reference Book. Springfield, Missouri: The Missouri Patriot Book and Job Printing House, 1873.

Morrison and Fourmy's General Directory of the City of Dallas, 1886–1887. Galveston: Morrison and Fourmy, 1887.

Red Book of Dallas 1895–1896. Dallas: Holland Brothers Publishing Company.

NEWSPAPERS, MAGAZINES, ARTICLES, THESES AND PAMPHLETS

Archives Israelites. Except from Vol. 26, No. 7. (April 1, 1865): p. 277.

American Israelite. Cincinnati, Ohio. Selected issues, 1875–1897.

Beau Monde. A Journal Devoted to Art, Drama, Literature, Music, Society, Current Gossip (April 16, 1898, November 19, 1898).

Brodsky, Ruth. "A Man and His Camera." *Dallas Jewish Life* (November 1994): 6–7.

Brown, John Henry. "Rabbi Herman M. Bien," *The Encyclopedia of the New West.* Marshall, Texas: The United States Biographical Publishing Company, 1881, 180–182.

Cockrell, Frank Marion. "History of Early Dallas." *Dallas Sunday News* (May 15, 1932 through August 28, 1932).

Cohen, Rabbi Henry. "History of the Jews of Galveston." *The Reform Advocate* (January 24, 1914), no consecutive page numbering for the articles.

Cohen, Dr. Henry, Dr. Ephram Frisch, and Dr. David Lefkowitz. *One Hundred Years of Jewry in Texas.* no place: Pamphlet Prepared by the Jewish Advisory Committee for the Texas Centennial Religious Program, 1936.

Cristol, Geraldine P. "The History of the Dallas Museum of Fine Arts." Master's thesis, Southern Methodist University, 1970.

Dallas Herald. 1858–1876.

Dallas Morning News. Selected years, 1885–1994.

De Sola Pool, David. "George A. Kohut." *Dictionary of American Biography.* ed. Harris E. Starr, Vol. 21. New York: Charles Scribner's Sons, 1946. 473–474.

Enstam, Elizabeth York. "The Forgotten Frontier: Dallas Women of Social Caring, 1985–1920" *Legacies: A History Journal for Dallas and North Central Texas* 1:1 (Spring 1989): 20–28.

Fair Leaflets: A Literary Souvenir of the Jahrmarkt. Dallas, Texas: Nolan Brown, 1898.

Gambrell, Herbert. "The Critic Club, 1908–1965," Dallas Historical Society, Hall of State, Fair Park.

Greenburg, Rabbi William Henry. "The Growth and Purpose of the Institutional Synagogue." Sermon, Temple Emanu-El, April 27, 1913.

Greenburg, Rabbi William Henry. "History of the Jews of Dallas." *The Reform Advocate* (January 24, 1914): 3–21.

Gurock, Jeffrey S. "The Emergence of the American Synagogue." ed. Jonathan D. Sarna, *The American Jewish Experience.* New York: Holmes & Meier Publishers, Inc., 1986.

Hill, Marilyn Wood. "A History of the Jewish Involvement in the Dallas Community." Master's thesis, Southern Methodist University, 1967.

"Immigration to the United States and Canada." *The American Jewish Year Book,* October 2, 1913–September 20, 1914. ed. Herbert Friedenwald and H. G. Friedman for the American Jewish Committee. Philadelphia: The Jewish Publication Society of America, 1913, 427–431.

The Jewish Texans. A pamphlet series dealing with the many kinds of people who have contributed to the history and heritage of Texas. San Antonio: The Institute of Texas Cultures, 1974.

"Jews in the United States." *The American Jewish Year Book,* September 17, 1917–September 6, 1918. ed. Samson D. Oppenheim for the American Jewish Committee. Philadelphia: The Jewish Publication Society of America, 1917, 412–413.

Klein, Rabbi Gerald J. "The Lefkowitz Years, 1920–1955." Rabbi Levi A. Olan Lecture, March 9, 1990, Temple Emanu-El.

Lefkowitz, David. "History of Temple Emanu-El, Dallas, Texas. . . "1873–1933," (4-page pamphlet).

Life. "Lofty Shrine." (February 25, 1957): 62.

Marks, Alexander. "George Alexander Kohut." *The American Jewish Year Book 5664*. ed. Cyrus Adler. Philadelphia: The Jewish Publication Society of America, 1903, 55–64.

Marks, Dr. Samuel. "History of the Jews of San Antonio." *The Reform Advocate* (January 24, 1914), no consecutive page numbering.

"Philip Sanger." *The Baptist Standard*. Baptist Standard Publishing Company: Published Weekly at Dallas, Texas, J. B. Cranfill, President, March 9, 1889: 5–6.

Ritz, David. "Inside the Jewish Establishment." *D The Magazine of Dallas* (November 1975): 50–55, 108–116.

Ritz, David. "Remembering Bloom." *D The Magazine of Dallas* (July 1985): 57–61.

Rosenberg, Elliot. "1843." *B'nai B'rith International Jewish Monthly* (October–November 1993), 12–16.

"Samuel Klein." *Memorial and Biographical History of Dallas County, Texas*. Chicago: The Lewis Publishing Company, 1892, 407.

Schechter, Abraham I. "Message of the President." *The Kallah: An Annual Convention of Texas Rabbis Yearbook*. Beaumont, Texas: March 1928–March 1929, 8–9.

Smith, Richard Austin. "How Business Failed Dallas." *Fortune*, 70:1 (July 1964): 157–163, 211–216.

Stolz, Joseph. "Joseph Silverman." *Central Conference of American Rabbis Yearbook*, Vol. 41. no place: CCAR, 1931.

Stringer, Tommy W. "The Zale Corporation—A Texas Success Story." Ph.D. diss., University of North Texas, 1985.

Tobin, Gary A. *Greater Dallas Jewish Community Study-Executive Summary*. Report printed at Brandeis University, Waltham, Massachusetts, August 1990, for the Jewish Federation of Dallas, Dallas Jewish Historical Society, Jewish Community Center.

Vanden Heuvel, William J. "The Holocaust Was No Secret." *The New York Times Magazine* (December 22, 1996): 30–31.

Winer, Mark L. "The History of Temple Emanu-El of Dallas, Texas, during the Nineteenth Century." History Paper, Hebrew Union College, 1969, Temple Emanu-El Archives.

Wise, Isaac Mayer, "The World of My Books." Translated, with an Introduction and Explanatory Notes, by Albert H. Friedlander. *Critical Studies In American Jewish History*. Selected Articles from *American Jewish Archives*. New York, KTAV Publishing House, 1971, 144-185.

Wohlberg, Gizelle. "History of the Jews of Waco." *Reform Advocate* (January 24, 1914), no consecutive page numbering.

Interviews, Taped Lectures, and Conversations

Taped interviews are in the Dorothy M. and Henry S. Jacobus Temple Emanu-El Archives. Untaped interviews and conversations are separately noted.

Adler, Samuel. By Norma Schlinger, Helen Stuhl, and Dottie Mandell, June 19, 1978.

Albert, Richard. Telephone conversation with Gerry Cristol, 1994.

Aronoff, Valerie. Telephone conversation with Gerry Cristol, 1993.

Bemporad, Rabbi Jack. By Carl Flaxman, August 15, 1975. Taped telephone interview by Gerry Cristol, May 19, 1994.

Berg, Rose Marion. By Gerry Cristol, June 15, 1994.

Bernstein, Frances. By Gerry Cristol, May 2, 1994.

Bloom, Sam. By Joan Loeb and Gerry Cristol, March 26, 1974.

Brin, Carol. Conversation with Gerry Cristol, 1994.

Bromberg, Henri L., Jr. By Shirley Tobolowsky, September 21, 1972. By Gerry Cristol, 1993.

Brooksaler, Irmgard. By Gerry Cristol, April 30, 1990.

Budner, Doris. Telephone conversation with Gerry Cristol, 1994.

Cohen, Rosalee. Telephone conversation with Gerry Cristol, 1993.

Davis, Leo M. By Gerry Cristol, October 25, 1994.

Diamond, Rabbi Barry. Untaped interview by Gerry Cristol, November 23, 1994.

Flaxman, Carl. By Gerry Cristol, April 3, 1974.

Flaxman, Edna. Telephone conversation with Gerry Cristol, December 21, 1994.

Florence, Grace. By Shirley Tobolowsky and Sharan Goldstein, March 27, 1974.

Funk, Joe. Telephone conversation with Gerry Cristol, 1994.

Goldberg, Irving. By Joseph Rosenstein, August 22, 1972. By Hortense Sanger and Gerry Cristol, September 21, 1994.

Goldman, Josephine. By Gerry Cristol, August 9, 1994.

Goodell, Sol. By Gerry Cristol, April 26, 1994.

Grossman, Irwin. By Gerry Cristol, March 15, 1994.

Harrison, Adlene. By Gerry Cristol, April 30, 1994.

Hexter, Emily. Taped telephone interview by Gerry Cristol, June 2, 1994.

Hirsch, Elizabeth Olan. By Gerry Cristol, January 6, 1994.

Hirsh, Bernard. By Joan Loeb and Gerry Cristol, October 17, 1974. Telephone conversation with Gerry Cristol, October 25, 1994.

Israel, Raymond. By Gerry Cristol, no date.

Jacobus, Gloria. Conversation with Gerry Cristol, April 25, 1997.

Jacobus, Henry, Sr. By Joan Loeb and Frances Tocker, March 19, 1974.

Jacobus, Henry, Jr. By Gerry Cristol, March 30, 1994.

Kahn, Fannie and Stephen. By Gerry Cristol, February 4, 1993.

Klein, Rabbi Gerald J. By Jerry Whitus, September 1972. By Gerry Cristol, May 24, 1988, June 2, 1988, August 25, 1994.

Klein, Hanne. By Gerry Cristol, June 10, 1994.

Kleinman, Harold. By Gerry Cristol, April 28, 1994. Telephone conversation with Gerry Cristol, October 14, 1996.

Kleinman, Ruth. By Gerry Cristol, May 17, 1994.

Kravitz, Jack. By David Zeff, Council of Jewish Federations, September 23, 1986.

Lefkowitz, Blanche. By Gerry Cristol, March 29, 1974.

Lefkowitz, Rabbi David, Jr. By James Alexander and Gerry Cristol, June 3, 1990.

Levi, Godcheaux L. Telephone conversation with Gerry Cristol, April 26, 1993.

Linz, Joseph Sanger. By Gerry Cristol, January 1974. Telephone conversation with Gerry Cristol, May 19, 1989.

Loeb, Helen. By Joan Loeb and Gerry Cristol, May 15, 1974.

Loeb, Joan and Milton. By Gerry Cristol, May 11, 1994.

Mankoff, Ronald. By Gerry Cristol, April 26, 1994.

Marcus, Minnie. By Polly Crossman and Gerry Cristol, November 29, 1973.

Meyer, Howard. "Art and Architecture of Temple Emanu-El." Panel with Rabbi Levi A. Olan, Max Sandfield and John Lundsford taped at Temple Emanu-El, February 10, 1974.

Michael, Carmen Miller. By Gerry Cristol, June 1, 1994.

Telephone conversations with Gerry Cristol, January 8, 1996, August 27, 1996.

Milstein, Sam. By Gerry Cristol, October 24, 1994.

Mintz, Rabbi Charles D. Conversation with Gerry Cristol, January 9, 1996.

Mittenthal, M. J. Conversation with Gerry Cristol, 1994.

Myers, Blossom. By Hortense Sanger, 1974.

Olan, Rabbi Levi A. By Hortense Sanger, August 5, 1972. By Gerry Cristol, July 22, 1974. By Helen Stuhl, March 22, 1978.

Philipson, Herman, Jr. Telephone conversation with Gerry Cristol, 1994.

Pollock, Lawrence S. Jr. By Gerry Cristol, May 12, 1994.

Pollock, Shirley. By Gerry Cristol, May 5, 1994.

Robbins, Rabbi Debra J. By Gerry Cristol, December 7, 1994.

Rosenstein, Joseph. By Gerry Cristol, June 8, 1994.

Rosenthal, Herbert (Buddy). By Gerry Cristol, April 29, 1994.

Salzberger, Paul. Telephone conversation with Gerry Cristol, May 28, 1997.

Sandfield, Carol. Telephone conversation with Gerry Cristol, 1994.

Sanger, Eugene. Telephone conversation with Gerry Cristol, December 22, 1994.

Sanger, Hortense. By Gerry Cristol, June 8, 1990. Other conversations, 1992–1996.

Sanger, Jane. Telephone conversation with Gerry Cristol, March 9, 1994.

Sargon, Simon. By Gerry Cristol, October 23, 1994.

Schaenen, Fannie. By Gerry Cristol, August 17, 1994.

Schlinger, Norma. By Gerry Cristol, May 26, 1994.

Shakno, Trudy. By Gerry Cristol, May 9, 1990.

Schindler, Rabbi Alexander. Conversation with Gerry Cristol, July 1994.

Silverberg, Philip. By Rose Marion Berg, November 14, 1974.

Sommerfield, Elissa. By Gerry Cristol, June 1, 1994.

Stern, Rabbi David E. By Gerry Cristol, December 2, 1994, and August 2, 1996.

Strauss, Annette. By Gerry Cristol, May 18, 1995.

Tannebaum, Nita Mae. By Gerry Cristol, May 31, 1994.

Tobian, Louis. By Jerry Whitus, September 1972. By Gerry Cristol, 1974.

Tobian, Milton. By Gerry Cristol, November 1975.

Tobolowsky, Shirley. By Gerry Cristol, April 5, 1994.

Tonkon, Max. By Gerry Cristol, May 31, 1994.

Wolfram, Rhea. Untaped interview by Gerry Cristol, November 26, 1994.

Yaffe, Gerda. By Gerry Cristol, 1994.

Yaffe, Martin. Telephone conversation with Gerry Cristol, January 1996.

Zimmerman, Rabbi Sheldon. By Gerry Cristol, April 14, 1994, May 10, 1994.

BOOKS

Abzug, Robert H. *Inside the Vicious Heart*. New York: Oxford University Press, Inc. 1985.

Acheson, Sam. "Temple Emanu-El Had Early School." *Dallas Yesterday*. Dallas: Southern Methodist University Press, 1977, 334–336.

Adler, Frank J. *Roots in a Moving Stream: The Centennial History of Congregation B'nai Jehudah of Kansas City, 1870–1970*. Kansas City: The Temple, Congregation B'nai Jehudah, 1972.

Alexander, Charles. *Ku Klux Klan in the Southwest*. Lexington: University of Kentucky Press, 1965.

Brown, John Henry. *History of Dallas County Texas from 1837–1887*. Dallas: Milligan, Cornett & Farnham, Printers, 1887.

Castleberry, Vivian Anderson. *Daughters of Dallas: A History of Greater Dallas Through the Voices and Deeds of its Women*. Dallas: Odenwald Press, 1994.

Cochran, John H. *Dallas County: A Record of its Pioneers and Progress*. Dallas: Service Publishing Company, 1928.

Cohen, Anne Nathan. *The Centenary History of Congregation Beth Israel of Houston, Texas. 1854–1954*. Houston: Beth Israel, 1954.

Congregation Shearith Israel 1884–1959. Dallas: Congregation Shearith Israel, 1959.

Diner, Hasia R. A. *Time for Gathering: The Second Migration, 1820–1880*. Vol. 2, *The Jewish People in America*. Baltimore: The Johns Hopkins University Press, 1992.

Evans, Eli. *The Provincials: A Personal History of Jews in the South*. New York: Atheneum, 1973.

Greene, A. C. *A Place Called Dallas*. Dallas: The Dallas County Heritage Society, Inc., 1975.

Greene, A. C. *Dallas: The Deciding Years—A Historical Portrait*. Austin, Texas: The Encino Press, 1973.

Harris, Leon. *Merchant Princes*. New York: Harper & Row, 1979.

Hertzberg, Arthur. *The Jews in America*. New York: Simon & Schuster, 1989.

Holifield, E. Brooks. "Toward a History of American Congregations," in *American Congregations*. ed. James P. Wind and James W. Lewis. Vol. 2. Chicago: University of Chicago Press, 1994.

Jacobs, Ginger Chesnick. *The Levin Years: A Golden Era 1929–1951*. Dallas: Taylor

Publishing Company, 1989.

Jick, Leon A. *The Americanization of the Synagogue, 1820–1870*. Hanover, New Hampshire: Published for Brandeis University Press by the University Press of New England, 1976.

Jones, Ted. *Dallas: Its History, Its Development, Its Beauty*. Dallas: Lamar & Barton, 1925.

Karp, Abraham J. *Haven and Home: A History of the Jews in America*. New York: Schocken Books, 1985.

Kohut, Rebekah. *His Father's House: The Story of George Alexander Kohut*. New Haven: Yale University Press, 1938.

Kolsky, Thomas A. *Jews Against Zionism: The American Council for Judaism*. Philadelphia: Temple University Press, 1990.

Korros, Alexandra Shecket and Sarna, Jonathan D. *American Synagogue History: A Bibliography and State-of-the-Field Survey*. New York: Markus Wiener Publishing, Inc., 1988.

Lay, Shawn, ed. *The Invisible Empire in the West: Toward a New Historical Appraisal of the Ku Klux Klan of the Twenties*. Chicago: University of Illinois Press, 1992.

Leslie, Warren. *Dallas Public and Private*. New York: Grossman Publishers, 1964.

Levinger, Rabbi Lee J. *A History of the Jews in the United States*. Cincinnati: The Union of American Hebrew Congregations, 1930.

Libo, Kenneth. *We Lived There Too*. New York: St. Martin's, 1984.

Linden, Glenn M. *Desegregating Schools in Dallas*. Dallas: Three Forks Press, 1995.

Lindsley, Philip. *A History of Greater Dallas and Vicinity*. Chicago: The Lewis Publishing Company, 1909.

Marcus, Jacob Rader. *United States Jewry 1776–1985*. Volumes 2–4. Detroit: Wayne State University Press, 1991.

Marcus, Stanley. *Minding the Store*. Boston: Little, Brown & Company, 1974.

Marinbach, Bernard. *Galveston: Ellis Island of the West*. Albany: State University of New York Press, 1983.

McCoy, John Milton. *When Dallas Became a City. Letters of John Milton McCoy, 1870–1881*. ed. Elizabeth York Enstam. Dallas: The Dallas Historical Society, 1982.

McCullough, David. *Truman*. New York: Simon & Schuster, 1992.

McDonald, William L. *Dallas Rediscovered*. Dallas: The Dallas Historical Society, 1978.

Meyer, Michael A. *Response to Modernity: A History of the Reform Movement in*

301

Judaism. New York: Oxford University Press, 1988.

Morgan, Ted. *FDR.* New York: Simon & Schuster, 1985.

Moses, Carolyn Holmes. *Hungary Sends a Dallas-Builder, The Story of Martin Weiss.* Dallas: Martin Weiss, 1948.

Olan, Levi A. Introduction to *Medicine for a Sick World* by David Lefkowitz. Dallas: Southern Methodist University Press, 1952.

_____. *Maturity in an Immature World.* New York: KTAV Publishing House, 1984.

Oppenheimer, Evelyn, and Bill Porterfield, eds. *The Book of Dallas.* Garden City, New York: Doubleday & Company, Inc., 1976.

Ornish, Natalie. *Pioneer Jewish Texans.* Dallas: Texas Heritage Press, 1989.

Payne, Darwin. *Big D, Trials and Tribulation of an American Supercity in the 20th Century.* Dallas: Three Forks Press, 1994.

Payne, Darwin. *Dallas: An Illustrated History.* Woodland Hills, California: Windsor Publications, 1982.

Philipson, David. *My Life as an American Jew.* Cincinnati: John G. Kidd & Son, Inc., 1941.

Plaut, W. Gunther. *The Growth of Reform Judaism.* New York: World Union for Progressive Judaism, LTD, 1965.

Resnikoff, Charles and Engelman, Uriah Z. *The Jews of Charleston.* Philadelphia: The Jewish Publication Society of America, 1950.

Rogers, John William. *The Lusty Texans of Dallas.* New York: E. P. Dutton and Company, Inc., 1951.

Rogow, Faith. *Gone to Another Meeting: The National Council of Jewish Women, 1893–1993.* Tuscaloosa, Alabama: The University of Alabama Press, 1993.

Rosenberg, Leon Joseph. *Sangers': Pioneer Texas Merchants.* Austin: Texas State Historical Association, 1978.

Sachar, Howard M. *A History of the Jews in America.* New York: Alfred A. Knopf, 1992.

Sanders, Barrot Steven. *The Caruths: Dallas Landed Gentry.* Dallas: Sanders Press, 1988.

Schutze, Jim. *The Accommodation: The Politics of Race in an American City.* Secaucus, New Jersey: Citadel Press, 1986.

Schiebel, Walter J. E. *Education in Dallas 1874–1966.* Dallas: Taylor Publishing Company, 1966.

Schmier, Louis, ed. *Reflections of Southern Jewry: The Letters of Charles Wessolowsky, 1878-1879.* Albany, Georgia: Mercer University Press, 1982.

Silberman, Charles. *A Certain People: American Jews and Their Lives Today.* New York: Summit Books, 1985.

Tarpley, Fred. *Jefferson: Riverport to the Southwest.* Wolfe City, Texas: Henington Publishing Company, 1983.

Wade, Wyn Craig. *The Fiery Cross.* New York: Simon & Schuster, 1987.

Wertheimer, Jack, ed. *The American Synagogue: A Sanctuary Transformed.* Hanover, New Hampshire: University Press of New England, 1987; reprint, Waltham, Massachusetts: Brandeis Press, 1995.

Wineburgh, H. Harold. *The Texas Banker: The Life and Times of Fred Florence.* Dallas: H. Harold Wineburgh, 1981.

Winegarten, Ruthe and Schechter, Cathy. *Deep in the Heart: The Lives and Legends of Texas Jews. A Photographic History.* Austin, Texas: Eakin Press, 1990.

The WPA Dallas Guide and History. Written and Compiled from 1936–1942 by the Workers of the Writers Program of the Works Projects Administration in the City of Dallas. Denton: University of North Texas Press, 1992.

Wyman, David S. *The Abandonment of the Jews.* New York: Pantheon Books, 1984.

Wyman, David S. *Paper Walls: America and the Refugee Crisis 1938–1941.* New York: Pantheon Books, 1985.

The Zionist Idea: A Historical Analysis and Reader. ed. Arthur Herzburg. New York: Atheneum, 1986.

303

INDEX

311